# PRAISE FOR *STEPPING OFF THE EDGE*

*"I invite you to read Sandy's book. Short stories are my favorite kind of reading, and this book is like that: a series of short pieces strung together. I like images and montages of images: I am very visual. Sandy presents things in little scenes that have different emotions. Reading it was like walking through a concert. Different instruments are played during each song; different kinds of sound rise and fall around me, producing feelings and images. That was pretty cool. She showed me glimpses of things, circles of things. That's the way I write my songs. The book wasn't like some scientific thing that takes the soul from the real meaning of healing and all the feelings going on. That's what I like about it.*

*"Sandy has a way of teaching that uses normal words so people can read and understand what she means. Some of the books you get at conferences use such professional language that unless you're a doctor, you can't understand what the person's saying. She doesn't do that, and I liked that. It made me want to know more about her."*

— BILL MILLER, Mohican-German musician, speaker, and artist; Winner of the 2005 Grammy Award for Best Native American Music Album; other awards including multiple NAMMY Awards; Spiritual Leader of the Gathering

*"This is a dynamic book. It's alive with Ms. Nathan's passion, and her presence is in every line, teaching and learning with you, helping you when you stumble, because she's stumbled, too. It's rich with energy and meaning."*

— GERALD DiPEGO, novelist-screenwriter; author of the screenplays for *The Forgotten, Phenomenon, Instinct, Angel Eyes, Message in a Bottle,* and other films.

*"A provocative and inspiring journey of discovery. It reads like a good novel."*

— LEONARD TOURNEY, novelist; author of *Time's Fool: A Mystery of Shakespeare* and *The Joan and Matthew Stock Mysteries.*

# ABOUT THE BOOK

When Sandy Nathan set out to write a book about her profound experience at the Gathering, a Native American spiritual retreat, little did she know it would guide her to chronicle a life of *Stepping Off the Edge*. Again and again, she takes the risks needed for her soul's growth and vividly presents her personal journey—one of growing into the courageous spiritual being she is. Sandy reminds us we all possess spiritual greatness: It is our birthright.

By walking with Sandy along her path we get more than a glimpse of a person: We get a revealing and inspiring view of her life. Her adventure and the understanding she adds as she writes help us use her experience to enhance our own development. This book does much more than tell about a life: It takes us by the hand (or sometimes by the nose) and leads us to the opportunity afforded by spiritual practice. And practice is the key word.

*Stepping Off the Edge* is alive with information and inspiration. It is a book about doing. It's more than a book that describes chocolate cake or even one that tells you how to make chocolate cake. It is a book that gets your mouth watering for chocolate cake and then lets you loose in the kitchen stocked with recipes and everything you need to make your own chocolate cake. With fudge frosting. And chocolate chips if you want them.

In this fascinating narrative you will encounter the basics of prayer, meditation, worship, spiritual retreat, and how a life can become dedicated to the pursuit of experiencing the Divine. You will even find how to domesticate your mind and make it an ally in your quest for inner knowledge.

It is said that the path to self-awareness is a solitary one. *Stepping Off the Edge* opens you to the possibility that it can be fun, challenging, and rewarding.

# ABOUT THE AUTHOR

While she has earned two master's degrees and had prestigious careers, Sandy Nathan found that these achievements served one primary purpose: to give her the discipline to practice what she preaches. In doing that, she found contentment. Sandy Nathan's multifaceted life expanded her view of her inner self and the outer world. Her clear and concise writing about her spiritual experiences demonstrates how to use inner experiences to create a fulfilling life. She is a writer, a rider, a wife, and a mother of three grown children. Sandy lives and writes on her horse ranch in the Santa Ynez Valley near Santa Barbara, California.

# STEPPING OFF THE EDGE

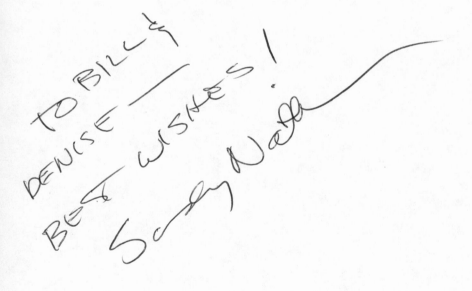

TO BILL &
DENISE —
BEST WISHES!
Sandy Nathan

# STEPPING OFF THE EDGE
*Learning & Living Spiritual Practice*

# SANDY NATHAN

VILASA
PRESS

SANTA YNEZ, CA

© 2006 by Sandy Nathan
Vilasa Press
PO Box 1316
Santa Ynez, CA 93460
www.vilasapress.com

ISBN: 0-9762809-8-1
Library of Congress Control Number: 2005925162

This book is sold with the understanding that neither the publisher nor author is rendering professional, legal, or medical advice. The publisher and author disclaim any direct or indirect liability, loss or risk, personal or otherwise, that is incurred from the use or application of the information herein. Attempts have been made to make this book as accurate as possible, but neither the publisher nor author guarantees its accuracy.

The examples presented in this book are based on true events. Participants' characteristics and incidental details have been changed to protect identity. The scenario in Chapter 6 is fictitious, though its content is not. Some material in this book has been previously published in *Spurs Magazine*, www.spursmagazine.com.

The feelings, thoughts, and opinions in this book are the author's. They do not reflect the views of the Holston Conference of Native American Ministries, which sponsors the Gathering, or the United Methodist Church, of which the Holston Conference is a part. Neither do the opinions herein express the views of Bill Miller and his associates, the Gathering staff or organizers, or those of Siddha Yoga Meditation, Swami Chidvilasananda, Swami Muktananda, or the SYDA Foundation, its officers, or staff.

The quote from Swami Muktananda on page 189 is reprinted with permission of SYDA Foundation, P.O. Box 600, 371 Brickman Road, South Fallsburg, New York 12779-0600, USA.

Publisher's Cataloguing-in-Publication

Nathan, Sandy.

     Stepping off the edge : learning & living spiritual practice / Sandy Nathan. -- Santa Ynez, CA : Vilasa Press, 2006.

     p. ; cm.

     ISBN-13: 978-0-9762809-8-9
     ISBN-10: 0-9762809-8-1

     Illustrated by the author.
     Contains an interview with Bill Miller, a Native American musician.
     Includes bibliographical references and index.


     1. Spirituality. 2. Spiritual life. 3. Meditation. 4. Good and evil–Religious aspects. 5. Psychology, Religious. 6. Indians of North America–Religion. 7. Internet addiction. 8. Recovering addicts–Biography. 9. Recovery movement–Religious aspects. 10. Writing–Psychological aspects. I. Title.

BV4501.3 .N38 2006                          2005925162
204--dc22

Printed and bound in the United States of America.

*To the Power that created and sustains the universe,*
*I offer my grateful heart.*

# TABLE OF CONTENTS

Acknowledgements                                        XV

A Note from the Author                                  XIX

**SECTION I. SOUL SURVIVAL**

1. Stepping Off                                          3
2. The Spiritual Path                                    19
3. Almost Makes the Day Begin                            33
4. A Demon                                               41
5. Free at Last                                          53

**SECTION II. WHO ARE YOU?**

6. You're Not Who You Think You Are                      77

**SECTION III. A PILGRIMAGE**

7. Departing for the Gathering                           109
8. Cross-Country                                         131
9. Busted Flat in Coker Creek                            141
10. Secrets & Faults                                     159
11. Singing Their Hearts Out                             167
12. Hitting the Trail                                    173
13. The Evil That We Do                                  187

**SECTION IV. AFTER THE JOURNEY**

14. Aftershocks                                          215
15. Time and Time Again                                  233
16. Scary                                                245

Epilogue                                                 249

## SECTION V.  THE GATHERING

What the Gathering Means to Me                                            255
   by Bill Miller
An Invitation to the Gathering                                           257
   by Vicki Collins, Director of the Gathering
Contact Information                                                       259
An Interview with Bill Miller                                            261

## SECTION VI.  RESOURCES

Books and Other Resources I Love                                        273

About the Illustrations and Cover Art                                    291
Notes                                                                    293
Index                                                                    295

## LIST OF ILLUSTRATIONS

1. Stillness                                                             17
2. Horse and Rider                                                       99
3. Nona Reed: Redbird Woman                                            129
4. Angels Don't Leave                                                   166
5. The Drum                                                             172
6. Twiggy                                                               243

# ACKNOWLEDGEMENTS

Authors typically acknowledge those who helped or inspired them. When I told my mother I was writing a book, she said, "Oh, *no!*" I was taken aback, but she explained that she knew how much work writing a book was, and she didn't want me to have to do all that. Isn't that sweet? I went ahead and wrote this anyway. She was right about the amount of work a book takes, but I think she'd like this one. Mom passed on a while ago, so I'm not able to show her the finished product. I'm sad about that: I miss her.

Acknowledgements are about circles of support, about one hand or heart touching another and allowing something to be born. In that, I certainly thank my parents: I wouldn't be here without them. I thank my extended family, my blood relations in California, Missouri, and Iceland.

My immediate family forms a closer circle of gratitude. My husband, Barry Nathan, was an unshakeable mountain during the production of this book. My daughters also contributed greatly: Zoë designed web sites for the Gathering and this book. My younger daughter, Lily, painted the portrait of Bill Miller that's on the cover. My son, Andy Tapella, and grandchildren, Jarrett and Cara, cheered me on from Idaho.

Families are relations of the soul as well as blood relations. My Native American "family" deserves special thanks. Vicki Collins, Director of the Gathering, the retreat I visit in this book, became like a sister. Vicki's insightful answers to my questions guided me to the Gathering. She taught me about American Indians, and steadily encouraged my writing of this and other books. I must also thank Bill Miller for the inspiration his music and message have given me at the Gathering and over the years. Thanks again, Bill, for our interview and your support. To the people of the Gathering, who inspired me and were just plain fun to be with, I send my gratitude and love.

Another level of family is the team that helped me produce this book. A book is more than pages between covers. It has an essence that takes a team to find and bring out. Many thanks to Ellen Reid, Book Shepherd extraordinaire; Leonard Tourney, Ph.D., editor; Sarah Chesnutt, cover design; Amy Hayes, interior design; C.E. Gatchalian, proofreading; Brookes Nohlgren, proofreading; Laren Bright, copy writer; and Gina Gerboth, of Pueblo Indexing.

As this book demonstrates, when you have horses your veterinarian becomes part of your family. I want to thank Greg Parks and all the vets of Alamo Pintado Equine Veterinary Clinic. They've saved our horses' lives many times and kept us sane to boot.

My academic family is especially dear. I *loved* school: That's probably why I kept going for so long. For those who became part of "My professor said—," a special thanks. Thank you, Fr. Austin Fagothey, S.J., Fr. Timothy Fallon, S.J., Mario Belotti, and Raymond Dennehy. Many thanks to Sarah Behman, who inspired me in some of my darkest days, while teaching me statistics and econometrics. Thanks to Len Kunin and Sue van Atta from my years at San Jose State University. From Santa Clara University's counseling program, many thanks to Bill Yabroff, Barry Hayes, Mary Anne Wakefield, and Jerry Kroth. From my time at the Graduate School of Business at Stanford, thanks to Richard Pascale, Kirk Hansen, and David Bradford.

In the innermost circle of all, that of my soul, I give heartfelt thanks to my meditation teachers, Swami Chidvilasananda and Swami Muktananda, for being inner sources of unending support and inspiration. My life made a quantum leap when I met them, and has kept on jumping. Thanks also to Swamis Shantananda, Vasudevananda, Durgananda, Kripananda, and Anantananda. And absolutely not least, I must acknowledge my dear ministers, the Revs. Sue Kelly and Jean Grover.

All of these people shared in shaping and inspiring me. Echoes of their voices can be heard in the book that follows.

—SANDY NATHAN, Rancho Vilasa

*It is best to perform our own duty though deficient*
*Than the duty of another well performed.*
—BHAGAVAD GITA 3.35


*Do your life.*
—SANDY NATHAN

# A NOTE FROM THE AUTHOR

I want this book to touch you and heal you. I'd like my writing to open your heart so that the love inside flows out and transforms your life. I want my words to make you laugh and cry and feel and become the person you were meant to be. I want to move so many of you that the universe of hopes and prayers becomes real and we live together in paradise.

Negotiation coaches tell us to set our aspirations high. Data shows that the higher a person's aspirations, the more he or she actually achieves. I set my goals high for this book. You can tell me if I attained them when you've read it.

Right now, I want to tell you about *Stepping Off the Edge*.

At first, what I wanted to write about was a Native American spiritual retreat called the Gathering. I wrote about that, but as I wrote I realized that what I was writing about was bigger. I was writing not just about a particular retreat or spiritual activity, but also about how we can all become mature, spiritual beings. What must we humans do to grow up? If that was too big a question, how did *I* grow up? I'm aware that I've grown up over thirty years of spiritual seeking. I'm aware of the bliss I feel on a daily basis. I'm aware of my balance and competency.

How did I achieve this state?

By what I do and how I live: Spiritual practice made me the woman I am. So I wrote this book about spiritual practice. This is a real "show me, don't tell me" book because you can't learn spiritual practice by reading a book. A book can tell you *about* spiritual practice, but doesn't give you its fruit. Trying to learn spiritual practice from a book is like trying to train a dog without having one. Spiritual practice is *alive* and requires a living body committed to learning. Given this, I use my favorite demonstration tools—*my* soul, body, and life—to illustrate the road to spiritual maturity. (A few of my friends chip in their stories, as you'll see.)

This book is my spiritual journey. It covers the basics of prayer, meditation, worship, and the practice of spiritual retreat. I also discuss what happened when I dedicated my life to experiencing the divine, and how to tame the mind ... I write about many things, using stories and examples that anyone can understand. The lessons are presented as interwoven vignettes illustrating a few years of my life and a lifetime's store of knowledge.

I suggest that we get going. Who knows how much time we have for our journey? None of us will come out of this earthly voyage alive; we'd best start now. We'll make the trip together—that's much better than going it alone, don't you think?

Sandy Nathan

SECTION ONE

# SOUL
# SURVIVAL

# CHAPTER 1

# STEPPING OFF

THEY FOUND CANCER ON ONE SIDE, but they got it in time. Then it showed up on the other side. Your child was stricken with a disease so disturbing that some people still won't look you in the eye. You've battled drugs and alcohol and the results of what your fellow human beings did to you. You never talk about your life: If people heard the outlines, they'd laugh. They'd call you a victim or a tragedy queen. But you have lived every minute of it, and no one knows how hard it's been. You have done everything to change how things are, but still the pain continues: illness, trauma, loss, despair.

Or perhaps your story takes a different turn: Born to success and all the right schools, you decide it's time to make it big. For the last seven years, you've worked harder than you knew a person could; no vacations, not even a day off. Not once, but dozens of times, you've awakened at your desk to find yourself blinking in the morning sun. Hobbies, friends, and family are memories from a past life. You've given it every dime you have, and signed a stack of notes at the bank. You know you will succeed—you have never failed.

The start-up fails. You're so bankrupt that you can't even cry. The Feds are hounding you for taxes.

You find yourself speaking into silence, "Why? Why me? Why at all?"

No answer.

On the other hand, some lives unfold like they'd been touched by a genie. From the kickoff to the final play, everything works. In elementary school, your science project wins the Grand Prize. Sailing through grade after grade, you captain every team. After serving your country with honor, you come home and start the business. Sure, you work hard and long, but success arrives like a flood. Years pass with champagne and congratulations and another round of applause.

Until one day, you look around. Your husband or wife has passed on; the kids are gone. Younger people run your business. Something lurks out there, a terrifying mystery. You're sliding toward it with no brakes. Questions keep coming: What did I accomplish? Was it worth it? Should I have done more?

You gaze into space and your reflection looks back, a hollow ghost.

What do you do when life gives you everything you want? What do you do when you get the crud on the bottom? What do you do when living in a human body hurts too much?

You do your life.

"You do your life?" you may want to scream. "What do you mean, do your life? I just told you about my life. It's a mess. I'm miserable. Why would I want *my* life? Other lives are much better. You can see them everywhere—on TV and in the movies. Some people have skinny butts and six-pack abs. Some people have great jobs and lots of money. Some people don't have my wife. Or her mother. I buy this book for help, and you tell me to *do my life?*"

I'm sorry. That's the most useful thing I can say to you and the only thing you can do—your life. That's the message of this book:

Your life is your spiritual path.

It's also the ultimate truth. Your life, as you complete the breath you're on right now, wherever you are, is *it* for you. You can't do anyone

4

else's life. If you don't want to do your life, all you can do is imitate a picture your mind got from somewhere and act it out.

Live your life or be a fake. If you copy someone else's life because it photographs better, you'll destroy the one chance you have at real happiness: your life. Brutal, I know. The alternative is worse:

Women with faces stretched like drumheads sport butterscotch hair and fingernails curved like beetles' backs. Puffed-up men wear muscles as camouflage. Kids with moussed spikes, pierced and tattooed head to heel, wag tongues with silver barbells. Guys in suits move so fast you think they're on speed. They're not: They're in the fast lane, making something of themselves.

If you look into the eyes of the people I described, people we all know, you can see who they are: living souls, the most valuable entities on the planet. Living souls longing to emerge and express themselves, souls that have always been perfect and know it to some degree. These are souls that weren't strong enough to battle the world's imperatives: *You must be thin; you must be rich; you must act like this.*

The spiritual path is the process of the soul reclaiming its dominion over the world's programming. Living this process feels like a battle to the death, because it is: Parts of the personality will die as others are born. The person being born and dying will feel all of it.

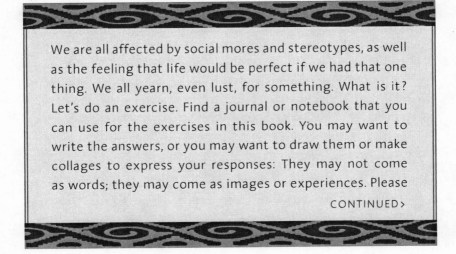

We are all affected by social mores and stereotypes, as well as the feeling that life would be perfect if we had that one thing. We all yearn, even lust, for something. What is it? Let's do an exercise. Find a journal or notebook that you can use for the exercises in this book. You may want to write the answers, or you may want to draw them or make collages to express your responses: They may not come as words; they may come as images or experiences. Please

CONTINUED>

record what happens when you do the exercise, including, "Nothing happened." That's fine.

Take a seat in a private place when you have some time to yourself. Sit quietly, taking a few breaths to start. A few easy breaths, emptying your lungs, bottom to top. Tell yourself, "Relax." Keep at it, watching the rise and fall of your chest. No hurry, and no need to perform. When you feel relaxed, think about what you really want. Take the first image that comes up. No right or wrong answers exist. Don't think I'm asking you for some high-toned spiritual answer, either. If what you really want is a yacht or World Series tickets, that's great. If you want a perfect partner, fine. A great body or a Ph.D., ter-rific. A best-selling novel, cool.

Let what you want play before your mind: See it, feel it. Ex-perience what you want with all your senses. Feel your longing for that object. Feel your desire. Focus on it. If you wish, add a few more things you must have for a good life. Money. A big house. Whatever you know would make you happy if you could get it. If you can imagine a circus of desires, all the better, though just one is fine.

Sit, experiencing the things you need to be happy, and feeling your desire for them. Allow the desire to intensify so that it fills your body. Now, imagine a great breeze blowing it all away. Whoosh! All those images disappear like sand before the wind.

Leaving you with desire. Pure desire, full strength, but with no object. Hold that experience and ask yourself a question: What do I really want?

CONTINUED>

Stay with the desire, the desire without an object, and see what comes to you. See what your soul longs to find.

**Some tips:** It may help to have a trusted friend with whom you're reading this book read the directions to you. If you can't get any clear images when you do the exercise, watch for them elsewhere. In dreams, at work, walking around the mall. What do you see when you remove the object of desire? If nothing comes, great. We aren't the same. This exercise may not be for you. If you find this or any of the exercises in the book disturbing or impossible, don't do them. Just read the text.

The world doesn't do it to us; we do it to ourselves. Having bought into the program, we can suffer for many years trying to attain what the world or others say we should. Souls are sturdy and can handle abuse. But if the soul/body/mind combo doesn't get past this delusion, something essential will die. The person will look alive, but be spiritually dead.

Recall seeing people you haven't seen for a long time—at a class reunion, perhaps. Can you feel how changed some are? How resigned? People who were lively youngsters once, full of dreams and jumping with life, seem dead. Recently, I ran into acquaintances I'd known thirty years ago and was shocked.

"How did they get so *old?*" I said to one of my friends. "We're the same age, but they were old. I don't understand it."

"Well, you don't look old," she replied. "Your face shines. You glow."

I was surprised, as I'm pushing sixty and definitely don't look the way I once did. I feel my glow, but I didn't know anyone else could see it. I feel really good most of the time, not that my life is perfect or I am perfect. My life has been very difficult in many ways, yet I feel more alive than I did as a child. How? Keep reading; I share my secrets below.

We are playing for nothing less than soul survival. The world of envy, hatred, fear, sadness, rage, corruption, and disease—the world in which we live—will destroy our souls. We will become ghosts sleepwalking across the planet, acting out hurts, scripts, and feelings imbedded in our bodies and minds. We'll join the millions of zombies spreading the gospel of bitterness and rage, preaching until we fall over dead.

How to avoid this? Face the inner and outer tasks before you and complete them well enough for the next set to arise. In living our lives, we share the same chores: breaking free of what Mom and Dad programmed us to attain, often with the best intentions. Getting clear of what society says we must be. Finding a way of life that works, learning to be effective partners or parents, or how to live in our communities if we don't marry. We have to learn to make a contribution to society and pay our bills. Those who are most fortunate learn how to find God.

I use the word *God* in speaking of the Divine. This causes consternation in many quarters. Some people have gotten involved in cults or other religious groups and have been seriously damaged. Others don't believe in God and are offended by the word. Still others believe in God, but only as defined by their religious affiliation. These people can't stand the views of anyone outside their definition.

CONTINUED>

Writing about God is fraught with potential for misunderstanding and polarization.

If I say *God* and this bothers you, substitute any words that work for you: Higher Power, Creator, Spirit, the Self, Universe, Great Mystery, Collective Unconscious, Buddha nature.

The word *God* is short and easy to type, so I use it. I have no idea what God is, except that God exists, moves things, creates and sustains them, and scares me to death. God is far outside our human sense of what should and should not be. I have no desire to convert you to my view of God, or anything else. Stay true to your heart and traditions.

To survive, everyone must find his or her essential core and live from it. Finding it is trouble enough, then you must maintain contact with it and follow its orders. You have to withstand the inevitable temptations from people who don't have your highest interests in mind: "Hey, let's go out for a few beers." When alcohol is your weakness. "You don't need to study tonight. Come on, have some fun." When you're trying to attain a degree.

Temptation doesn't have to be external. I carry mine in my head and computer. The console sits there before me, undulating. I can awaken what lies inside with a click of a mouse: A world of Native American jewelry and Persian rugs, a world as magical and deadly to me as a cobra's bite. I picked up a little addiction on an on-line auction in my travels. Spiritual survival involves mastering everything the universe throws at you. Hazards arise from inside, outside, all around.

What fuels my glow? Spiritual practice, which starts with finding your spirit. What's that? The first definition of *spirit* in my dictionary is, "A vital force that characterizes a living being as being alive." My father taught me about spirit in 1964:

I walked down the aisle as if chains were hauling me, all the while knowing that I had to do what I did. The casket was muted bronze. They kept it closed for the public, but opened it so we family members could say goodbye. When I saw my father's face, I wondered why the plastic surgeons had made such a fuss, wanting photos of how he had looked before and talking about reconstruction so urgently. I didn't think he looked that bad—just a little mashed. He was wearing a white shirt and one of the custom-made suits that his bodybuilding necessitated. I stood before him, absorbing what was there. My hand extended, and I touched the body of this man I adored. I had to touch him to make sure it really happened. Cold and rubbery, my father was dead.

Where was the volcano of energy he had been? Where was the intelligence and wit? The charisma? Where was the drive that knocked down mountains and put houses in their place? What did this lifeless husk have to do with the man I knew? How could that vital power die? How could it disappear?

My father taught me that spirit is the difference between a living person and a dead one. My father taught me that the soul is immortal. My father taught me to use the time I had on earth well. He was forty-five years old when a drunk driver mowed him down. He and the man who killed him taught me that what you do with your soul when you're in your body matters.

We've defined *spirit*, how about *practice?* A practice is something that you do repeatedly in order to improve strength and performance. A practice also is an established custom or habit, and what you do when acting in accordance with the beliefs and customs of a religion.

Spiritual practice is a way of strengthening your soul. It's a way of your essence taking control of your being. Once that happens, you will begin to do and be what you've always wanted. You perform spiritual practices every day so you'll be strong enough to handle the inevitable challenges. You don't have to go anywhere, join anything, or even tell anyone you're doing it. You just have to do it.

Originally, I planned on writing this book solely about the practice of spiritual retreat. I love retreats and have attended two or three a year since the 1970s. As I began pondering and researching, observation revealed something important. Retreats aren't the only practice I do. They haven't been for a long time but, once, they were my sole sustenance.

In my early days on the spiritual path, I'd go on retreat and attain a sense of peace and contentment. A blast of nirvana. Feeling fantastic, I'd return home. After a few days of floating bliss, the people around me were just as annoying as ever, my husband was how he always was, and the kids did their usual things. It was all the same.

I wanted to manage my loved ones, to haul everyone to a retreat so they'd say the right words and support my illusion of spiritual superiority. They wouldn't go, choosing to be themselves instead of the exceptional beings I knew they could be with a little help. I pined away, a mystical princess in a land of toads.

Making a growth leap, I realized: "I'm making everyone who doesn't think like me into a metaphysical frog. That's against everything I want to achieve." I began to incorporate other practices into my life on a daily basis. You'd be amazed what it did for the people around me—they straightened up right away.

Our lives are all ours—they won't go away. We need techniques to get through the daily grind, not just keep us going until the next dramatic pick-me-up. We can't run off to a retreat, personal growth seminar, or *anything* that gives us a high and think, "I feel great. I've done my duty."

Living for the highs misses a crucial point: Every day can be an ocean of bliss. Spirit is available wherever we are; we must tune in to it. That involves cleaning out the old house, letting in the light, adding new furnishings and whoopee! The party is on. We never knew what a party life could be.

Of course, remodeling the old rattrap of our inner house takes a lifetime and costs everything we have. We must give up our egos, everything we think we are or wish we were. But let us not be daunted by length of the road. The trip is worth the price.

Permanent bliss is the essence of spirituality. Every day matters.

What can we do to feel good all the time? Many thousands of books on spiritual practice have been written. They boil down to a simple precept:

Do what takes you closer to your goal; don't do what takes you further away from it.

Many great minds have promulgated esoteric systems setting out how to live properly. These require fancy concepts, Universal Laws, Sub-Galactic Rules, and Itty-Bitty Good Ideas. When you get through all that, Saint Thomas Aquinas said it best: "Do good, avoid evil."

That's something we can all remember. As I grow older, I like simple ideas. I can remember them. Keep going in the right direction, eventually you'll reach your destination.

Thousands of spiritual practices exist, often with telephone-book-sized instruction manuals. If you want that detailed instruction, it's available. What I do here is lurch through my life, demonstrating what I do. I do the following practices on a regular basis: pray, meditate, worship, contemplate, go on retreat, repeat my mantra, read holy and inspiring books, hang out with positive people that bring me up, vigilantly observe the contents of my mind and behavior, exercise control of both, exercise, use my environment to promote my spiritual evolution by displaying pictures and sayings that motivate me, abstain from drugs and alcohol, and eat right. Oh, yes. I also donate to organizations that support me spiritually.

"My God! That's a lot."

We're playing for our souls' survival, remember. Do you think taking a vitamin pill once a week will do it? This is a full-time job. And it packs a reward.

We don't talk about the reward much in this world where opulence is implanted and wrapped in Spandex, where *bigger, faster,* and *more* are the prevalent gods. "He who dies with the most toys wins" is a bumper sticker you see in Silicon Valley, where I was born and raised. What does this world know of the rewards of spiritual life?

Once, I stood next to a monk I admire greatly. He owns nothing, has no income, and has spent most of his adult life on retreat—whether talking to thousands or meditating alone. He wasn't doing much, just talking to a few people in a hallway. Something radiated from him, something that calmed my soul and shocked me with its subtle power. Purity of being. He had attained something truly valuable. Stillness and contentment. I looked at him and saw no *me* and *mine,* no *us* versus *them.* His was a soul with the dross burnt off. I felt better because I'd stood by him. That's what I want. You get it from spiritual work and contemplation.

Where are you going? Why are you here? What is the purpose of human existence? Why do we suffer? Where is justice?

These are the questions a contemplative asks. These are the questions our brains are constructed to ask. Scientific research has indicated this: Human brains are made to look past the material world into the world of meaning. We are the only species on the planet hardwired to do this. A purpose-filled life is not the property of any tradition or denomination— it's part of our operating equipment. It's our birthright.

How do we claim it? If you look around the world or watch TV, most people don't seem to know an inner world exists. Reality TV shows people screaming hysterically for bigger and bigger prizes. If you've tried for that monk's state, you'll know how hard it is to turn away from the snares of the world. Yet that's our job.

How do we do it?

We don't do it alone. We are not alone in this process. God exists, Creator exists, the Beloved exists, longing to help us if we give the tiniest show of interest. Like the blades of a scissors, our personal effort and the power of grace cut through the knots that keep us stuck.

What causes us to look up? What causes us to walk the path? Pain, usually. Pain is a highly effective motivator. Some people in pain mask it with drugs and addictions and get lost, at least for a time. Others find their pain dropkicks them into the spiritual realm. If your life doesn't motivate you with massive doses of pain, give thanks. A person with a less dramatic life can be strongly drawn to the Divine. Some people feel the call in gentle ways, and respond to subtle insights with focused and effective behavior.

Whether you're motivated by a sledgehammer or a feather, the spiritual path requires work. The work of spirit is spiritual practice. Usually we're better at one or two practices, and they become the basis of our daily routine. But what does this mean? How does living it feel?

⋘⋘⊪◉⊩⋙⋙

In front of our house, there's a path. It runs to the hay shed, around the main barn, through the lower pastures, up and around the little stable and back to the house. I walk that circle every day, many times. I've done it for years. I've come to see it as a meditation walk, a prayer walk.

The gravel crunches under my feet. Some days, mist dampens my cheeks; others, the sun scorches my neck and I wish I'd worn a hat. Always, the ranch amazes me. Oaks erupt, sage tumbles, and the undulating hills reveal the truth of California. I walk on the path as hawks soar overhead and smaller birds hop and twitter. The space is enormous, every inch beautiful. I see everything: plants, flowers. New molehills. Anxious squirrels. Dropped feathers. I check the horses on every pass.

Her belly is swollen, bursting with the life inside her. I look at the mare's hollow buttocks and caved-in flanks. Will it be tonight? No, I judge, looking at the rest of her; the foal won't come tonight. Three days, most likely. Farther along, I talk to a youngster with a skinned knee. "How are you doing, little Teco?"

They come to the fences, all of them. Ears pricked like sickles, focused on me. Their bright dark eyes are full of intelligence. Not human intelligence, but a kind that suits them. I can't imagine living without horses.

I walk the path, every day, many times. The sun and sky soar to the cadence of my footfalls. Life becomes very quiet. I can observe my thoughts and watch my mind. The mind is the chatterbox inside, the thing that talks, constantly repeating its litany of what it must have to survive. Other inner voices have become apparent with years of watching. We have many parts, many tongues. I walk, listening to the crunch of each step, observing the world inside along with the outer landscape.

As the sun beats on my shoulders, something else touches me. I feel it, funneling down through the top of my head, filling me. Filling the whole universe. It knows everything; it *is* everything. I participate in its knowing, just from its touch. Something exists above and outside me, something so good that I can't think of it without crying.

We move, the hawks and horses, my feet and mind, around the path, the everlasting circle. Something informs us all.

Within my skull, a blue light flashes. Powerful beyond imagination, piercing, brilliant, it scintillates. I see it inside my head; I see it outside of me, a glint, a flash. The blue light is to me what the larger presence is to all that exists.

I walk in the moving sphere, mind talking slowly, speaking slowly. Lots of space everywhere. I can see the parts of my mind and soul displayed, not in clinical array, but lovingly. That mind is me; its sometimes infuriating contents, also me. I can intervene now, I can say, "No, that's not true." I can mend a part that's hurting, give a good word. All the while the light shines down, and the booming unity fills my heart. The blue jewel shimmers or hides, and I walk, blessed.

This is contemplation.

Contemplation is the doorway to mystical experience, the purpose of human life.

Will the door open? Will we see the other side? Will it reveal its bounty? That other world, which created and supports the one we see, operates on its own rules. Totally free, it can't be bought or influenced, cares nothing for awards or achievement, money or the bottom line. It comes and goes where it will, attracted to those who love it and want to be free.

It opens for those who love it most.

I want to share my path with you; I want to walk with you like we were old friends. Two wise friends who know the magnificence and desperation of this time on earth, who like to amble and chat. Won't you join me as I walk? It will be an interesting journey, covering new terrain. Sometimes we'll be silly; other times, awestruck, gentle, or sad. Won't you walk with me and hear my story?

I want to tell you what happened when I stepped off the edge of the ordinary and gave my fate to the stars.

# STILLNESS
Buckskin dancer at the Gathering

CHAPTER 2

# THE
# SPIRITUAL
# PATH

STANDING AT THE EDGE OF THE precipice with the wind whipping your clothes, you stare into the vastness before you. You have to jump, must jump. Your life won't be right until you do. You're terrified.

That's how taking the next growth step feels, isn't it? Stepping into oblivion, stepping off the edge of the universe. You've prepared, done all the necessary steps to be ready, and have your support network waiting. Taking a deep breath, you leap ... and enter the freefall.

As you plummet, shirt and pants flapping, a skydiver with no 'chute, it's good to know that this is how the spiritual path lives. How it looks is another matter. Everyone's path is different. While your specific precipice may have different landmarks, the process is the same. Approaching the edge, wavering, the leap, the fall ... being caught as you land. Hopefully, the universe will catch you—always, that doubt, until grace comes through.

The trail of a long leap I made not too long ago provides the meat for our investigation, our philosophical discourse. What looked like a simple step proved an acrobatic departure worthy of the wildest amusement park. The ride dropped and spun, ejecting me onto another shore, only to set up another spiral after a short quiet stretch. A perfect interlude to illustrate soul survival. Here we go!

Eyebrows plastered to my hairline, face frozen by fright, I grabbed the steering wheel and punched it. I was doing about eighty when I entered the cement chute. Images whizzed past: painted monsters, messages in writing I couldn't understand. Something shattered in front of me; my vehicle bucked and shuddered as I swerved. They were right behind me, countless others, screaming in pursuit. No fear, no slowing, no escape. Drive or die. I blinked, eyes stinging from the noxious air.

The only time I truly came close to death was near my destination: Someone pulled out and almost rammed me into a pylon.

Driving on the Los Angeles freeways is always like that.

I ripped myself out of the car and rummaged for my stuff. I'd made it, so far. I had to crane my neck to see the top of the building. It erupted into the sky, a tower of mirrored glass and steel. California Hulk: I knew the architectural style. A uniformed bellman emerged from the hotel's entrance. Upscale California Hulk.

My fellow attendees flooded the lobby. I did the obligatory clothes check: Did I look as hip as everyone else? Yes. I made my way into the room that would give me the keys or seal my fate.

The ballroom was furnished with long, cloth-covered tables on each side of a central aisle with a large dais in front. The lights on the central stage were brighter than I expected. Many more people sat along the rows: a formidable crowd. I steeled myself to do whatever was necessary to succeed in this place.

Why had I made that wild journey?

Out of desire, chiefly. Desire for fame, wealth, and recognition. Adoration, if I could get it. Visions of loyal fans finding great value in my words goaded me. Wanting to save the world with my wisdom pushed me. Fear of failure figured in: Would I die without leaving my mark? Fear that *they* were right about me. Or that my deepest fears about me were right. Beckoning behind it all—my mental image of the radiant person I could possibly be. Hope pulled me to L.A. These feelings swirled in a stew smelling like lust.

◄◄◄►O►►►►

In the previous chapter, we talked about the spiritual path. Different images come to mind when we think of the human longing for the Divine: A painting of a Zen monk leaning on a stick broom, face alight. Ecstatically dancing Hindu monks. Dervishes whirling. The poetry of saints from around the world. The words of Jesus. Moses. The Buddha. Krishna or Mohammed. Thousands of the faithful marching toward a holy goal. Contemporary men and women searching inside and out for a right way of being and living.

We don't usually think of spirituality in terms of the tangle of emotions I listed. We think of spirituality as ascetic and blissful, not driven by primal forces and powerful feelings.

Some people experience the call to grow as a force almost too powerful to be controlled. Do they know why the raging flood inside directs them one way or another? Why it's a flood for them and a nudge for others? Can they explain it so others can understand?

I'll give it a try. I've felt the power within me—and without me—for many years. It goads me. Someone once asked me, "Why do your spiritual experiences have you running down the hall at night to do things you should have done? Mine don't." He wasn't being complimentary; he was saying, "What's wrong with you? Why don't you have a nice, manageable spiritual life like mine?"

Given this, what was I doing in L.A. that weekend?

◄◄◄►O►►►►

Answering requires some history. If a bad time is called *the pits*, the 1993 to 1995 interval of my life could be characterized as a *proliferation* of the pits, even a *glut* of pitful living. I went on a spiritual retreat, working as hard during those ten days as I hope you will work with this book. I did *everything* at one hundred percent intention: all the prayers and meditations, all the worship activities, the classes and contemplations. When the retreat was over, I felt like a miracle had occurred: I was renewed and ready to begin again. Little did I know that the miracle hadn't begun.

Several days after returning home, I felt an electric "Zap!" inside my head, a shock traveling from one side of my skull to the other. As I stood dumbfounded, a book was injected in my brain in less than a second. I couldn't speak: I didn't know such an experience was possible, much less that I would have it.

Running to my computer, I began to write. For nine years, I hardly stopped writing—that first book was part of a series. The series begins when a great Native American holy man meets the richest man in the world, a Silicon Valley billionaire. They meet at a Native American spiritual retreat. I'm from Silicon Valley: I haven't the faintest idea why whatever put that book in my head filled it with Indians—but there they were, refusing to leave.

As the pages and drafts piled up, I felt like I was sitting on top of an oil well: That gusher kept spouting. Writing was so pleasurable that I often preferred writing to riding my horse. If you ride, that gives you an inkling of how good I feel when I write.

A few years ago, I realized that I needed an editor. Effortlessly and unexpectedly, a terrific editor came to my aid. Finally, the flood of words slowed and I realized it was time to find a publisher. Or an agent, or something.

I began reading about publishing, agents, self-publishing, and book promotion. Almost all the articles and books said, "Ninety-nine-point-nine percent of fiction submissions are rejected." I was sure I'd end up in the point-one percent that made it. My fiction was divinely inspired. How could I fail?

I felt that way until I started submitting query letters.

Queries—a publishing industry term—are sent to literary agents or publishers to tease them into asking for a sample of your work. That way, your sample doesn't find its way into the garbage can immediately. You have three sentences in which to pitch your deep and complex novel and wow the agent. They have to be snappy sentences. For instance, Dickens's *Oliver Twist* might be pitched as, "In an emotionally wrenching tale of turnabout and unfair play, young Oliver discovers that life is rough in Jolly Olde England."

If your query is sufficiently enthralling, you will be invited to submit a sample of your book. It has to grab the potential publisher in the first five pages. This leaves out Tolstoy, Doestoevsky, and most Nobel Prize winners: They don't get off the starting blocks fast enough.

The publishing industry has seven categories for fiction. If your book doesn't fit into one, they don't know what to do with it. Also: If you submit a book, your name better have nationwide recognition. Literary agents don't care about your straight A's, your GRE scores, or how much the National Science Foundation loved your treatise on sewer extensions.

I discovered all this the way you'd expect: by getting rejected. Some of the rejections reached levels of sadism usually confined to serial killers.

Something was at work here, but was it spiritual? Well, I did get the idea for the book after a retreat. I have an enormous drive to be published. But all this about query letters and agents, all that trying and striving: Is that spiritual?

Yes. Everything is spiritual, no matter how warped it may appear. Everything we humans do is the fruit of our longing for who we are: our larger selves, the people we are meant to be. We need to cut out the tainted bits, that's all. Sometimes the tainted bits are the key to liberty.

Writing was no longer fun. Working with my editor was tedious and dull. I feared I'd die before seeing my work in print. I kept having horrible experiences with members of the publishing industry. The worse it got, the more I wanted to be published. I couldn't stop trying, nor was I getting anywhere with my efforts.

I felt like a clove of garlic when you squeeze the garlic press's handles and little white squiggles come out. Extruded. Stinking and barely recognizable.

An email came in January 2003: "Attend Mark Victor Hansen's MEGA Book Marketing University! It's so BIG, it's MEGA!!!" The email was timed so I had one day to sign up and get the special discount. I recognized good marketing when I saw it. Also, I'd heard of Mark Victor Hansen.

Have you? Chicken Soup? Ring a bell? Mark Victor Hansen and his business partner, Jack Canfield, have sold more than *one hundred million* copies of the *Chicken Soup for the Soul* books. Hansen and Canfield are acknowledged as world-class personal coaches, helping thousands to achieve peak performance. I needed that. Plus, every important person in the book industry was listed as a presenter.

The *Chicken Soup* books were the main reason I went to the MEGA University. When I had my knee replaced in 2001, a nine-inch gash looking like it came from *Frankenstein* ran down the front of my leg. I hurt so much that I trembled with pain *after* taking my meds.

For weeks, I gobbled those happy *Chicken Soup* books like popcorn. They were evidence that *something* turned out right.

I signed up for Mark Victor Hansen's seminar with grave reservations. I'm a native Californian and did the New Age/Human Potential Movement groups of the 1970s hard. I know what happens at big self-help seminars and it's not pretty. Fearing that I'd be convinced to sign up for a lifetime course I didn't want by excessively happy, fast-talking people in shiny clothes, I left my credit card and checkbook in the car. And entered book utopia.

The desire to see our names on book covers, or sell the books if our names were already on them, brought us together. Lust for publication/riches/fame motivated us. Or at least me. In a massive, upscale hotel ballroom packed with semi-hysterical, wannabe authors, Mark Victor Hansen and the rest held forth—cheerful to the point of exploding, although not all of them wore shiny clothes.

Mark *is* a world-class motivator, using the same positive techniques as my dog trainer, with the same good results. The seminar provided seminal insights.

One highlight came after Mark introduced the Senior Head Honcho Editor from Some Major Publisher. The room leaned toward her, panting. Clutching her briefcase to her chest, the editor looked scared. She mumbled a few words and headed for the rear door. The ballroom tilted as legions of rejection-crazed writers leapt after her.

I led the pack. We cornered her in the rear of the room, but she cleverly opened a door and escaped to the hallway, where hundreds of other would-be authors trapped her, called telepathically from all over the hotel. Trembling slightly, I spoke to my possible Portal to Publication.

*"Would you look at my novel?"* My voice shook as I proffered a manila envelope with its exactly fifteen, double-spaced, left-justified, twelve-point, Times New Roman font, professionally printed sample pages.

*"I don't do fiction."* She looked at me as though I were leprous. I slunk away, MEGA-rejected. People engulfed her and carried her away.

Transformational moment #1: I learned that fiction is hard to sell. I was about to learn more: Dan Poynter got up to speak next. Have you heard of him? Dan is known as the "guru of self-publishing," having written the book on the subject—fourteen editions, actually. What Dan said that got to me was this:

"Writers of fiction are very interesting people and fun to talk to at parties. Writers of nonfiction drive better cars."

Clearly, publishing anything that wasn't nonfiction would be very difficult. (Though this is silly. Much fiction is actual experience that the author's unconscious has jumbled up so that the people who did it don't recognize it, preventing them from suing or ostracizing her. Much of fiction is nonfiction.) I thought furiously:

"What do I know a lot about that I could turn into a book?"

Casting about mentally, it hit me:

"What about *The Horse Book?*"

We live on a horse ranch. I've ridden since I was ten years old. We've bred horses for almost twenty years. My web site and *Spurs Magazine* contain many articles about horses. What's on the Net is not The Good Stuff. The really good stories I've kept in my computer for the day I got old. I would disgorge them then. I looked in the mirror:

"Honey, you *are* old."

I decided to write *The Horse Book*, making a desultory and incomplete attempt at a book proposal and sending out a few emails asking experts for input.

When Mark Victor Hansen's agent rejected me the second time, this effort piddled out.

⋘◄◄◄►►►⋙

Yearning, rejection, pain. I was learning, but not enough to amount to anything. This is the spiritual path?

Yes.

⋘◄◄◄►►►⋙

After my moment of insight about nonfiction, I went back to being crazed.

Imagine a circus juggler—the kind that uses long sticks and spins plates on top of them. One stick, two sticks, three, four, dozens. They're balanced all over the guy's head, shoulders, and elbows. Nose. That's how I felt. Editing, writing, jumping from one story to another. Writing query letters in hopes that one would hit. Demented.

Not everything happening was negative. Some readers really loved my book. But no matter what minuscule crumbs of encouragement I got, everything positive seemed to dribble away.

⏵⏵◈⏴⏴

We often think the spiritual path is supposed to be pretty and uplifting. No, it's usually just how it is. Different for everyone. The way I see it, the spiritual path is like the business cycle: What goes up must come down. That is, unless the management is really on the ball, which it usually isn't. Even with the ups and downs, if we work hard, we can find an upward growth trend. Spiritual practice is what you do on the wild upside of prosperity as well as the descent: It allows you to remain stable no matter what the outer you is doing.

Let's take another look at the spiritual path using a different kind of map, that of personality theory. A personality theory describes how a complete person works. This means it models and attempts to explain personal traits that endure over time: attitudes, behaviors, emotional patterns, social roles, and anything else that distinguishes an individual. Why study this? We'll see.

I'm going to describe part of the work of Dr. Abraham Maslow. Maslow was the father of humanistic and transpersonal psychology. These psychologies seek to illuminate and clarify the higher ranges of human experience, such as mystical and religious experiences, and the drive to grow and transcend. An important part of Maslow's thought, the Needs Hierarchy, is summarized in Table One.

# TABLE ONE – MASLOW'S HIERARCHY OF NEEDS

## THE BASIC NEED LEVELS

The four basic needs were found in Maslow's writings from the 1950s. Arranged from lower to higher.

| PERSONAL NEED | CHARACTERISTICS OF PERSONAL NEED |
| --- | --- |
| Biological/Physiological | A person at this level is primarily concerned with physical survival. |
| Safety | The desire for security and safety becomes the prevalent driving force. |
| Attachment/Belonging | A mate, friends, and a place in a community become life goals. |
| Esteem | The life of a person seeking the lower type of esteem revolves around status, recognition, and dominance. A higher type of self-esteem revolves around mastery of skills and independence. |

## THE HIGHER NEED LEVELS

The self-actualization stage shown below was part of Maslow's original work. Later theorists added the other higher need levels as extensions of Maslow's theory.

| NEED | CHARACTERISTICS |
| --- | --- |
| Cognitive | Thinking, learning, and theorizing become the driving forces. |
| Esthetic | Esthetic and creative pursuits are the goal of life. |
| Self-actualization | The self-actualizer appreciates the universe, pursues personal goals, and cultivates the highest levels of humanity. |
| Transcendent | A person at this level has all the qualities of the previous stage, maintaining the mystical states of peak experiences continually or almost so. These are the great teachers. |

The table at left isn't a developmental model, which assigns an age range during which a person ought to have mastered each stage. Maslow suggested that we must meet our lower needs consistently before we can advance to higher levels. He felt that very few people reached the self-actualizing stage—perhaps two percent of the population. Those who attain the transcendent level are rarer than rare.

Does this mean that ninety-eight percent of us are duds? Not in my book. Many people spend their lives overcoming the results of abuse, neglect, disease, addiction, and calamity. In overcoming these trials, people attain great merit, even if they don't look impressive in terms of theory. Maslow's chart is a useful tool, but not the whole truth.

Why is this information important? Simple: We're talking about the spiritual path. That's it. The chart presents the path in clear, unambiguous terms as laid out by one of the top minds of our time. If you don't like Maslow's theory, you can overlay Erik Erickson's eight stages of development, Freud's five stages of psychosexual development, Jung's developmental spiral, and whatever else pleases you.

The chart *is* the spiritual path, minus the pseudo-mysticism that often accompanies the term. I'm not a "woo-woo" person. Some invest spirituality with trappings of crystals and channeling and the sense that *the path* is for a precious few. This drives me wild. The spiritual path is why we're here. Everyone feels the urge to develop personally; we are a purposive species. Without gross abuse, we will develop according to our spiritual nature. All we need to do is grab onto a little nurturance and we're off like a dynamo. Maslow's chart and the work of other theorists give us a logical structure on which to hang our experience.

While our task as human beings can be conceptualized rationally, it's lived in flesh and blood by each individual. That's where the mystery appears. The way each of us evolves is as complicated and awe-inspiring as the birth of a universe.

**AN EXERCISE:** Why do you think I made that stampede to Los Angeles? I'd like you to get out your journal and jot down what stage of functioning you think motivated me. Was I trying to belong? Achieve? Meet some intellectual imperative? Enjoy an aesthetic thrill? Was it a peak experience?

Next, I'd like you to look at your life. Take some time and observe yourself. What do you want? A family? Job? Peace of mind? What are you going for? Professional acclaim? Security? Whatever it is, that's the edge of your growth. If you feel called to do something, it will be from that edge. This exercise has no right or wrong answers. One can't push one's self to a higher level: Every level is fine. Being honest about it is the important part.

We're on the spiritual path. Theories of personality are road maps. If you're on a trip, you look at the map to see where you are. That's what we're doing.

In pursuing our developmental drives, we sometimes do stuff that seems foolish. Even if publication and writing mean nothing to you, I think you can see yourself somewhere in my antics. Notice the compulsive quality of my craving for publication. Nothing wrong with it: Pure life force is behind that drive. Pure growth energy. Also, I got really good information.

The problem wasn't with the publishing industry: I wasn't ready. I needed to develop as a writer, learn the ropes, and make some contacts. An excellent, professionally written book proposal would have helped.

I think everyone has something similar going on. It's embarrassing to look at it and admit it, but crucial if we are to grow.

Our unique bundles of neuroses create our lives. Our problems are really spiritual growth opportunities. That we don't like it doesn't matter. What we do in response matters. What we do in response can sometimes be amazing.

# CHAPTER 3

# ALMOST MAKES
# THE DAY BEGIN

ODDLY OR INEVITABLY, A MAN WE'LL come to know well appeared in my life. I'd never heard of him; our worlds had no reason to intersect. Yet there I was, shopping in a little town near my house, Solvang, California (the Danish capital of America). While I stood at the counter of a western store, I became aware of music on the sound system. Haunting, wonderful, sophisticated. I was captivated.

"Who is that singing?" I said.

"Wuh?" said the lady behind the counter. Then, "I dunno." She rummaged around and pulled out a CD with a picture of an Indian on it. "It's that New Age stuff." She and her fellow employee made disparaging faces.

I bought the CD, took it home, and listened to it. Bill Miller—the Indian on the cover—blew my mind. This was around 1996; I was in one of those states where coincidences appear to signify something. Bill's music and message knocked me flat; that I should run into his music at that time was very odd. Synchronistic. *Synchronicity* is psychologist Carl Jung's term for unrelated events that appear to be related but clearly aren't caused by each other. I felt myself entering that spooky super-reality of spirit.

I was in the initial rush of my writing craze, writing my way out of the pits. I had written drafts of books that featured Indians as major characters. Eerily, Bill's photo on the CD cover looked the way I imagined one of my heroes would look—exactly. His voice was the same, too. In that productive and off-center period, Bill Miller's music crashed into my psyche.

Music can do it, and there's theory behind it, too. Neuro Linguistic Programming is a psychological school that explains the different ways people use their senses—hearing, sight, and touch—to navigate life. NLP practitioners say that sound is more involving than vision. Music is a vibration that enters the ears and moves the entire body. Listening to music is highly personal, unlike the cool distance that one maintains with the visual arts. The greater the musician's skill, the greater the impact.

I was so excited by that first CD that I wrote Bill Miller a fan letter— my first to anyone. I mailed my letter to every address on the CD.

It was about thirty pages long, as I recall. A gusher. I don't know if he ever got it: I never heard anything from him. Thinking about that letter now puts me into paroxysms of embarrassment.

What would impel me to write a thirty-page letter to a perfect stranger?

A few people have the ability to cut to the soul's core and release its encapsulated pain. Some people have the ability to heal with a thought, a word, or a glance. Some can heal without our even meeting them. Some people are so positive that seeing them in front of a room scratching their noses can enable us to do things that were impossible before.

Bill is one of those. He expresses deep truths through his music, and these allow his listeners to touch their own truth—or pain. Touching the core prompts listeners to share their lives and feelings, in ways ranging from highly appropriate to extremely inappropriate.

In saying this, I must make it clear that my letter was a philosophical discourse rather than an ingratiating missive from an admirer. No, I was too sophisticated then and now to fawn. I wish I had that letter; I could probably get a chapter out of it. Even its absence is inspiring; Bill has that much wallop. Which serves to introduce a snare: infatuation.

Depending on how the infatuation is handled, one of the developing soul's greatest potential hindrances is obsession with another human being. There's nothing wrong with admiring virtuous people or having mentors and spiritual teachers when the relationship is healthy. I'm talking about the kind of relationship—no matter how one-sided—where the other person seems grander and more glorious than anyone else. He or she is the embodiment of virtue and everything good. This is someone you think about every day—often for hours. Whose web site you visit at every opportunity, or more often. Whose picture you display at home, work, and in your car. Who could solve your problems, if only you could talk to him for a while, or, better yet, move in with him.

A person whose house you cruise—or would like to cruise, if you knew where it was.

I'm writing about the people who make your eyes misty and your knees shake. The group could include almost anyone, from public figures like entertainers, musicians, teachers, ministers, rabbis, and meditation masters, to people no one notices, like the girl in the bus or next door.

You may feel yourself blush as you read. Nothing to be embarrassed about: Everyone has felt this way about someone. (You can even write about a few special infatuations in your journal.) I remember some from my teens that were so sweet, and seemed so important at the time.

If we all have infatuations and they're sweet in retrospect, what's the problem?

Two things: First, infatuation knows no boundaries. It doesn't care that its object is married, has children, personal responsibilities and needs.

Infatuation is centered on the person who has the infatuation, not the needs of the beloved/admired one. It may result in inappropriate and unseemly behavior, such as stalking or breaking into a home or hotel room. The person with the infatuation thinks, "I have to talk to him," regardless of his energy level, time constraints, or personal situation.

At its worst, infatuation can result in the wanton behavior associated with rock groupies. It can result in death. My family experienced this indirectly. A man became infatuated with a young woman. After he stalked and terrorized her, she obtained a restraining order. In retaliation, he went to her workplace and killed seven people, one of whom was my daughter-in-law's uncle. When someone you love is murdered, the pain doesn't go away. It affects everyone in the victim's life as long as they live, not to mention killing the victim.

As potentially deadly as infatuation is to the object of adoration, it is equally damaging to the one harboring the desire. How?

When I was earning my M.A. in counseling, one of my professors pointed out that some people seem to believe that if they can't be the person they admire, they can attain their state by having an intimate relationship with them. What he said was considerably stronger than this, but my words capture the essence. This is not only erroneous— it's potentially disastrous. Personal development does not rub off. You have to do your own work, which means setting goals, training yourself, and becoming your dream. It's a lot of trouble, but the only real choice.

"You fall in love with what you're becoming," the same professor said. "You fall in love with what you're becoming" is the positive way of looking at infatuation. When you fall in love with someone, you see qualities in that person that your soul longs to develop and express. Attaining those qualities is your next growth step. Analyzing what attracts you to a person will give you the key to your next direction. As Maslow's chart indicates, the growth edges of our lives change as we fulfill one level of needs after another.

For instance, when I fell in love with my husband in 1974, what attracted me was the purity I saw in his eyes—and what he had done with his life. He'd done everything I wanted to do but was too chicken to try. He was a member of one of the first Peace Corps "classes," serving in Brazil from 1964 to 1966. From there, he trained other Peace Corps volunteers, and worked in antipoverty and community development programs all over the United States. He had lived his values. I fell in love with him. Although my husband is good-looking, had I fallen for his looks instead of his purity I doubt we'd be together today.

Whenever you feel that buzz, that hype over someone or something—we don't just fall in love with people—look inside and see what part of you they/it mirrors. What value or quality is personified? Courage? Power? Mastery of a skill? Beauty? Freedom? Truthfulness? Does the person touch something in your soul that no one else has? One of the higher personal values is undoubtedly involved. Identify that value and develop it in yourself.

You can have your cake and eat it, too: You can stay a fan while behaving appropriately and developing yourself.

My daughter, Lily, wrote the clearest statement that I have seen of "You fall in love with what you're becoming." In the following passage, she writes about her relationship to art and life.

*In high school, I would walk down the halls with my eyes half-closed in meditation. Wandering amidst the herds of adolescents. Misery, lust, jealousy, love. Wandering amidst the hot lava of youth. It was in those halls that art found me. That art took me by the hand and whispered into my ear, "There is a way out. You may become a creator and then you may tell the people the secrets you hear."*

*So art found me as a freshman in high school. It found me, held me up, and has not let me go.*

*There was a young Mexican man called Manuel. He came to the high school at the very end of my steamy freshman year and he shared his work with my art class. I wanted to touch his face, his paint-stained hands. I wanted to know him, to trust him. Part of me wanted to be him. He painted with so much passion that I thought I would faint while reading his diaries and viewing his art. After being introduced to his work, his lifeblood, his empathy, his loving, red heart, I decided that I was falling in love with what I hoped I would become: an artist. So that was the planting of the seed.*

*Manuel said with his beautifully accented voice, "You can do it, you may become anything you want. Believe in yourself."*

*With tears in my eyes, rolling down my face, I heard Manuel. I set out to fill the pages of my own diaries. To cover my own canvases. To tell my own stories. That was five years ago. I have been sailing my vessel across stormy seas. I have breathed and closed my eyes and prayed in the eyes of these deluges. I have spat in the face of my own misfortune and then I have embraced that misfortune for all that it taught me and made me see. The ocean is glittering. The tides are swift, then slow. I paint with cloud-covered skies. I paint with the sun burning my face.*

*I want to show Manuel what I have become. I want him to touch my face, as I have always wanted to touch his. I want him to see that I have charcoal rubbed on my face and neck. That my hands are stained with oil paint. That I have paintings in my bathtub, and everything I touch becomes covered with pigment. I scrub my cheeks but the paint does not rub away. So I walk through town with a painted face. I live and breathe art. It shall be written on my gravestone: "She became what she fell in love with: an artist."*

Wouldn't you rather write that, or paint it, than remain someone's fan? You can develop yourself and express your talents and still be deeply affected by other people. Mature regard for another is whole and freestanding; it has a different quality than the dependent, worshipful tone of the fan's adolescent adoration.

Paradoxically, by developing yourself and breaking the hold of infatuation, you're more likely to be interesting to your *enamorado* if you ever do spend time with him or her. What do you think Manuel would think of Lily now, if he could see her paintings or read her words? She never saw him again, but it's fun to think about what his reaction would be if he saw the swan she's become.

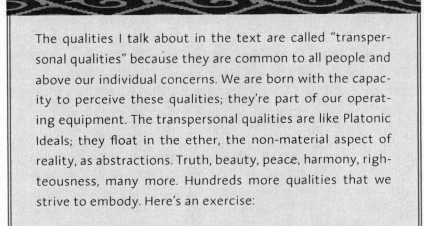

The qualities I talk about in the text are called "transpersonal qualities" because they are common to all people and above our individual concerns. We are born with the capacity to perceive these qualities; they're part of our operating equipment. The transpersonal qualities are like Platonic Ideals; they float in the ether, the non-material aspect of reality, as abstractions. Truth, beauty, peace, harmony, righteousness, many more. Hundreds more qualities that we strive to embody. Here's an exercise:

1. When you have some uninterrupted time, sit quietly. Relax by breathing slowly, feeling the air pass into and out of your body. Take long, deep, slow breaths, not pushing yourself.

2. When you feel relaxed, call someone you currently are infatuated with into your mind's eye. If that's too exciting and you can't stay centered, recall someone with whom you were infatuated in the past. See the person in front of you. What attracts you? Is it a devil-may-care joy? Freedom from constraint? Power and self-assurance?

CONTINUED>

Purity? Intensity of purpose? Truthfulness? Kindness? Appearance—was the person beautiful, or did he or she have some physical quality that reminded you of someone else? Can you identify what quality attracts you?

3. When you can name the quality or qualities, see if you can feel them in yourself. Do you feel your courage? Do you feel your creative capacity? Whatever it is, can you make it yours? You don't have to let go of the object of your past or present infatuation. Let him or her just hang out in your mind while you allow your soul to tell you how you can make that quality yours. How can you make it yours, right now, in your present life, no matter what it might be? What do you need to do? Take a class? Set time aside to write or practice an instrument? Volunteer somewhere? Start a business?

4. Stay in the place of peace and serenity as long as you can. When you must attend to your duties, come out carefully and slowly to the real world. Write down the ideas in your journal. This is your path, given to you by your heart. Cherish it, and follow it.

# CHAPTER 4

# A DEMON

*Led astray by many imaginings, enveloped in a net of delusion,*
*attached to the gratification of desires, they fall into a foul hell.*

—BHAGAVAD GITA, 16.16

EACH HUMAN LIFE UNFOLDS ACCORDING TO its *own* development theory. Each soul holds scars from time uncounted, and memories impressed upon it before history began. Life's river surprises us with eddies and currents that raise us high and dash us low. Underwater vegetation undulates, branches and fronds waving, leading us down tangles that go nowhere or pointing us straight at our goal. Astonishing creatures teem in our depths: parts of ourselves we don't know because they haven't surfaced before. Some are demons that would devour us; others, angels ready to rush to our aid. Each of us carries a private universe within our skulls and skins.

Even with this worldview, I was surprised by what happened next.

I continued to write and suffer. Seeing my unhappiness, my husband approached me with the sweetest expression.

"Does getting published matter so much, Sandy? Can't we go back to when you wrote for *me?*"

Hmmm. I thought hard, realizing something.

Ladies: Do you want your man to regard you with shining eyes and an earnest heart? Write. Yes—write. Scheherazade was no dummy. She knew how to keep him involved and herself alive. For eight years, Barry toiled during the day while I wrote. At night, he bounded up to our room, saying, "What do you have for me to read?"

He'd read my new stuff, laughing or crying at the right parts, engrossed. "Wow. That was really good." And then he'd correct a word or two, or give me a great new idea.

Eight wonderful years.

I thought about what he was proposing: going back to that bliss.

No. It wasn't all right with me. Getting published had become political: I believe that people should get paid for their work. I'd worked for eight years, producing really great stuff—for nothing. It wasn't fair.

Somewhere, it had dawned on me that if I'd signed on at McDonald's for minimum wage and translated all the hours I'd spent writing and editing and drafting query letters into time working at the Golden Arches, I'd be a wealthy woman. Not only that, I'd have made more than I probably would on a first novel as an unknown writer, assuming the book could be sold.

That wasn't right. Artistic people should make lots of money.

I deserved to be published. I would be published. I would do whatever necessary to get published. Including—well, whatever was legal and moral.

"No, Barry, we can't go back to the way it was."

I continued my literary crusade while he spent his days outside, working our horses and keeping up with the ranch. I assuaged my loneliness by discovering new things to do on a computer. I learned how to surf the Net, checking out a few favorite sites from time to time. One day, while I was happily taking a break from productive activity, I made a discovery.

Bill Miller's web site said he had one of his paintings up for auction on eBay.[1] In addition to being an extraordinary musician, Bill is a talented painter. The painting being auctioned was pictured; it was magnificent. I had just the spot for it.

I'd heard of eBay: Every living creature on the planet knows about eBay. I'd just never been there before. I typed eBay.com into my search engine, made up a user name and password, and slid into Bill's auction. I gasped at the painting's color and line, the sophisticated design.

Unfortunately, I couldn't afford the starting bid. I vowed to keep watching. Maybe they'd lower it. Maybe Bill would call me up and just give it to me. I sat facing Bill's painting on my computer screen. It was a simple step to, "I wonder if eBay has other stuff for sale?" I typed something into the search box and clicked.

In a nanosecond, I found myself face to screen with fourteen single-spaced pages of listings of turquoise and silver jewelry. Mostly Native American silver and turquoise. I love this stuff. Hours later, when I had bid on hundreds of beautiful objects I couldn't afford and didn't need, I realized that I was in what is known as a "red-light area" in Weight Watchers'[2] parlance. Except they talk about "red-light foods."

Days passed. My writing output, normally an impressive twelve to twenty-seven pages a day, dropped to four or five, then quit. This bothered me, as I was completing the draft of a novel. It also bothered my family and editor. I couldn't help it—I was stuck. Something had arisen from my depths and grabbed me.

On a pre-eBay morn, I'd bound downstairs, run to my computer and see how many hits our web site had racked up the day before. I'd answer emergency emails from my kids, such as "Mom, I'm stranded in New York City ... I don't have any money ... What should I do?" Pre-eBay, my web use revolved around events that materially impacted my life and that of my family.

Not after the Force got me. "Oh, my God! Did that auction close? Did I win?" Every day, I spent hours looking at auctions. My head hurt. My shoulders were stiff. I got less exercise. Was crabby. Sleep-deprived. But I was learning fast. I learned how to use the site's organizing features. I could look at my favorite areas with a minimal time commitment. I also signed up with a service that let me use my credit card on-line. That was a thrill—I could buy anything with a few clicks.

All of it was wildly exciting, a wonderful new game. I knew I was possessed from the start. In five to seven days, I was a full-fledged addict. The thrill of the chase. Learning how to beat the lurking unknown bidders ready to pounce at the end of every auction. The deals—if there's anything I love as much as a good book, it's a good deal. And they had 'em, and good stuff, too. I made new friends: Lots of fun people I could chat with could be found on eBay.

One morning, I came down early, intending to break free. Instead of hitting the computer, I sat in meditation. I went as far inside myself as I could, which wasn't too deeply—an auction was closing. I prayed to my spiritual ancestors, real ancestors, teachers, anything in/out there: "Please! Help me!" And though I prayed for freedom on one level, I really was praying that I would win both the amber and silver necklace and the old pawn silver bracelet. And the three-piece watchband, belt buckle, and ring set for my husband's birthday. Even my inner life had a silly, lust-riddled glaze.

Well, whatever's in or out there heard me: In that meditation, my first meditation teacher, who'd been dead for many years, appeared in my inner world shouting, *"Freedom follows renunciation."* Which I took to mean, "If something is getting in the way of your spiritual development, give it up." An inner voice I knew well gave me specific instructions: No eBay until five p.m. the next night. Over twenty-four hours of abstinence: It seemed like an eternity. At five the next day, I could check my bids and check out the new stuff. I could bid on that squash blossom necklace I'd barely lived without for fifty-five years. But not until five the next day. I was not supposed to think or talk about eBay. If I made it through the initial abstinence period, I could continue to check in with eBay once a day and bid in a controlled fashion. Otherwise, I'd have to give it up forever. Yogic discipline is rough. But still ... it could have been worse.

It *was* worse, as it turned out.

Another teaching came in that meditation: Turn your difficulties into nectar. Not just lemons into lemonade—go all the way to nectar. Nectar, the elixir of life. Ambrosia. Sustenance. Turn your difficulties into something that nourishes, sustains, and delights you. Something delicious and irresistible.

Nectar would be a long time coming. I didn't hold out until that five o'clock deadline; I was back on-line long before then. And I didn't give up eBay.

As the hours I spent watching auctions consumed my days, I experienced the most intense agony. Although I've complained about the horrors of being unpublished, hanging out in my skin was pretty nice, before my addiction. Most of the time, I felt high energy and motivated, sometimes almost obscenely happy. Gratitude came unbidden. Appreciation for beauty rose like a flood. My writing roared from some deep inner well. My meditations were wonderful, like walking through a crack in reality into a marvelous world. A column of light would rise up my spine and I'd experience blissful visions, colors, and sounds. When I was with my family, I was really with them: present, heart and soul.

After I became addicted, the connection to that inner wellspring was broken. I could feel every loosening thread, every tearing of the fabric of my life. My soul, or some cheap resemblance of it, turned from living my life to needing to possess Native American silver jewelry. I learned fast, mastering the system. Rather than losing to snipers, people who bid in the last seconds of an auction, I became a sniper and the winner of pretty near whatever I wanted.

I could watch myself sit down at the computer, planning on just a little look-see. I'd get up hours later, bleary-eyed and intoxicated. I watched my awareness go from clear and alert to cloudy. The interaction between the buzz of the computer, the flickering lights, and the tantalizing images did something to me. The thrill of the chase and contemplation of victory produced a tangible change in my nervous system, mesmerizing me. I became a shopping machine, absolutely aware of what I was doing. I knew it was ruinous.

I tried to stop and couldn't: That's the definition of addiction.

I found myself in a buying haze, where budgetary constraints and our income did not apply. On-line credit cards and financing were available at a click. I clicked. Getting more and more stuff became the goal, not enjoying what I'd purchased. Where I'd normally give myself a budget of forty-five dollars for jewelry over three months, I was spending far more than that every week. I don't know how much I spent over the years this went on. I don't want to research my records and find out. I don't want to revisit that time, except to warn others.

I will talk about the *silver chicken*. A charming object came up for auction: an enchanting silver and turquoise bolo tie representing some kind of fowl, maybe a chicken. It was adorable, a delightful piece of Native American artistry. The seller confessed that he didn't usually deal in jewelry, but had found it at a sale. "I'm no expert, but looks like silver to me. The turquoise seems real. It's got markings on the back." A photo on the auction ad showed them: It had stamped markings of some sort, but nothing that said *sterling*, or 925, or an artist's name.

I had to have it. So did someone else. We got into a bidding war: I won, bidding many times what I intended. I was so sick of getting beaten, I would *have* that bolo tie, no matter what it cost me!

Only after winning did I read the auction ad again. "Looks like silver ... *seems* real ... " The markings on the back weren't for sterling—I knew that. I took a printout of the ad to a western store and talked to a salesperson. She scoffed: "Is that seller going to take it back if you don't like it? Do they guarantee their goods to be Native American?" Uh, no. The shop's sterling bolos were nothing like the charming chicken, not in manufacture or style. Some cast white metal jobs looked similar, but they were one-tenth what I'd promised to pay for the chicken. I also realized that I hate bolo ties. I'd never wear one, and neither would my husband. What had I done?

*Remember the silver chicken.*

My stomach churned as I faced the computer screen later that day. Damned if I was going to pay what I'd agreed, but an auction is a legally binding transaction. I contacted the seller and spelled out what had happened at the western store. "I know I made a mistake, but the bolos similar to yours are cast metal and cost a tenth of what I bid for yours."

I lucked out. The seller was very nice, reiterating that he knew nothing about jewelry. He let me pay a tenth of the auction price for the bolo. I didn't get out of the auction. He wrote, "Many sellers on eBay wouldn't let you out of your bid."

I have the *silver chicken* and will keep it forever to remind me of what can happen when lust takes over. Seeing it in the flesh, or metal feathers, revealed that its turquoise is plastic, and its silver probably is, too. The thing is uglier than you can imagine, and it's mine, all mine.

When I'd purchased so much jewelry that I couldn't justify any more, I switched categories. I'd see things that I didn't need, but vaguely wanted. Mohair blankets, for instance. The whole family got them one Christmas. East Indian statuary was another buying favorite for a while. Crosses— almost every room in our house sports a cross. I don't know what all else. I was into Persian rugs at the end—my purchases were escalating in price.

How did my husband and kids take all this? With more forbearance than I could muster if the roles had been reversed. Barry brought out the credit card bills and showed me the damage each month. I learned that when I pushed those buttons to charge an auction to my credit card, the amount actually ended up on our card. And we had to pay with real money.

My husband was upset with me, but he knew I had gone somewhere that he couldn't reach. He didn't pull a screaming fit, which is admirable, because it would have driven us farther apart and not stopped my buying.

What about my relationship with my kids?

In those days, my younger daughter and I walked together every evening. We laughed and talked over the day. We discussed what we had done and felt, talked about our horses. Her writing and mine. Our joined universes. We walked, as close as mother and child could be.

After I became addicted to eBay, my connection with the world around me dimmed. The glory of the hills faded. Massive shoulders of earth, blasted with oaks, sage, and tumbleweed became unreal. Fresh grasses waving as we passed seemed distant. My daughter, the horses, dogs. Life. Everything was removed from me.

One day, I realized that an invisible, unbreakable wall separated me from the world. I could look through the glass, smile, and pretend. I laughed with tinselly tones and vacuous brightness. An empty shell walked the hills.

My daughter could tell my joy at being with her was feigned. Something very powerful inside me wanted to fly back to the computer. To look at more jewelry. Place bids. Check my auctions. To run from her company to that of an electronic screen and my own greed.

I was enslaved. The universe that I had known existed on the other side of some wall created by my nervous system. I could not touch it. In place of the rapture that lived in my heart, I had a silly hysteria. An agitated desire. Something inside, not my deepest soul, something far baser, wanted to recoil into that computer just like a window shade retracts when you let go of the string.

I smiled at my daughter, partly there. I worked on my book, partly there. I was lost. And I knew it. Knowing what was happening and being unable to stop, I despaired.

I became a master of subterfuge, keeping a computer screen with my writing on it ready to click and cover the eBay screen if anyone walked into the room. "Don't worry, I'm just checking an auction," I'd say if they caught me. "It's all right. I'll be right off." In an hour. My family told me they were worried about me, and I sloughed off their concern. I downloaded notices that I'd won auctions and erased the emails, then got a separate email account so no one would know what I was doing.

How could they not know? Every time the mailman arrived it was Christmas. The box was jammed with presents I'd bought myself. The mailman and my husband joked darkly: His wife had a habit, too.

<hr />

You may say, "You've done all this spiritual practice and written this book about how to keep from being run over by the world. How could you become an addict? How can you admit it?"

Anyone can become an addict. I think that becoming addicted is an area where human beings excel. We have the traditional addictions to substances—drugs and alcohol. Everyone knows about those. Now, we've got the new, behavioral addictions: gambling, work, sex, relationships and love, spending, shopping (not the same as spending), codependency, compulsive overeating, compulsive achievement, anorexia, bulimia. The list of things professionals know we can get addicted to keeps growing.

The on-line addictions are relatively new. When therapists first began seeing clients with on-line addictions, the presenting problems were work- and relationship-related; these were masks for the real problem, which was spending hours on the computer plucking away at some addiction. Theorists currently are studying and defining on-line addictions as primary illnesses.

Why should I become addicted? Because that's what human beings do, and my personality is perfect for on-line addiction. I'm obsessive, which is great if I want to finish a book or get a job done, not so great if I'm looking at a list of five hundred necklaces and won't stop until I've seen every one. I don't stop when that mesmerizing buzz occurs, as my brain and the computer interact. Throw in a competitive situation (an auction) with someone from Silicon Valley, land of compulsive achievement, and a cultural tradition of mistaking things for love: I was an auction addiction waiting to happen.

If I'd known about the possibility, would I have avoided the problem? Don't know. I was attacked by one of those inner gremlins that we don't know exist until they've eaten us. If other people with a potential for the problem read this and avoid what happened to me, then we'll know information can produce change. Alas, history shows the human species hasn't demonstrated much ability in learning from others.

As a spiritual person, how could this happen to me? I smile. Years ago, I was on the Board of Directors of my church. People used to come to me with questions after Sunday services. A very good church member was having a terrible time. Legal troubles, relationship troubles, you name it. "Why is this happening to me, Sandy? I tithe, I study, and I work hard. I believe. Why should these things happen to me?"

"Why not? Do you think being spiritual makes you immune? You think you get a free pass because you love God?" I wasn't quite so obnoxious, but that's it. We have time bombs lurking within us that don't manifest, until they do. Living is like swimming in the ocean: some of the denizens will eat you alive.

Good people become addicts. I've talked to a few:

"I never thought it would happen to me." Sleek and stylish, her expensive good looks said she was a professional. "We live an active life. There's always a party or reception. We both work hard: There's lots of stress. We entertain. It was just wine, I didn't see how it could hurt me. I didn't know how much I was drinking. My family had an *intervention* … I was so ashamed. I tried to quit and couldn't. I had to go to a recovery center to quit." Tears filled her eyes. She hadn't realized that the active ingredient in the wine she loved was an addictive drug.

Nice people become addicted. People in pain use substances and behaviors to self-medicate, producing problems they didn't see coming. When I look at the homeless people down on lower State Street in Santa Barbara, I think, those were *nice* people, too, once. Some of them are mentally ill, a segment of the population we try to ignore. Some are drug addicts and alcoholics. Who knows how they got that way?

# CHAPTER 5

# FREE AT LAST

*The first step in combating addiction is understanding its processes.*

—SANDY NATHAN

THIS IS WHERE WE *GET DOWN*—and tackle addiction. The previous chapter illuminated my experience with on-line auction addiction. While this may have been engrossing reading, it may not have done anything to free you of your addiction(s) or make you the person you came here to be.

You don't have any addictions? Well, bless your heart! Isn't that nice.

Are you sure you're being completely honest? If it's not a full-fledged, couldn't-stop-if-I-tried-and-I-already-have-tried addiction, do you have little *tendencies* that might benefit from pruning? That little shopping itch you scratch a bit too often, perhaps? This is the place to turn the tables on the beast.

How can I write this if I've just confessed my auction obsession? I beat my addiction, that's why. I haven't been on eBay or any other on-line auction since September 2003. If I did it, so can you. A plan follows.

You may want to get your journal out as you read about what I did. If you have an addiction, some word or phrase may stand out for you and be useful. Jot that down and write about it later; see where your mind leads you. If you aren't battling an addiction, you may want to try the following tips on other troublesome areas of your life. Modify my techniques to suit yourself, or do something entirely different. The important part is getting free.

Practically from my first log-on to eBay, I knew I was in trouble. I didn't know how much trouble until I tried to stop. Breaking the bonds that kept me bidding took everything I had spiritually, psychologically, and mentally. It also took a couple of years.

I had the luxury of taking as long as I did to break free because I managed my habit so that I didn't blow my marriage or finances. If your problem is more severe, don't fool around. Get into a twelve-step program, seek professional assistance, or get medical care immediately. The material I present doesn't substitute for professional treatment.

*Don't fool around if you've got a severe habit: Get help now.*

How does a writer approach addiction? By writing. One of the things I did when the auction bug bit was begin a series of articles about eBay on my 'zine, *Spurs Magazine*. Entitled *An Ode to eBay*, the series eventually consisted of nine articles covering buying, selling, economics of auctions, addiction issues, financial recovery, and recovery resources. Producing the series was "writing therapy" for me, and it's paid off. The first article on buying, "Buying on eBay 1: Negotiation Theory & Handling Sniping," has become one of the Net's top sites on eBay buying strategies. The article on Addiction Issues is also ranked number one by many search engines. As a whole, the series gets many times more hits than anything else on *Spurs Magazine*. In addition to giving me a way to capture and express my insights, *An Ode to eBay* gave me great data.

For instance, the articles on buying get more than ten times the number of hits as those devoted to kicking addiction. Does this mean eBay addiction is rare? Or that people would rather learn how to win than address their auction-related problems? Or does it mean that my buying articles are so effective—they're directed toward buying in a non-addictive manner—that people don't need the material related to kicking? Who knows? My statistics seem to indicate that reading about buying is far more popular than reading about kicking.

Since posting the articles on eBay addiction, I've had other feedback. People have emailed me saying things like: "I'm leaving my husband/wife. Our credit cards are maxed out. We're in so much debt; I don't know how we'll ever get out. I can't walk through the house for all the junk. All he/she does is sit in front of that computer. I'm so lonely I could cry. We never talk anymore. Whenever we go anywhere, he/she has to check his/her auctions."

If any of these words apply to you, you have a problem and need help.

I need to emphasize something else. Do I consider eBay at fault or to blame for what happened to me? No, not in any way. eBay didn't make me do any of the stuff I've described: I did it. The only reason I'm talking about "eBay addiction" is that eBay is the largest on-line auction by a long, long shot and is the one that I preferred. I'm sure I could have gotten addicted to any on-line auction just as easily.

Rather than casting blame on or disparaging the corporation, I must say that eBay is a superbly effective organization that has created a revolution in consumer economics. It has produced highly efficient markets for some goods and has contributed to the welfare of its buyers and sellers, not to mention its stockholders. My contacts with eBay personnel—which happened when I was attempting to resolve problems with people from whom I'd bought—were exemplary in terms of "people handling" and effectiveness. eBay is a true cultural and economic phenomenon deserving of praise.

Unfortunately, the combination of stimuli it represents are dangerous to some people. Equally unfortunately, I'm one of them.

What's the real reason to break free of addiction? It's not fun. Addicts are not having fun. The addict may get a temporary high after shooting up or winning an auction, but the joy is illusory and followed by pain.

*Addiction is not fun.*

Addiction is synonymous with bondage; the addict is not free. Addiction is the antithesis of our essential state, freedom. It will gall us as long as we're enchained.

I've said anyone can become addicted, even spiritual people. The essence of spirit is bliss and freedom. In my experience, a life devoted to spirit delivers the greatest joy and absolute freedom. So how can a spiritual person be addicted?

With enormous pain, just like anyone else.

The good part about being a spiritual person with an addiction is that: (1) you will know you are not free and that feeling better is possible, and (2) your spiritual practice will provide you with tools to break free, if you choose to use them. Addiction motivates you to *real* living spiritual practice!

In beating my addiction, I used everything I know, including material from psychology, twelve-step programs, yogic self-examination,

*Conscious awareness empowers the soul.*

and even economics. In the beginning, the most important practice was detached self-observation, or the Witness state. This was also the *only* practice I could use in the beginning: All I could do was observe my behavior, thoughts, and feelings as I bid away, out of control.

The Addict was one of the first entities my interior observation revealed. If you are familiar with recovery programs or terminology, you will have heard of the Addict. It is the part of the personality embodying the addiction. It seems like a separate person inside you. I think the phenomenon is biological: Addiction strikes at the cellular/chemical level. Since we're human, we experience the chemical reaction as a part of our personality, as a separate voice and will. A very powerful will.

The Addict is like the monster at the bottom of the murky lake in a horror movie. You know the scenario: The hero and heroine are walking peacefully through the woods, when everything turns dark and sinister. They're standing by a scummy lake when a monster leaps out, huge and overpowering. It grabs the heroine and careens down the road, swinging her by the feet to clear its path, while the hero runs hopelessly alongside. That's how the internal Addict feels, except you're the hero and heroine. And the Addict. And you feel just as much the put-upon innocents as the couple in the movie did.

For me, mastering addiction was a matter of refining my observation and drawing detailed portraits of what I saw.

## WHAT DOES ADDICTION DO?

1. Addiction separates the soul from the source of its being, from itself, from other people and things.
2. Addiction replaces reality with a glittering false world. Addiction promises satisfaction, but cannot deliver it.
3. After separating the soul from reality, addiction tries to kill it.
4. To become free, the soul or "core of being" has to become stronger than the addict.
5. The first step in combating addiction is seeing it and understanding its processes.

## STEPS TO FREEDOM

My process of recovery was like being on a teeter-totter: At first, the Addict was heavier and more powerful than I was. My end of the teeter-totter flew into the air. My feet dangled and I railed against my enemy, without enough weight to put myself back on the ground.

As I observed and gathered information and tools, I took on more power. The teeter-totter became more evenly balanced. As I observed and had insights, my behavior didn't change; it seemed like nothing was happening. Then—wham! A quantum jump would occur and I'd be in control. That demon found itself dangling off the ground, powerless.

## STEP 1.   OBSERVATION AND THE WITNESS

One of the most basic spiritual practices is self-observation. Being spiritually aware means that you can view the world with a detached, non-judgmental gaze. That neutral gaze must take in both the outer world and your inner world. In the witness state, you observe everything that happens inside you. Years of meditation and yogic observation stayed with me throughout my bidding craze. I couldn't stop what I was doing, but I could watch it.

## STEP 2.   GETTING TO KNOW THE ADDICT

Earlier in this book, I talked about our various inner voices; we all have parts, subdivisions of our personalities. In graduate school, I studied deep complexes and drives, but had never felt the power of one of them until I experienced my Addict. Observation of my thoughts and behavior yielded an anatomy of the Addict.

- **The Addict hides.** The Addict wants to pretend everything is fine and there's no problem. This is an enormously powerful defense mechanism. *Denial* is the primary symptom of addiction. The Addict doesn't know it has a problem.

- **The Addict blames and assigns fault to others.** I wanted to whine, "It's all eBay's fault. They should warn people." Perhaps, but eBay didn't make me buy all that stuff. Shifting responsibility for one's behavior onto others is a characteristic of addiction.

- **The Addict is intoxicated.** The Addict lives in a drunken world. The drunkenness might come from drugs or alcohol, or from indulging a behavior. To see this with on-line auctions, log on to any auction site and look at anyone's feedback. Most read like this: "Ralph, you're the greatest! The best on eBay! A+++++++ transaction. WILL BUY AGAIN!!!!!!" What these words mean is: "I got my *silver chicken* (that wondrous object I had to have) on time and in one piece. Ralph was polite during the transaction." The over-the-top verbiage is *auction high*.

- **The Addict is uncontrolled.** The Addict goes for the high compulsively and impulsively. The Addict can't stop, nor does he or she want to stop. The First Step of all the twelve-step programs boils down to: "We admitted we were powerless over our addiction—that our lives had become unmanageable." The First Step is the biggest and the hardest.

## STEP 3. NOTHING IS WASTED IN SPIRITUAL LIFE

On the spiritual path, everything you've done counts. Every experience gives you tools needed for success. In my first career, I was a research economist. I have a bachelor's and a master's degree in economics. I was working on a Ph.D. when I realized that it was the wrong field for me.

Given what I've done the last few decades, that education may seem to be wasted effort. Not true. Economics gave me mental discipline. It also demanded a mathematical, statistical, and scientific rigor that is invaluable for spiritual study. A research economist must focus abstract theories on the real world. As an urban economist, I spent years sleuthing out patterns of urban development and devising ways to measure things like urban sprawl.

I studied the problem of on-line addiction like the trained researcher I am. I read everything the experts said about on-line addiction. When I wrote the eBay series on *Spurs Magazine*, I read all the books listed in its bibliography. The books took the edge off the Addict by giving me facts and techniques, but they didn't stop the addiction. I had to get the right me back on top.

In the same way that nothing is wasted in spiritual life, sometimes it's hard to tell if a particular character trait is a flaw or an asset. I'm a cheapskate: I'm always trying to get a bargain, and I don't spend any more than I must for anything. My *cheapness* was an asset in my auction addiction, helping to control my buying. I realize that I sound like I went hog wild with my buying. I did and I didn't. I bought a lot of stuff and I spent a lot of time watching auctions and looking at things, but I never went for the really expensive items. I kept the total amount I spent to a semi-affordable level because I pride myself on frugality. Or cheapness. This was also one of the attractive traps of the auction: eBay has the best deals anywhere, but a good deal on something you don't need is a bad deal.

> *A good deal on something you don't need is a bad deal.*

## STEP 4. WHAT WAS I REALLY BIDDING ON?

Asking this question was a quantum leap. One day, I noticed what I was bidding on. That may seem obvious, but it isn't. When a friend told me her husband only purchased electronic stuff on eBay, something inside me clicked. At that time, I mostly bought Native American jewelry. Why? Why didn't I buy computer stuff, or Marilyn Monroe memorabilia? Obviously, the things I bid on had emotional meaning to me. What was I trying to buy?

I remembered exercises I'd done in graduate school in counseling. What was behind my fascination with turquoise jewelry?

To find out, I sat myself down and relaxed, drifting into meditation. I recalled the image of an antique squash blossom necklace I wanted desperately. The necklace hovered before my mind's eye, an exquisite piece of Navajo workmanship. I kept my focus on it, exposing it to the lens of my soul. Why did I want it so badly? What did it symbolize?

As I watched my inner "screen," an imaginary scene flamed behind the image of the necklace. The scene was so real it was as though I were in it. In a southwest desert landscape, a traditional Navajo family worked around their hogan, living a life of great simplicity. They were tranquil, peaceful, and idyllic; the exact opposite of my harried, computer-bound, performance-obsessed existence.

That's what I wanted when I bought American Indian jewelry: tranquility. Peace. I wanted nirvana. I wanted a break.

I repeated this exercise for the other types of things I'd bought and my favorite ways of wasting time on-line. What was I trying to buy when I went for mohair blankets? That was easy: fuzzy warmth. Cuddles. How about East Indian statues and crosses? The peace of God. How about Persian rugs? Their ornate patterns and brilliant colors satisfied my aesthetic needs. One of my favorite non-eBay on-line pastimes was looking at pictures of dogs on animal shelter web sites: What's more loving and warm than a cuddly dog?

What I needed was not all the stuff I was buying, I needed more comfort and ease in my life. My auction addiction was a misguided attempt to buy *stuff* to satisfy needs that weren't material. I would *never* get what I needed on eBay or through any other retail outlet.

I knew this, but couldn't break the Addict's hold. The insight percolated inside. That Navajo family remained in my mind as if they were whispering to me, "You need simplicity. Rest. Serenity."

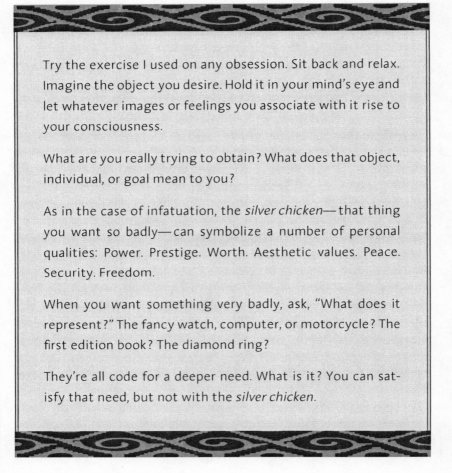

Try the exercise I used on any obsession. Sit back and relax. Imagine the object you desire. Hold it in your mind's eye and let whatever images or feelings you associate with it rise to your consciousness.

What are you really trying to obtain? What does that object, individual, or goal mean to you?

As in the case of infatuation, the *silver chicken*—that thing you want so badly—can symbolize a number of personal qualities: Power. Prestige. Worth. Aesthetic values. Peace. Security. Freedom.

When you want something very badly, ask, "What does it represent?" The fancy watch, computer, or motorcycle? The first edition book? The diamond ring?

They're all code for a deeper need. What is it? You can satisfy that need, but not with the *silver chicken*.

## STEP 5. GET HELP

About this time, I realized that my do-it-yourself approach to recovery wasn't working. I consulted a financial recovery expert and looked up the local Gamblers Anonymous and Debtors Anonymous numbers—but didn't follow through. Had the problem lasted much longer, I would have committed to one of these programs. Something else happened that cracked me open.

## STEP 6. AT THE RIGHT TIME, DELUSION CAN BE PIERCED

Even though I'd had a bunch of insights, I'd still find myself drifting to the computer and logging on to eBay, even when I didn't want to, even when I'd resolved to quit. I felt hopeless and like nothing was happening. Nevertheless, conscious awareness empowers the soul. Portions of the psyche outside our awareness are activated, insights build up, and when the time comes, change can happen quickly.

*At the right time a few words, a gesture, a thought can pierce delusion.*

Even a small stimulus may trigger a big change. Mine came when a man I admire greatly, a mentor/father figure, said, "It's a *tragedy.*" He was speaking about me. "Your being on eBay the way you are is a *tragedy.*" His face and tone said more than his words; my involvement appalled him. I was applying my talents to something far below my capabilities; I was wasting my life.

Those words broke the Addict's back.

How? I felt a shock of recognition: I had said those exact words, with the same tone, about someone who was an obviously out-of-control addict. The other person's tragedy was clearly apparent.

When that man I regarded so highly said those words about *me*, it shocked me to the core, breaking through my denial. I already knew that I had a problem, but someone else seeing it made it a *real* problem.

That was the beginning of my real recovery. I erased all my auctions and bookmarks and quit eBay for the first time—but I had won only the battle, not the war.

## STEP 7. GOD DOESN'T TAKE A POWDER

Have you ever prayed desperately, only to get no response? Despite appearances God hasn't deserted you, but simply isn't visible. In India, this is called the power of concealment, one of five divine powers. I don't like this power very much. I wish God had blown up the computer right after I saw Bill Miller's painting. But that didn't happen, so I got to write this chapter instead.

All my spiritual work, the power of grace, and God were there all along. I had kept up with my spiritual practice as well as I could, making gifts to my favorite organizations right on time and continuing to go on retreat several times a year. I tried to meditate. That one got clobbered. But what I did was enough.

*Spirit is working, even if nothing seems to be happening.*

I'd go on a spiritual retreat, and stay off eBay for a while when I got back. Slip back. Go on retreat. Quit, slip back. Over and over. I finally realized that I can't go near eBay at all. I had to totally abstain.

## STEP 8. FREE AT LAST

How did I kick completely? I went on a spiritual retreat. Later in this book, I write at length about a Native American retreat called the Gathering. I haven't been on eBay since attending that retreat in 2003. My experience at the Gathering was very powerful. While I was there, I didn't consciously work on my addiction at all. Discovering it was gone when I got home was an unexpected benefit.

*A powerful spiritual experience can knock out addiction. If you have such an experience, regard it as a gift and a blessing. Don't waste it!*

A retreat can work miracles. When you go on a retreat, you are out of your usual environment. No phones, no Net access, no computers. That's part of the reason a retreat works: Behaviorally, you're cut off from your usual sources of gratification, allowing you to feel the full extent of an addiction. This cutting the ties is so effective that some retreat centers are called "rehabilitation or recovery centers." The latter provide a slightly different type of retreat, but a very effective one.

The best recovery or retreat centers are places that allow something else to enter, namely spirit. A retreat is spirit's playground. It's the place where addiction is unplugged, the Addict yanked out of power, and the true Self installed where it belongs in the personality: in control, but subordinate to the experience of the Divine.

That's what happened to me. The Gathering came when I was open to spiritual change. My soul leapt forth in the vacuum. Spirit took control and that was it.

I *can't* log on to eBay now: Something inside catapults me off the computer, usually into a different part of the house, or outside. I *can't* go back.

I'm very aware that my recovery will last as long as I abstain. If I logged back on, I'd be back where I was in hours. How long would Spirit let me dangle before intervening again? What would I lose? *Would* Spirit intervene again?

## BENEFITS AND COSTS: A USEFUL CALCULATION

Okay, the addiction is mastered. How about a post-game analysis? A bit of cleaning up and adding up? Cost/benefit analysis is one of the many wonderful tools economists possess. Cost/benefit analyses are typically commissioned by governments to determine whether a development project should be funded, or to pick the most socially advantageous project if more than one are being considered.

Concepts from cost/benefit analysis provide a way of evaluating an outcome that provides useful insights. This can be used to keep the Addict away. In the case of my problem with auctions, cost/benefit analysis asks: What benefits did my auction activity bring? What did it cost? What else could I have done with the time and money? Are the benefits greater than the costs? How much greater? Enough to clearly support continuing the activity? That's the bottom line cost/benefit analysis produces.

This reckoning is a great spiritual practice.

I'll run through my costs and benefits and let you do the same for a troublesome area of your behavior.

## COSTS: WHAT MY ADDICTION COST ME

1. **Financial Cost:** I'm not sure exactly how much I spent on auctions. Enough money to publish this book very nicely. Enough for the vacation I need so badly. I'm letting myself off the hook here: To be thorough, I should go back through my records and calculate the exact monetary cost.

2. **Emotional Cost:** My addiction created tension and distance from my kids and husband. In a pure cost/benefit analysis, the economist renders non-financial costs such as emotional, aesthetic, and environmental costs into dollar amounts, which are then compared to the similarly constructed dollar amounts associated with benefits. Non-financial costs are hard to put in terms of money, which is one reason that cost/benefit analysis is a flawed analytical tool. Vitally important factors, such as environmental costs, can't be turned into rigorous monetary terms. (For example, one can attempt to put a dollar figure on the environmental cost of removing all the oak trees in California, but this is an intellectually constructed amount, not real money. Few will pay attention to such a construct. Real money talks.) So, how do I measure the cost of the sadness in my daughter's eyes as I truncated our daily walks to run back to my computer? How do I measure my husband's frustration and hopelessness as he showed me what I'd charged month after

month, only to have me continue to spend? It's impossible to render personal distress into monetary terms, but it was as real as the packages that came in the mail.

3. **Professional Cost:** The novel I was working on was finished a year later than it might have been. I wasted time and talent that could be put to more productive and profitable use. Monetary cost of this? Like the emotional cost I imposed on my family, this is unknown, though certainly significant. Another term from economics is *opportunity cost*. The opportunity cost of a course of action is what you lose when you take it. What you could have gained from putting the time and resources into another avenue. Something to remember always: Every time you make a choice you lose the fruit of everything else you could have done with your resources. That's opportunity cost.

4. **Personal Cost:** I lost my soul, temporarily. Writers write from their depths. My deepest heart was waylaid and an imposter took over. Whatever I did write in that period was not as profound or true as it might have been, including the eBay series on the Net. That was funny, but incomplete. My pain doesn't show: This experience *hurt*.

So I end my cost calculation, the first half of our cost/benefit analysis. The technique provides a useful way of thinking about things, and it also demonstrates its inherent weakness. An analyst cannot reduce complicated issues that impact human beings and the world into monetary terms. Economists try to do this with such rigor: When I was an economist I felt deification of mathematics was almost an illness. The most abstract mathematical constructs were most praised, despite the fact that they assumed away the real world on the first page.

*Opportunity cost: Every time you make a choice you lose.*

I'm interested in the real world; I'm interested in modeling—drawing pictures of—the real world as clearly and with as much impact as possible. I left economics in part because I felt that art and literature do a more accurate job of describing reality than do mathematical models. Some of the models I studied were so difficult that perhaps only one-tenth of one percent of humanity could understand them. Yet who can fail to understand the cost of the Iranian revolution described by Azar Nafisi in her *Reading Lolita in Tehran*? No set of equations could convey the devastation of a world the way Nafisi does with simple words.

Are we therefore excused from continuing our look at costs and benefits? Oh, no. An imprecise, but logical, examination yields fruit, too.

## BENEFITS: WHAT MY ADDICTION GAVE ME

That an auction can yield benefits beyond the goodies won seems paradoxical. This is just one of those little anomalies of spiritual growth.

1. **Fear:** Fear is good. We should be terrified of some things, addiction especially. I had no idea my Addict existed, yet there it was, totally careless of the welfare of others and myself. We all contain such parts. In the sixteenth chapter of the *Bhagavad Gita*, Lord Krishna sets out the demonic qualities that humans can and do exhibit. He warns us to be vigilant lest these take control. All the religious systems that I know warn of what can happen if our inner evil is unleashed. Fear of our inner demons is very useful.

2. **Respect and Compassion:** I now have much greater compassion for people who suffer from addictions, and far greater admiration for those who are actively working on recovery. I had no idea how hard that process is.

3. **Experiencing My Own Lust:** We often think of lust in sexual terms, but that hardly touches lust's possible attachments. When I was actively addicted, I experienced what might be termed the "seat of lust" in myself. I *was* my desire, my want, my lust. Realizing this punctured my inflated opinion of myself. For instance, I'm concerned about the environment. We have a number of forces operating in the rural valley where I live that could degrade our environment. Some people have cut down two- and three-hundred-year-old oak trees to make their rows of wine grapes straight, for instance. Straight rows are easier to cultivate and yield more grapes. Before experiencing my own lust, I saw the vintners who cut the trees—or wanted to cut them—as monsters. In another area, certain people want to circumvent local and county ordinances and create massive development in areas currently zoned as cow pastures. I saw these people as greedy thugs. Now, I see them as human beings possessed by lust, just as I was.

4. **Essentially, We're Not So Different:** The people I noted above demonstrate what can happen if a mind or will is allowed to run rampant. Swami Muktananda, my first meditation teacher, taught that everyone is the same: No sect, race, sex, or other division of humanity is better than another. We all contain the same parts. It's what we do with the parts that matters.

5. **Lots of Native American Jewelry & Other Stuff:** As a result of my auction participation, I've got drawers of lovely jewelry and other great things. I have squash blossom necklaces in every color stone. Jewelry I've not worn since sniping it away from someone else.

6. **Nectar:** As I finish this chapter, something wells up inside: nectar. In that early-morning meditation years before, I had been told to turn my addiction into something that isn't just

sweetened bitterness, but flowing bliss. I was told to transform it into sustenance for others and myself. The nectar's back inside me. When you have a problem, if you work it all the way through to the end, it yields its fruit. Bliss and power. Which will last as long as you abstain from the addiction.

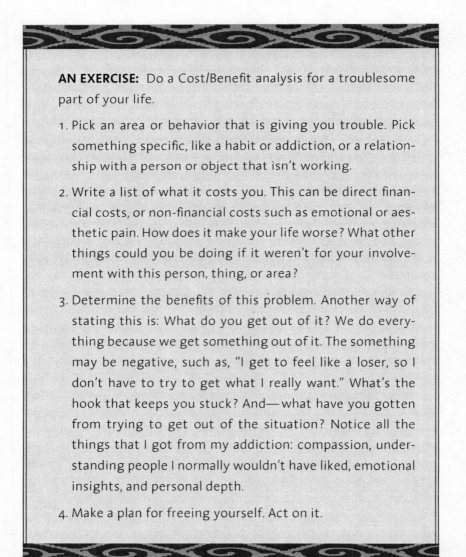

**AN EXERCISE:** Do a Cost/Benefit analysis for a troublesome part of your life.

1. Pick an area or behavior that is giving you trouble. Pick something specific, like a habit or addiction, or a relationship with a person or object that isn't working.

2. Write a list of what it costs you. This can be direct financial costs, or non-financial costs such as emotional or aesthetic pain. How does it make your life worse? What other things could you be doing if it weren't for your involvement with this person, thing, or area?

3. Determine the benefits of this problem. Another way of stating this is: What do you get out of it? We do everything because we get something out of it. The something may be negative, such as, "I get to feel like a loser, so I don't have to try to get what I really want." What's the hook that keeps you stuck? And—what have you gotten from trying to get out of the situation? Notice all the things that I got from my addiction: compassion, understanding people I normally wouldn't have liked, emotional insights, and personal depth.

4. Make a plan for freeing yourself. Act on it.

# TIPS FOR CONSCIENTIOUS AUCTION PARTICIPATION

## LEARN AND APPLY THE PRINCIPLES OF FINANCIAL SOBRIETY

If you choose to participate in on-line auctions, here are some guidelines to keep your bidding healthy and constructive. You may find the principles useful in other spending-related personal challenges.

1. **You do not need the silver chicken.** You do not need that wondrous object that has captivated you. If you can get something in an on-line auction, you can live without it. Also—a better and probably cheaper one will come up later. Letting go of your object of lust is a valuable spiritual practice. Personal growth occurs when you realize that the universe has registered your desire for the silver chicken and will provide it when the time is right. Or give you something better that you actually need.

2. **Set a maximum amount you will pay for your desired object.** Do not exceed this, no matter what. Losing what you want because it's outside your budget is a powerful spiritual practice. This curbs/controls greed. Think of what the world could be like if greed were controlled. When you give up that thing you must have, you are actually doing something good for the universe.

3. **Set a total budget for your auction expenditures per month (or week).** Do not exceed it. Figure out your allowable disposable auction funds by attending to your personal finances. Add up the total number of auctions you're in. Determine the total amount you'd have to pay if you got everything you've bid on. If this equals the national debt, you're in trouble. The total amount should be within your monthly auction budget. These are the principles of financial sobriety.

4. **Money you charge is real money.** Many sellers accept credit cards or have neat on-line services that will charge your card and give them the money. Of course they do. Sellers would be dumb not to. But—if you use credit—you'll still have to pay for the item. Just tomorrow, not now. Can you afford it?

5. **You can get some real bargains on the Net—if you've done your homework.** Know what you really want and need; don't get hooked on a whim or infatuation. Know what the item costs in stores, and what quality is being auctioned. If it's a real deal, go for it—within your budget.

6. **If you get burned.** I talked to a man who stopped buying on eBay because the quality of the items he purchased wasn't what it appeared to be in the picture. If this happens, eBay offers recourse, chiefly filing a negative report on a seller if you can't work it out with him/her. If you have put the item on a credit card, you can also protest via the card. Many sellers offer money back guarantees to buyers. Patronize these sellers.

7. **Is this how you want to spend your money?** How do you want to spend your hard-earned money? Do your budgeting and post the monthly "blow on auctions" figure on your computer. Put pictures of your kids around your computer, so you can look at them as you bid: Joey's shoes vs. the gold-plated weed whacker. Sally's orthodontist vs. the hula skirt worn by Elvis's co-star in *Blue Hawaii*. Jill's college vs. "Assorted Memorabilia." Which is more important? Not only that—is the auction important at all?

8. **What does the world get from you spending your money on the silver chicken?** How about if you gave your money to a worthy cause? One that would effectively spend it to save lives and make the world a better place? Put a picture of your favorite saint or a religious symbol by the screen with the kids

and your budgeted amount. Seeing the sacred, can you bid at all? Don't you really want to spend more on charity?

## DOES YOUR SPENDING SUPPORT YOUR SPIRITUAL GOALS?

# WHO ARE YOU?

## THE HOOP DANCER

weaves an illusion.

# CHAPTER 6

# YOU'RE NOT WHO YOU THINK YOU ARE

THE DOORBELL STARTLES ME—I've lost track of the time. I met you when I was speaking at a conference a few days ago. You wanted to come over and talk about—things worth talking about: Why we're here; who we are. How we get lost; how we find ourselves. I told you I didn't have much time, but you said you'd be grateful for whatever time I had. Who could turn away such a seeker? I open the door.

"Come in. I'm in the middle of packing. Let's talk in my room while I finish." I don't usually bring visitors up, but I've got to get going. Through the open doorway, I notice the swaying treetops. Leaves cartwheel along the walk, driven by the wind. "The weather's changing. Can you feel it? Something's brewing." We climb the stairs.

"Sit here." Pointing at a fat chair, I smile at your expression as you look around the room. "I write over there." The alcove behind your chair is jammed with overstuffed chairs, chests, and tables. Disheveled manuscripts spill over them. A baker's rack holds the computer. Binders bearing unborn novels huddle in the corners. The clutter does not flummox you. Rather, it's the crosses, feathers, hunks of amethyst and crystal, and statues from India that assault your reality. You've wandered into a disordered, foreign opulence.

"Some people go into culture shock," I remark, pointing to the folding screen behind you. Its panels are filled with photos of people. You stare at white-bearded figures in beads and loincloths. "Saints from India. Don't worry about them."

Your jaw drops as you survey the rest of the room. Sequined and mirrored, the bedspread and wall hangings twinkle. Paintings of blue men with cobras or flutes look down from the walls. Statues of sensuous deities recline on chests. Candles and incense, crystal lamps, hanging jewels. Books everywhere. Clothes spill out of a suitcase.

You feel a little drunk. I hasten to explain: "I meditate in here. You're feeling meditation energy; you'll get used to it. Let's see, you wanted to talk about how a person can lose his true self, and what to do if that happens." You nod too quickly, looking for a way to escape.

I smile. "It's easy. Have you ever been in love?" I take your blush to mean yes. "You got knocked over by it, right? Whoever you usually were disappeared, and your 'I'm in love' self took over. How long did it last?"

"Six months."

"That's about right. Then you noticed her flaws and the glow deserted you. What I want to say is: Not only was your in-love self not the real you, neither is your regular self."

"What do you mean?"

"You aren't who you think you are. No one is. We're phonies."

"*What?*"

"We wander through life playing roles, wearing masks to fit the occasion. Only a few of us get wise enough to realize we aren't our masks."

"All the world's a stage ... and we're just players playing our parts. Or something."

"Yes. Shakespeare said it perfectly." I look at you appraisingly. You've retreated from what I'm saying into gawking at the statues and photos—

Buddhist, Hindu, and Christian. Native American totems, a fan and rattle. A carved buffalo. You seem more disturbed. "It's how I'm made," I explain. "I've always seen more than one side. Now, let's get back to ... "

"If you're going to try to convert me to any of this ... forget it. I have my own religion ... "

"I don't want to influence your beliefs or traditions in any way. I do want to share a theory with you. When I was in graduate school, I found a theory that explained experiences that I'd had for many years. It forms a model that all religions can fit in, without being a religion itself." I pull books off the top of a chest, tossing them on the bed. *The Tibetan Book of Living and Dying; Living Buddha, Living Christ. Play of Consciousness. Interior Castle.* "The concepts and experiences in these books fit within the theory's framework, but they're still Buddhist, Hindu, and Christian." You're poised to flee.

I look around, trying to find a way to make it clear. "A personality theory is like that closet." We can see the clothes and other items hanging through the open door. "It has special compartments to store different things. The closet's structure is fixed, but you can put *anything* into it.

"A model of personality is like that: a structured container. You put your memories, personal problems, hang-ups, goals, and strengths inside. The model organizes the data in it, but doesn't influence it. When you find a theory that makes sense of your life, it's a powerful experience. Knowledge is power.

"The theory I'm going to talk about gives you a place to hang your religion's words and ideas without changing them. Everything has a place." I point to the books on the bed, pulling in a breath so I can say more.

You have other ideas: "I thought we were going to talk about people getting lost. What is all this *closet* stuff?"

"Hang on a moment. We talked about how being in love can knock you off center. Can you think of any other times that you've acted like a different person?" You shake your head. "Try this: Imagine yourself sitting in your living room, alone, just hanging out. Close your eyes and see yourself sitting there, doing whatever you do when you're by yourself. Close your eyes, it's okay." You close your eyes reluctantly. "Spend some time with this: Really imagine it. How do you look and act? How do you feel? Notice what you're wearing, and how you sit. You're just chilling out. Now throw in your wife. You're married, aren't you?" A nod. "That's different, right?" A vigorous nod. "How do you sit and act now? Are you as relaxed? Do you fart? Or belch?" Your eyes pop open. I smile. "Notice what you *don't* do when your wife's there.

"Okay. Lift the two of you to your mother-in-law's house the first time you met her." You jerk. "That's very different than just the two of you, isn't it? Now imagine yourself at work, talking to your boss. You have a project due, and it's not done. What's that like? How do you speak? Stand?" Fear registers on your face. "Now, see yourself in your church, temple, or wherever you worship. You're talking to your rabbi, minister, or priest. How do you feel? Act? Dress? Think? Talk?

"Don't go into overwhelm. Open your eyes." You seem a little dizzy. We look at each other. "We have different *acts* for different places; we almost act like separate people. This is not DID, Dissociative Identity Disorder, which used to be called Multiple Personality Disorder. That is caused by trauma: DID is caused by having to endure unendurable terror and pain with no escape. Dinner with your mother-in-law isn't that bad." We laugh. Good, you're loosening up.

"The roles we play are our brain's shortcuts so we can make it through the day. 'Put on this suit at work, this one at Mom's, this one at *her* mom's', and so on. Imagine how much effort it would take if you had to reconstruct yourself everywhere you went. 'I'm at the doctor's. How do I act? I'm at work, how do I talk to my boss?' You'd never get anything done. These different selves are called 'subpersonalities' in psychosynthesis, the theory I want to share with you.

"Roberto Assagioli, the psychiatrist who created psychosynthesis, was a contemporary of Sigmund Freud. His personality model allows for spiritual experience and the higher reaches of human consciousness. Assagioli's description of the subpersonalities provides an explanation for what happens when the Addict takes control and how we feel when we're in love. And how the world works, if you look.

"Most people have no idea they're anything *but* the roles they put on. Their subpersonalities run the show. This happens naturally: Right from the start, everyone's better at some things than others. The subpersonality in charge of that activity becomes very strong. For example, what do you do for a living?"

"I'm a geek: a computer programmer." You swagger a little.

"A good one, I bet?" Another swagger and a nod. "Okay. I bet your computer geek subpersonality has gotten you a lot of goodies: a job, money. Friends. Maybe your wife?" A shy affirmation. "I expect that your geek would get pretty upset if computers were outlawed and anyone who used one was put in jail."

*"That would never happen!"*

"Right. It would never happen. Why are you upset?" You're ruffled, even as you deny it. "Your computer geek would scream bloody murder if it couldn't work, just like my writer would have a fit if I couldn't write. Any role can take over. You see it clearly in bodybuilders, glamour girls, intellectuals, artists, losers—a chronic loser can be as powerful a subpersonality as the guy who has to win. All of this denies the totality of the person. In yogic terms, it's called *false identification*: You're identifying your essence with what isn't the true you.

"None of the things we fight and die for—nationality, race, ethnicity, and sexual identity, even religion—is who we really are."

"What are you saying? I love my country. I'd die for it. I love my religion, too. I thought you weren't going to put down religion, but you're saying it's not real. I thought you believed in God! I came here for you to teach me about God, not this bullshit!" You're out of your chair, aimed at the door.

"Wait a minute! I never said any of that; you're distorting what I said. But you're right, I *don't* believe in God." I'm serious. You stop dead, appalled by what I've said. "Let me explain." I put my hand to my heart like I'm making a pledge—"To me, belief is: 'I *believe* despite the total lack of evidence that what I believe is real. I *believe* even though I've never had an experience of what I believe and don't know anyone who has. I believe because someone told me I had to believe or bad things would happen.' That's superstition. You *believe* in the Easter Bunny or Santa Claus. 'I believe' is very dangerous. People have been manipulated into doing horrible things by believing in abstract ideas." You're staring at me, puzzled and hostile. "Sit down, I'll tell you more. You believe in God I take it?"

You nod vigorously.

"Guess what—you can't prove that God exists ... "

"That's why you have to *believe!*"

"You can't prove that your *elbow* exists, either. Or your body. Or me, this room, or the world. You can't prove that *anything* exists, much less God. All you can ever know is the learned interpretation of electronic impulses fed to your brain by your sense organs. You're trapped in your nervous system and can never get out, not to experience God or anything else."

"That's bullshit!"

"Sit down. Listen to me. Okay, when I write, what happens?"

"You sit at that computer and type."

"Type what?"

"Words. Sentences. Books."

"What are those?"

"They're letters on a page."

"Yes. What are 'letters on a page'?"

"What are you talking about? You're making me crazy."

"Let me break it down for you. My writing reduces to a pattern of markings on a page that we call 'letters'. We've learned to make these into words, which are symbols our brains have constructed for concepts and actions. My writing is a bunch of squiggles interpreted in an agreed-upon way. That's all. Think of it this way:

"We know the world through our five senses: sight, touch, smell, hearing, and something else. I can't remember the last one—I'm getting old. Anyway, because we can only perceive reality through our senses, we can never know anything in itself. As it exists in itself: the nuomenon, to use Kant's terminology." You look more confused.

"Try and understand it this way: I'm sitting at my computer, typing. I hear the machine whine. Sound waves strike my eardrums and are zapped to my brain as a series of electrical impulses. They register on my brain cells in a pattern I call 'the noise the computer makes.' My fingers type: Same thing—nerve impressions on my fingertips run up my arm to my brain. They form a bunch of neurological imprints I call 'I'm typing.' My eyes see the screen, the room, and look out the window at that mare in the pasture. Same thing—light strikes my retina, is transformed into unbelievably complex series of nerve impulses that go to my brain, where something says, 'Computer screen, desk. Horse in pasture.' That's reality.

"Do I know that the computer, keyboard, or horse exist? Or even my own fingers? Or me, or you? No. I can never know if anything really exists because I am trapped inside my nervous system." I pull out some books by the neurologist Oliver Sacks. *Awakenings. An Anthropologist on Mars.* "The neurology of perception is astonishing. People create their realities with an incredibly complex learning process based on minute electronic impulses. That's all we can know.

"What does this mean about God? If I can't say my *fingers* exist, if I can never get to the thing in itself—the horse as she exists apart from the electronic data my brain uses to construct my experience of her—how can I say God exists? How can I ever experience God?"

You look stunned.

"That's right, you can't experience anything in itself. In philosophy, that's called the Kantian Dilemma ... A guy named Immanuel Kant wrote *A Prolegomena to Any Future Metaphysic* explaining all this. It was once on the Catholic Church's 'Read at your peril' list. If you really get what Kant said, it will shatter your reality."

We sit silently as you struggle.

"But I came here because you said something at that conference that sounded like the truth. I want to know the truth. I want to know God. I could feel God when you were talking. And now you say no one can know God, and that you don't believe ... " Tears glisten.

"You're a good student," I say softly. "I'll tell you what brought you to me. It's not my graduate degrees; it's not the jobs I've held. It's not my resumé and what awards I've won. What brought you here is what you feel when you're near me. I am the way I am because of my experiences of God. I don't want to *believe* in God; I want God coursing through my veins. I want to see blue and white patterns of electricity enveloping my body like lightning. I want to feel God's being surge up my spine. I want to feel the earth *as* my toes. Not under my toes, *as* my toes. I want to feel one with everything that exists, to the end of the universe. That's what my life is about." I pace, enflamed.

"I've had those experiences, and I want them to stay with me. I want them to embrace me; I want to walk along holding their hand like a child holds its parent's. God is not abstract to me, not something to *believe* in. God is real! God is as real as this room to me. As real as you. Or me. Realer," I laugh. "Maybe you're just a phantasm of my brain, but the love I feel inside, the visions: those are real, and I don't care what any scientist or philosopher says."

"You just said that we can't know anything, even God."

"So what? Does that change how I live my life? I still experience what I do. The hell with science and philosophy. It's my brain—I can call my experience whatever I want."

"Then you *do* believe?"

"No, I *experience*. I *know*. The transcendent state doesn't stay with me all the time, but it's there sometimes." I lean toward you. "I started having mystical experiences when I was tiny. I didn't know what they were until I could put words to them. When I got older, I had experiences of Jesus once in a while, mostly when I wanted to kill myself. He saved me many times. Jesus is as real to me as this." I slap my hand on the bureau, making a resounding smack. You jump. "That's the basis of religion for me: That God is realer than the physical world, not some concept someone talks about.

"But that wasn't the end of it. Jesus came, and then the others," I wave at the pictures and statues around the room. "The rest became real to me as I studied them." I smile. "*If you contemplate, they will come.* Sounds like a slogan for a movie. But I don't know how they'd make a movie of *this* story!" Your laugh comes out a bark.

"God courses through my veins like molten gold. God wakes me up in the night, pushes me, informs me. Moves me. I am burning with God!" I settle myself down. "That's why you came to me: because you could feel that. There's no need to believe when God's roaring up your spine.

"Of course, the experience disappears sometimes. That's when I believe like everyone else." I shrug apologetically.

"Oh! You *do* believe in God! You said it!"

"Yes, I do, only when I have to. But I'd rather have the real thing."

"You *do* believe!"

"Yes, but don't forget what I said. It's based on experience."

"And faith that it will come back."

"Yes." You seem to be feistier than the others. "Look, I've got lots to do. Shall we debate, or do you want to hear what I've got to say?"

"Sure. I'll listen." You sit enthralled, my buddy now that I've said the right two words—*I believe*. It's like politics: If you say one word, half your audience will love you. They'll listen to you as if you were a prophet. Say another word, and they'll walk out, while the other half applauds. Democrat, Republican. I believe, I don't believe. Do people listen? Do they want the truth, or platitudes?

"We were talking about roles people play. Who are you if you're not the roles you play? Take away the geek, the husband, your religion, and whatever else you think you are. The truth is: Anything on this earth that you think you are, you *aren't*. You aren't that, or that, or that." I point at your shoes, your watch, and your body. "What are you?"

You chew on the question, at first looking puzzled. "What's left if I'm not anything?"

"Nothing. Nothing is left."

"I'm *nothing*?"

"Yes. You're nothing. That's all we are in essence ... nothing."

"But you said you *believed*. You said, 'To hell with philosophers, God courses through me.' How can I be *nothing*? How can you believe that?" You're confused to the point of devastation.

"Oh, I don't believe it, my friend. Don't think that. I've *experienced* my nothingness. Don't sell yourself cheaply. Don't believe anything. See if it fits experientially. When I was discussing my on-line addiction, what was the first thing I did to overcome it?"

You think for a moment. "You said you couldn't stop it, but you could watch it."

"Yes. That's what I could do: Watch it. The Witness is who we really are. The stage upon which the play of life is acted. We're nothing but conscious awareness, which sees everything but isn't anything. We're nothing."

"That seems kind of extreme."

"It's very extreme." I go to the bookcase and throw more books on the bed. *Psychosynthesis* and *The Act of Will*, books written by Roberto Assagioli. "That's what it boils down to: Essentially, we are contentless consciousness. Disidentified consciousness, no longer identified with or attached to any of the roles or limiting concepts that bind us to this body, in this place." I pat my chest, and point to the room's floor. "Of course, almost no one gets that far. Most of us whack off a few attachments—quit thinking, 'I am my money, I am my car, I am my job,' and give up the quest. Only the big boys and girls have the guts to see it all the way." I throw out *The Collected Works of St. Teresa of Avila* and *The Collected Works of Saint John of the Cross*. "The really great humans go for the big prize. The rest of us learn a thing or two, and consider ourselves done."

"We should go all the way to *disidentified consciousness?*"

"Yep." I pull out *The Splendor of Recognition: An Exploration of the Pratyabhijñā-hṛdayam*. "We need to recognize our essential selves, where we came from, what we're still part of. Look at the place where your thoughts arise. Meditate on that. You'll find yourself there."

"The place where my thoughts arise?"

"Yeah. Focus on that. Or notice the place where your breath arises or subsides. That's a good one."

You look puzzled. "That's nowhere."

"Yes. Focus on it."

"I thought you were going to explain how you lost control of your life, and how you got it back. I thought we were going to talk about spiritual growth and power."

"If you can really focus on the place where thoughts arise, you'll have as much power as you can handle. If you withdraw your energy from false identifications like your geek-self or the Addict and focus it on your real identity, the power within you will be magnified. The Self and the will," I point at *The Act of Will*, "are intertwined. As the true identity develops, so does the will. That's not willpower in the Victorian, mind-over-matter sense. It's will, as in how you live who you really are. People whose wills are developed are very disciplined. They can focus like lasers and have almost limitless energy. They get the job done; they know why they're here." You look boondoggled.

"This takes time. I heard this for the first time when I was in my early thirties, after searching for truth since I was very young. I'm fifty-nine now, and I consider myself a little bit above a beginner.

Understanding these concepts takes time, and living them ... well, it takes a lifetime. That's what we're talking about: living spiritual practice. Not spiritual life as a hobby, but a profession. Your life's work. That you're asking these questions is fantastic: Almost no one gets as far as you." I look at the clock. "Let's finish our session."

"You're going somewhere?"

"Yes, soon. The wind's changing." I ponder what I've said so far. "Okay, the will and the Witness act together. They are the true you. But they are not all of the true you." Bliss overcomes me as I think of the rest. I force myself to concentrate. "What else is there? What did you come here to discover?"

"God," you stammer.

"Yes. That's what's left. You and I call it God; Assagioli called it the Higher Self. Other traditions call it different names. I experience it up here," I wave my hand above my head. "It acts like a lens, directing the energy and knowledge of all the universe through us. It is our connection with the Divine, with all that is. When you touch the Higher Self, you touch God.

"When you touch God, you reach the highest levels a human being can. Some people do it. Here they are, the flowers of humanity." I toss out books of poetry by Rumi and Mirabai, writings of a half-dozen saints of as many traditions, ending with *Black Elk* and *Black Elk Speaks*. "When you touch God, you become like these people, saints intoxicated by the experience of God." Energy swirls around me as I speak. "They are the mad lovers of God, who appear so bizarre to our eyes. They live in permanent contact with the Divine.

"And that is what Maslow and later theorists of his school said. Saints live in the Transcendent level of the Needs Hierarchy. Personality theories complement each other; you don't have to choose between them. It's not an either/or world; it's both/and. Inclusive."

You're thinking intently. "Let me see if I get what you're saying. I'm nothing physical, just pure consciousness. The Witness. That's connected to my will."

"They're intertwined. In many ways, the will *is* you. Your will is the part of you that finally puts you on a diet and sees that you stay on it, without beating yourself up. Will allows you to give up a bad habit. It's the power to focus and control your behavior. It's very important in personal development: You *can't* have a consistent spiritual practice until your will is sufficiently developed. The will is the part of you that puts you in your meditation chair every day. It's the part that knows—silently, often—that you're here for more than hanging out with friends. Your will is the part of you that brought you here to talk to me."

"My will?"

"Your will."

"How does it develop?"

"It's built-in, part of your operating system, like everything I'm talking about. For some reason, some people tend to pay more attention to it than others. Those are the ones who develop personally and spiritually, the ones who move up Maslow's Needs Hierarchy. The ones that get what they really want in life. You can develop the will like a muscle."

"How?"

"By doing exercises for it. The will and the Higher Self aren't the ego. The ego is about: 'I'm the greatest; I matter so much.' The ego wants things that puff it up. The will and Self don't care about any of that. They're totally different systems. The will and Self reach for the light, you might say. They're interested in personal, non-material goals and growing to what they were meant to be. Even as babies, some part of us knows what we were meant to be. The Self and the will are not punitive as they pursue that goal: They don't beat you up if you make a mistake. Personal development is not run by the ego."

"What exercises do you do?"

"Whatever you do to develop either the will or the Self can't be related to winning anything or making yourself look good. One whiff of that, and the ego will jump out and take over. Many of these exercises you have to sneak into. To develop the will, choose to do something that doesn't serve the ego at all. Do it every day, in a proscribed manner. The exercise lies in the choice to do it, and in doing it.

"An example: take a box of toothpicks and throw them on the floor. Then pick them up carefully and put them in the box. Do this every day. Why? To do it. The exercise serves no useful purpose but to develop the will. One of my counseling professors had a big rock in his backyard. Every day, he'd pick it up from one corner and move it to another. All around the yard, day after day. The activity meant nothing; he did it to develop his will. He thought it a great exercise, until he noticed his neighbor watching him over the fence, looking at him like he was crazy … That was the end of that exercise." We both laugh.

"A lot of higher education is like moving that rock. The value of the coursework is developing the discipline to do something just because you've decided to do it. I can't remember much of most of the courses I took, but I have developed the will to do what I want. I can write books and see them published—prodigious tasks. I can maintain a spiritual discipline.

"The more you develop your will, the easier it will be to cultivate and maintain good habits. The more you develop your will, the harder it will be to indulge in bad habits. Even though you may slip, temptation is more easily overcome. Growth is a self-reinforcing upward spiral. That's the power of the will."

"And the will is connected to God—or that Self?"

"Yes. They touch the Higher Self. The more you clean yourself out, and get rid of your psychological baggage, your hang-ups, your complexes, your sad litany of what people have done to you—the closer you'll come to your real Self, and the more contact you'll have with God."

"That seems too easy."

"It's not easy at all. The subpersonalities are energetic bodies containing your psychic power. Every single one of them will scream bloody murder when it gets shoved out of its number one position. They think they're dying and will fight to stay alive with everything they've got. They'll toss up every fear you've got. Cleaning up your complexes requires facing your demons, nothing less. You'll have to develop vigilance and watch every thought. You'll work harder than you can imagine, and you'll destroy who you are in the process. At the end of the path, who you are now will be dead."

You're staring at me, openmouthed. Maybe I went too far.

"Dying isn't so bad, really. It's less painful than limping through life thinking you're a dummy, or chasing one relationship after another. That's what we do if we're not enlightened. Act out scripts. You aren't any of those: You're God's agent on earth."

You smile.

"That's what many religions say, too. We're here to serve and worship God and take care of God's earth. This is just a different way of saying it. Fit your beliefs and religion within the closet's spaces, my friend. See what happens if you turn your attention to the place where thoughts arise within you." The light in the room is darkening; the day has slipped away. I look around. Is it my imagination, or is the air thicker and fuller? Are unseen entities present? Is someone whispering to me?

"Do you ever feel the unseen world?" Your expression says: What is this crazy lady going to say next? I keep going. "When you start cleaning yourself out, getting rid of the stupid, worthless distractions that fill your time now, you will become aware of more things." You look ready to bolt again. "Listen, the other day, a very nice, normal young man like yourself told me that he had gotten through the hardest times of his life because he could feel his grandfather holding him up. His grandfather died before he was born, but his spirit came to keep him going. Have you ever felt that?" Your head swivels from side to side: no.

"Well, stick with me and you will." I laugh heartily. "I thought it was weird when it first happened to me. I told one of my friends about it—she's an ordained minister, so I thought it would be safe. She said it happened to her all the time: psychic messages from people who are dead. I asked her what she did with the messages. 'I tell the person they're meant for.' 'Don't they think you're weird?' 'They're so grateful, it never comes up.'"

I light some candles, warding off the night. They flicker, light bouncing off the mirrored hangings and the statues. "Something else happened to me once. I've never told anyone." This time I look at you, searching for reassurance. Your open look gives it to me. "There's a little lake over there." I point in its direction. "It's an old Chumash holy site. They still do ceremonies there. Years ago, someone built a resort next to the lake. The resort is closed to the public now, but we went there when it was open. It's set in a pine forest, far off the beaten track. The lake is small and murky. It looked like something from a horror movie; all it needed was some creepy music. The area definitely had something bizarre about it. We hiked all over. I got separated from my husband and daughters. I walked past a cabin, and then saw a barricade with a sign saying it was a Chumash ceremonial area and restricted to invited guests. Fine with me, I wasn't going to intrude."

I look at you to see how you're taking this. You're rapt. "I shot out of there, hiking down the trail. A man's voice stopped me in my tracks. The voice was loud and very insistent, as though he were telling me something important. He was behind me, but when I looked around, no one was there. He spoke absolutely clearly—in his language. An ancient, indigenous language. I couldn't understand it, but I could have written the words down, his voice was so plain. I didn't have anything to write with, but the words were so clear, I thought I'd never forget them.

"I did, of course. Can't remember a single one. I bet I could have taken them to someone in the tribe and had the message translated." I look at you. "Weird, huh?" You look at me. I can't decipher your expression. "It's part of the spiritual path. The unseen becomes seen."

"What do you think he was telling you?"

"It was a warning. He was saying we have to be extra vigilant in caring for the earth, and for each other. He was warning me of danger to the planet." I shiver. "So, of course, I didn't write it down. This was so weird; it was creepy."

"Does all this seem supernatural?"

"Yes. My education doesn't allow for irrational occurrences: I studied economics and statistics. Parts of my brain don't have any room for this sort of thing." You're asking something else, I can see. "You mean, like, is it demonic? No. It doesn't feel demonic. Demonic is what I've seen people do under the influence of drugs, alcohol, and mental illness. You read about people in major corporations stealing billions of dollars from stockholders and their employees' pension plans and getting away with it. Laughing to each other about the old ladies they're ripping off. Did you see that in the paper about those traders? The ones behind California's energy crisis? Enron? They were recorded *laughing* as they manipulated natural gas prices, knowing that they were destroying a state's finances and harming millions of people. *That's* demonic. No, this doesn't feel that way." I look at you. Our relationship has changed. I'm not the teacher anymore. I'm just me, talking about the mystery of life.

"I feel my ancestors around me. I can feel my mother and my father." My eyes fill with tears. "It's hard to talk about them; my dad died long ago, and my mom not so long ago. I can feel them, wishing me well. Whatever negative feelings that once existed are gone; they wish me well. That's all we wanted when they were alive. Something about death changes everything ... I feel my dad's Icelandic heritage, and my heritage from my mom. Crowds of departed people come to me, sometimes." I wave at the books on the bed. "All of those saints are real to me. And all of those." I indicate the statues and paintings all around. "My real ancestors and my spiritual ancestors, too." I glance at you. "You should meditate: Meditation opens up a world of such richness, it's all I can do to stand it." I smile. "I think we run from the bounty that has been given to us into addiction and waste, because we can't deal with life being as good as it could be." We share a smile.

"When Alex Haley wrote *Roots*, he made himself stronger by honoring his ancestors, and he showed the rest of us what we need to do. I have a friend who's a healer—Sudama Mark Kennedy. His healing work focuses on our relationships with our ancestors. Sudama's also the leader of a band, Dreamtime Continuum. And he has a master's in Religious Studies. A multitalented guy. Anyway, he studied a form of Hawaiian healing, Huna healing, that focuses on healing your relationship with your ancestors. When I heard about it, I didn't think it was too far-fetched. That's what Freud and all the other shrinks are about, right? They just don't go as far back.

"When Sudama first told me about his healing work, I was in a restaurant having dinner with my daughter and a friend. Sudama joined us. He told us how we need to clean things up—let go of grudges and feuds, those deadly hatreds that we carry around—not just inside ourselves, but with our ancestors going back generations. We pack many generations of psychological crud around with us. The blood feuds you read about are the most dramatic example, but you know the sort of things we carry. 'Aunt Elaine stole Aunt Betsy's boyfriend. Betsy hated her the rest of her life.' I know stuff like that about my family, I'm sure you do, too."

"Yeah. *Families* ... " You roll your eyes.

"Sudama said we need to clean that up. That's what he does with his healing."

"How?"

"He gave us a demo as we ate dinner. He was on the other side of the table and didn't touch us. He said he felt tension in both my friend and me about the male side of our lineage. He asked us to close our eyes and to focus on that. I felt like a war was going on inside me."

"Really?"

"Yeah. And the next thing, a wave of relaxation swept over me. I opened my eyes, and I was almost facedown in my salad. So was my friend. Something powerful had happened. I don't know what it was."

"And your relationship with your father changed?"

"Yeah. Unscientific, but plausible. Sometimes I feel like I've got a whole crowd around me. Whether this is true or not, we need to preserve our ancestors. They have so much to give us—stories, if nothing else.

"My aunt Elma tells about the world she knew, starting with San Francisco before World War II. When she talks, she makes the foggy streets real. You can hear the gulls crying, and see the women in their pompadour hairdos with funny hats pinned on top. They look like skewered croissants in photos. She talks about the end of the War, and my father coming home and starting the business. That world doesn't exist anymore. We need to collect our family stories; they're our real treasure.

"We're losing our culture—all of us, not just Native Americans and other minorities. Our country is turning into a bunch of malls run by corporations. Popular culture is about having stuff and turning one's self into Barbie or Ken. We need to save our cultures and traditions. We need to express ourselves: Our real wealth is our art, our souls' product." The wind rattles the window. I jump, knocked off my rant. "It knows how to get your attention, doesn't it?"

"What?"

"The earth. When you're cleaning up inside, you become more aware of people—and you become more aware of the earth. I've read articles saying that energy currents exist in the earth. That power spots exist where energy and psychic powers are stronger. Once, I would have said that was crackpot stuff. Now, I wouldn't, not all of it. Certainly, that Chumash site had something going.

"Do you feel like that in some places? There's a kind of click, like you insert a key in a lock and it fits. Everything's right, and you can't say exactly why."

"I've felt that. At my grandfather's farm."

"When I went to Iceland back in the '60s I thought I'd ignite, the feeling was so strong. My dad's family was one hundred percent Icelandic, dating back I don't know how many hundreds of years. I saw those cliffs and the starkness. The freezing ocean, rock, and air. Just seeing it, I felt like part of my soul fell into place."

"You felt complete."

"Very." You're a fast learner. I'm about to learn how fast. You raise your hand to interrupt.

"I understand what you're talking about, I guess. But something bothers me. Say we find out we're just this Witness—and then something breaks open above us." You gesture overhead. "We make contact with God, and all this good stuff comes to us. How do we keep it coming? You said you got addicted on-line and that it could happen to anyone. Why? How can everything fall apart after you've done so much work? How can a person keep it together? How does this spiritual thing work?"

"Those are the sixty-four-thousand-dollar questions! Are you old enough to remember that TV show? Once, that was a lot of money." I sit back, thinking. "Well, let's see. The process works because that's how we're made. Scientists say our brains are made to search for meaning, to ask the questions you're asking. All of our biology and psychology is aimed at the experience of what you and I call God.

"The other side is, God wants to come to us even more strongly than we long for God. My meditation master teaches that our relationship to God goes in two directions. First, all creation and, therefore, all human beings belong to God. We belong to God totally and absolutely and always have. Understanding this was no problem for me; I'd heard it in a dozen places since I was a child. I also know it from my spiritual experience. I've given myself to God in prayer and meditation many times, at increasingly deeper levels.

"Surrendering to God wasn't easy, but it wasn't as hard as comprehending the second part of her teaching: God *belongs* to us. Just as we belong to God and always have, whether we know it or not, so God belongs to us. This absolutely blew my mind.

"The relationship goes both ways? God *has* to come if I call? This was really hard for me to accept—I expect that many people feel that way. God loves *me*? What if God really got to know me? Don't I have to work like crazy to earn God's love? Can things just come to me without my beating myself to death?

"These thoughts are hard to get rid of since our determination can waver at any time. Yeah, we can get addicted. People who have been on the path very seriously for a long time—like me—can get run over by a weakness they didn't know about. Also—we can have an accident, get some disease, or be blown up and the whole process goes bye-bye. No human brain equals no human experience. It can happen at any time."

"How do you keep that from happening? How do you keep God around?"

"God's always around: You can't get rid of God. That power is everywhere. Knowing it is a matter of awareness."

"Well, how do you keep that awareness and stay on the straight and narrow? How do you make sure that God loves you?"

"God will always love you. We can't lose God's love. What we need to do is stay cleaned up so we can feel that love and so our souls stay strong enough to resist temptation. That's why I talk about living spiritual practice. We need to live a certain way, mindfully. Full of prayer and worship. Would you like to know the essence of worship? It's so easy."

"Okay."

"Say you meet someone irresistibly attractive." I point to a statue of Lord Krishna, the flute-playing deity who embodies the love of God. "You meet someone so attractive that all you want is to live in his or her presence. You want that person to love you back. If you met the Goddess," I point to a statue of Shakti, divine energy in its feminine aspect, "how would you treat her so she sticks around?"

"I'd be good to her!"

"I bet. What would you do?"

"I'd spend a lot of time with her; I'd buy her whatever she wanted. If I couldn't afford it, I'd work harder and earn more. I'd take her places. I'd always act the way she wanted, even if she wasn't there. If she wanted me to get a better job or go back to school, I'd do it. Whatever she wanted, I'd do. I'd even give up watching football if she wanted. I'd love her. I'd worship her ... "

"You'd adore her."

"Yes."

"That's the basis of worship: love. God wants our prayers, our hymns, and our praises all the time. 'Oh, dear Lord, I praise Your name. I love You, I worship You, I adore You.' God wants our worship. Wants us to build a little remembrance to show we care: a temple or cathedral to hang out in while we're worshipping. God wants us to do the work we're shown to do. And God wants us to live in a way that befits us as divine creations. If you take one step toward God, God will pick you up and take you to nirvana, if that's what you want. All we have to do is listen and do what we're told.

"Here's a great example of the way God wants us to behave. You've heard of Martin Luther? The guy who started the Reformation?" You indicate you have. "I heard the following quote attributed to him: 'The proper relationship between man and God is shown by the relationship between a horse and its rider.'

"You know we have horses, right? You noticed them on the way in?" The flat front part of our ranch is divided into pastures, each of which holds at least one horse. Between the pastures' occupants and the sign by the front gate, which proclaims we are a Peruvian Paso horse ranch and bears the image of a horse head, you'd have to be dead not to know that we have horses.

"Yeah."

"When I heard that quote, I went, 'Luther must have known horses, because that is right-on.' Some horses listen to the rider so intently it seems the rider's will is their own. Look at this picture." I pull a framed photo off the wall.

## HORSE AND RIDER

"This is my husband riding one of our geldings, Corcovado, or Corco, in a show. Notice anything?"

You stare at the photo. "Your husband's wearing a poncho."

I roll my eyes. People who don't know horses don't *see*. "The important thing is that Corco has his ears cocked back. See that?" I point to the photo. "The direction a horse's ears point indicates his focus. He's listening to Barry with as much focus as a horse can muster.

That's the *horse* part of what Luther was talking about. Our horses are judged in part on a quality called 'brio' in Spanish. Translated, this means 'spirit' or 'willingness to please the rider.' This is a perfect example of how Luther said we humans should be.

"When I was young, I rode reined stock horses. They are so willing that all I had to do was pick up my reins and my horse would tremble in eagerness to do what I wanted. I felt I could control one mare's breathing with my thoughts. I needed to simply *think* what I wanted to do, and she would do it.

"That's what Luther is talking about: a mind dedicated to doing the will of its master. A perfect servant. How many of us come close?" I shrug. "Our minds wander, we forget. We turn away: 'I'd rather go clubbing every night than feel the bliss.' We throw away our birthright for cheap trinkets."

"How can we stop?"

"Spiritual practice is the best way to wake up. You need to do a consistent, daily practice. Make it a discipline. Horseback riding gives some tips. What do you do when you get bucked off?"

"I don't know. I've never been bucked off by a horse."

"By other things, I bet." You smile. "You get back on. That's how you master fear, by going through it. Assuming you're not in the hospital, of course. Getting bucked off of anything can be painful. There's more that horses can teach us. Their brains are about the size of a walnut, I've been told. If they can learn things, we should be able to learn, too. When I'm riding a horse, I collect him. That means I take a hold of his mouth— lightly, just maintaining my contact—and squeeze lightly with my legs. His back will round up, and I'll have his attention. See my husband in the photo? The horse is perfectly collected."

You look.

"Once you get him collected, he's like a ballet dancer. He's balanced, and can stop or turn in any direction easily. He can do whatever he's told and knows how to do. That's the perfect stance we should have on the path. Our stance matters. If you're riding along, your horse may get bored, or fall asleep. I've had them fall flat on their faces because they're not paying attention. Sort of like people. To keep a horse listening to you, you move in the saddle, wiggle the reins, or squeeze with your legs. Just a little wake-up, and there he goes, perfectly collected and doing what you want again. We need to wake ourselves up, or God will do it for us."

"How? By shaking things up? Sending an earthquake?"

"Don't laugh! This is earthquake country. The fault's right over there, on the other side of those mountains." Your eyes widen. "But back to our discussion, something wakes us up. We never know what it will be. When it happens, we need to be prepared. Hence, prayer and mantra. Two tools for soul maintenance."

You have a silly grin. "Mantra?" You roll your eyes back and put your thumb and forefingers together, mocking a meditator in the movies. "That's so *California*."

I poke you with my finger. "Yeah, *mantra*. The word was invented in India, not California. It means 'sacred word'. You already have a mantra, I guarantee it."

"No way."

"Yes way. Say you hit your thumb with a hammer. What's the first thing you say? Think it, don't say it."

A sheepish grin.

"That's your mantra. The first thing on your mind in an emergency. Or—what do you think about all day long? What does your mind rattle on about? Who did what to you? How rotten your boss is? How you can't trust men or women, or both? How people will lie when they can? How life has cheated you? These are the kind of mantras that ordinary people repeat. Unconscious people. They produce lousy results. Look at the world. Look at the news. That is the product of the typical mental activity of our species. Most of it tells a hangdog story of disaster and dashed dreams. You should ask people who are getting what they want from life what they think about. People who look like that." I point to a photo of a radiant woman.

"Here, read her book." I pull *My Lord Loves a Pure Heart: The Yoga of Divine Virtues* off the shelf. "She thinks about virtue—you can see it in her face. She also writes about it. Look at this." I take you over to my computer. It has signs plastered all around it: My life is my spiritual path.

"That's what I'm writing about: I want to stay on course. This is my life, and what we're doing. Every part of it is focused on God, on attaining what God has for me. This is living spiritual practice." Behind us are mock-ups of covers for a half-dozen books I'm writing. "Those will be books someday, I know it." I frown. "I've got to put something up about sales levels and how much I'll make. 'Ask and ye shall receive.' You have to be specific. What we repeat, what we trigger ourselves to believe, what we wave in front of our faces, is our mantra. Conscious or unconscious, we reap our mantra's fruit.

"I use a traditional Sanskrit mantra from India. It means I bow to the omnipresent aspect of God that dwells in every soul. I got it from my teacher in 1975; I've been using it a long time. It runs in my head by itself."

"How do you use a mantra?"

"You repeat it all the time, out loud or silently. It should be so much part of your consciousness that when disaster strikes, that's the first thing that comes out of your mouth. The mantra will protect you; I've tested it out.

"A few years back, my horse spooked and leapt halfway up a steep hill. It happened very fast. I reined him to turn him back down, but instead of just turning, he spun and started to fall. He was falling down the embankment, going full speed. His shoulder would have landed on a hard-packed, rocky trail. I couldn't pull my leg out of the way fast enough. The instant I realized what was happening, I *yelled* my mantra at him. Miraculously, he pulled himself together and didn't fall. We went on to have a fine ride. If he'd fallen, I'd have broken my leg under him, no doubt. Maybe worse—my leg and hip. Friends have had that happen to them. A mantra protects you—that's just one of many examples I could give you.

"If it's against your traditions, you don't have to use a Sanskrit mantra. I've heard of people repeating a Hebrew phrase. The name of God in any tradition should be fine. I've tried using mantras out of books with no success. I couldn't stick with them. I think you need to be given a mantra by someone with great spiritual attainment for it to really work. You could ask your minister, rabbi, priest, or other clergy for a phrase to calm your mind. I'm sure they could suggest something helpful."

I open *My Lord Loves a Pure Heart* and read it out loud. You listen quietly. I hand the book to you and you glance through the pages.

"This room is my altar. On the path, you need an altar." I survey the room slowly. "A place to focus your devotion, where you do your practices. Everything in this room is a balm to my soul." You don't answer and I turn to find you sitting in your chair with your eyes closed. Your feet are flat on the floor and your hands rest on your thighs. Your face is relaxed, attention drawn deep inside, into territory you've not explored.

Good, I think, looking around. A pile of clothes surrounds my suitcase. I haven't packed at all. I finish the job, putting this in, leaving that out. I hold up two outfits: one simple and elegant enough for anywhere. The other, purple and green velvet, trimmed with braid and mirrors. Something a queen would wear, or a sorceress. Which one? Be both. Do both. I fold them quickly and close my bag.

The wind batters the window. I look up, noticing the stars. Day is gone, replaced by the dusky transition. Time to leave. Tiptoeing over, I smile at your unlined face, remembering when I wore the smooth skin of youth. "It's time," I whisper. You start, called from far away. "Come back slowly. That's right."

You look into my eyes, which glint with whispers of the unseen. After touching the inner world, you glow brighter in the darkened room. Candles flicker and wane. Our eyes catch, joining us. You look disorientated, drunk. A bit afraid. "Are you a witch?" you stammer.

"No. I'm a housewife. We clean up the mess. That's what I'm doing." Your brow knits. "Oh, yes, my friend. These are perilous times. We need many good wives of the soul. Many good shepherds. Evil walks all around, mighty evil, heavily armored and armed."

"Must we fight evil?"

"Oh, yes. Fight for our survival."

"How?"

"As I have shown you, starting with yourself. When you've found out who you are, when you've found your job in this life, when you feel the connection to everything else every minute, show others. That's all anyone can do."

"Is that enough? Will that save the world?"

"I don't know. I don't know if those who can't curb their addictions, who are mad with lust, who love their mind's phantoms and delusions can be stopped. But if they can, it's only by the truth. We need to show them that, and watch that we hold on to truth as a lifeline. And now, my friend, the day is gone and it is time for you to follow it."

We walk out of my room onto the landing. The stairs curve downward, falling an eternity. The ordinary world is far away. I touch your arm. "One last thing. What is the greatest skill? The highest learning?"

You think before answering. "I don't know."

"Listening. If you listen, you will know everything. You will hear the voices inside you and the voice of your own heart. You will hear the longing of others, their fears and joys. You'll imbibe the bliss of the universe and feel the planets turn. All that from being silent and listening. Listen, all the time."

We descend. The hall is darkened, its mirrors reflecting starlight and gods. The wind buffets the house. I open the door for you. "A change is coming, can you feel it? It's time to move."

"Where are you going?" You look alarmed.

"On a pilgrimage."

"Can I come back?"

"If I do."

The door closes and you are blown away.

# A
# PILGRIMAGE

# CHAPTER 7

# DEPARTING FOR THE GATHERING

HAVE YOU EVER FELT THE NEED to *move*? Not to travel, hunkering from one place to another dragging your baggage. Not to relocate, doing an end run hoping to escape the mess you made, only to discover that it arrives before you.

Have you been called to *move*? Has something called you? A place? A person? An experience you knew you were supposed to have? Something that felt like, *Oh, yeah. That was it*, afterwards?

For me, the call arrived simply, in a letter from a friend. Had it landed with a flaming elephant, it couldn't have had more impact. "It's a Native American spiritual retreat in the Cherokee National Forest in Tennessee!" I could feel my friend's excitement as I read. When I got that letter back in 2001, I felt like something reached down, grabbed my heart, and said,

"Go!"

Not only did the retreat, called "the Gathering," feature a magnificent forest location and workshops on American Indian culture, but Bill Miller was the headlined musician and speaker. The combination was worth the trip.

Also—purely by coincidence—I had just completed the first draft of a novel that takes place at a Native American spiritual retreat. I'd been working on it for, oh, six years. Maybe finding out about the Gathering at that time meant something ... Whatever grabbed my heart followed it with a swift kick in the derrière.

I made my plane reservation and was ready.

What happened was: My knee fell apart, and the tragedies of September 11, 2001, transpired. No Gathering for me. I was supposed to *move*, but not then. Doors open, and doors close. I had to wait until the doors opened again.

Two years and a full knee replacement later, I made it to Coker Creek, Tennessee, and the Gathering in September 2003. Did it live up to my expectations? Was it worth the approximately 2,389.6-mile trip? Definitely.

Whatever grabbed my heart and got me to the Gathering goaded me to write this book. It kept upping the ante: First a little book, then a bigger one. Then this book. I wrote and wrote, a

*The Gathering changed my life.*

simple treatise becoming an unruly monster. Imagine me wrestling with a manuscript, shoving it into a pile as its pages attempted to bolt, holding it down with one knee and jamming it into order—that's not far from the truth. So here we are, with you holding the finished product, ready to make a pilgrimage with me.

A pilgrimage is a journey to a holy place, undertaken for religious reasons, a journey to a place with special significance. It's one of the most venerable spiritual practices, occurring worldwide since the dawn of man. What happens on the way to the holy site is often as important as what happens when you arrive. This is the story of how

I got to the Gathering, and what happened inside and outside of me once there. It's a story about a specific retreat, as well as the process of making a pilgrimage and going on retreat.

Dates become vague when spirit starts to play. Thirty years ago, I was a newcomer to spiritual journeys. If an event was slated to begin on a given day and end on another, I thought it began on the advertised date and ended on cue. I soon realized this wasn't so. The retreat began when I thought about signing up, jumped into the starting gate when I wrote the check, and was screaming down the stretch when I stuck it in the mail. Every hang-up, problem, and personal issue I had going was triggered by that action. By the time I got to the retreat, I was a thirty-Kleenex mess.

When I got home I'd attained answers and peace, for a while anyway. Expelling the mess I brought to a retreat seemed to allow more muddle to surface. The process wasn't finished until it had wrung the juice out of me, which could be six months after the dates on the flier. By that time, I was getting ready to go on the next one. When does a retreat begin? When does this pilgrimage begin?

The Gathering I'm going to describe happened in September 2003, but this tale might have begun in the late 1930s, when a beautiful young woman named Clara Ella Byler bolted from her family home in Missouri's Ozarks.

Why my mother left for Garfield, Oklahoma, with Aunt Ethel Bybee remains a mystery. She hit Kansas City and a couple other towns before heading out to Los Angeles. There, she found my father, an auspicious meeting from my point of view. My pilgrimage might have begun then, or perhaps in 1945, on the day I was hauled out of her, screaming. Or it could have begun in 1995, when that book was injected into my brain and I began to write.

Whenever you say a pilgrimage begins, wherever you feel called to go, one thing's certain: You'll take yourself with you. All of you. Recall our discussion of subpersonalities, the little hunks of your psyche that think they're *you*? They will accompany you on your pilgrimage or retreat, each with his or her concerns. One may be concerned about safety, while another is concerned about achievement. This is normal. Did you know that they talk, as well as behave differently? They have distinct inner voices and attitudes, which you can observe if you're sharp. Sit quietly and listen to the voice in your head. You'll hear a voice after a few seconds, maybe saying, "What is she talking about?" Or, "This is weird."

That's known as your *mind*. It talks all day long, setting out its view (a fractured view, since you have many different parts, according to many theorists), telling you what it needs to survive, and how you must be if disaster isn't to befall you. The mind is a collection of survival programs. By ceaselessly repeating stuff it learned before you were five, your mind seeks to keep you safe.

Going on a pilgrimage implies traveling to a different place geographically, to a strange place, perhaps. Your mind may have something to say about this. One of the things you learn from a pilgrimage is that you don't have to listen to all that. Pay no attention to the shrieking in your head and keep doing what will get you there, making sure that you're not taking stupid chances. In this way, you can explore new cultures and ideas. Places, too.

In going on a pilgrimage, we do something else that's unusual: We go to a new, elevated inner space. That's the purpose of a retreat or pilgrimage, to elevate the soul and touch God, or at least have an expansive experience.

What do you think those little subpersonalities will think about your journey to transcendent consciousness if they believe they are the beginning and end of your existence? That nothing exists but them and their level of reality? What if you have a transcendent experience and the ego—who you think you are—gets knocked aside by a direct experience of God?

The shrieking that occurred when you changed time zones and saw cacti instead of palm trees will be multiplied a millionfold. Transcendent experiences can be very unsettling.

The solution to the screaming voices and cognitive dissonance is finding the one inner voice you should heed—the Voice. It's pure, simple, direct, and does not mess around. When I hear that Voice, I do what it says immediately, asking, "Is there anything else you want me to do?" That Voice has never steered me wrong; I've gotten into trouble only when I didn't follow its orders.

An acquaintance gave a perfect definition of spirituality:

"Either you hear the Voice, or you don't."

What more can one say?

The hallmark of the Voice is its fruits. If you do what it says, or follow the hints it leaves around, positive results occur. It's not silly, capricious, shallow, self-centered, selfish, or stupid. It takes into account not only your good, but the good of others. Remember the Transcendent level shown in Maslow's Needs Hierarchy? That's where this Voice originates, not from any subpersonality or ego state. When you hear it, it feels like God speaking. I think it is.

Reaching the Voice takes work. First, we have to recognize it among all the pretenders inside. Dominant subpersonalities will try and take this identity over, too.

"Hi, I'm Saintly Sandy. Glad to meet you." That's my Spiritual Seeker subpersonality imitating the real thing. The spiritual charlatans we've all met fall in this trap. A lower portion of the personality is trying to assume the voice/role of something it's learned gets lots of goodies, especially after a spiritual experience or two. The Voice can't be faked.

Second, having connected to our Voice, we need to work hard to stay in a pure enough state to recognize and heed it. That is why we do spiritual practice.

Want to map your inner territory and subpersonalities? This exercise requires the skills of a sleuth. Your subpersonalities won't jump out to be counted. You need to observe yourself. As you move through your day, notice changes in your thinking, differences in posture or muscle tension, and new thoughts or attitudes. Keep your journal handy and track yourself through your life. Record what you see. You might start observing who you are during the majority of the day. This will probably be who you are as you earn your living. Watch yourself, and look for the things I mentioned: posture, language, and attitude. I know when I'm in my professional *persona*—another word for subpersonality, literally meaning the way I present myself to the world—I'm on top of the universe. No fear, no doubt, just highly effective performance. That's why work addiction is so prevalent: You don't feel pain. Check out your other roles: keep watching. Are there times you feel like the underdog? What role do you assume in your relationships with various people? Submissive? Aggressive? Don't challenge these roles: They're there for a purpose, adapting to the life you live now. Don't attempt to dismantle them because you think something else is better. Just keep this as information, watching the ebb and flow of identity. I invite you to listen to your own inner voices.

The voices and Voice I talk about above are not psychotic voices, the kind that urge people to jump off roofs to show they can fly. Such voices are not healthy. They lead to disaster. They're not much fun, either. I know several people who have had psychotic episodes and heard this kind of diseased voice.

"I can't tell you how horrible it was," one sufferer told me.

The Voice isn't Freud's superego, either. You know, the mock-up of Dad you carry in your head, telling you that you should have done better—even if you just broke the world record. Well, that's one superego. The superego is the conscience, cobbled together from memories of subpersonalities that triumphed or at least survived in your life. We're not talking about *that*, either.

◄◄◄►◉◄►►►

As I prepared to go to the Gathering, everything was the same. I had the same eBay addiction, which remained tamed until I logged on. My passion for publication drove me dawn to dusk. Said passion was complicated by the fact that I now had a literary agent. Isn't that what writers pine to have? An experienced person with connections to peddle their words and cheer them on? To send their scribbling to editors who can put it in print, and see they get paid, too? Yes, it is. Did having an agent make me happier? We shall see.

My looking-at-dogs-on-the-Net thing was backed off. When my younger daughter left for school, I wandered around the ranch feeling like my heart had been ripped from my chest. Empty Nest Syndrome was far worse than I imagined. Tolerating the loneliness and quiet house for a week or two, I did the only possible thing. I headed to the pound and adopted the cutest little black dogs in the world. Proudly, I brought my darlings home, sure that their bright eyes, smiles, and wagging plumed tales would charm my husband. They didn't. To Barry, a dog is a black Lab or a Great Dane. Anything smaller is an affront to his masculinity. Sammy and Raj were objects of disdain.

Everything was the same, as it always is in spiritual practice. Going on a pilgrimage simply means you get to pack and travel in addition. Would my little dogs be there when I got back?

Fortunately, the call to go on a spiritual journey has an origin. The universe wanted me to go to Tennessee. The Voice began guiding my movements before I left. The closer the Gathering got, the louder the Voice became. Also all the other voices, the fragments of my ego dedicated to preserving my existence by endlessly repeating what didn't work earlier: my *mind*, as we say in enlightenment circles. It became a broadcasting station blasting in my head, with various points of view making sure that I did/brought/thought everything needed to succeed in Tennessee.

From my compulsive worker: "You'll have a whole week there. Take some chapters from your novel and edit them. Also, take the outline of *The Horse Book*. Print out everything you've written about horses: You can edit it. Hurry up!"

My *clotheshorse, compulsive packer,* and *she who worries about leaving home* also took their turns.

Right before I left, the Voice knocked them flat:

*"Take everything for the horse book. Do not bring the novel. Do not work on anything until I tell you."*

I did as I was told, and got on the plane.

⋘⋙◄◗►►►

A pilgrimage necessarily involves going from here to there. Most subtly, it involves going from one inner state to another, higher state. On the physical plane, it means hauling one's body and stuff to wherever the action is. This can be a real problem, as it was in 2001 when all the flights to Tennessee were cancelled, and I couldn't get to the Gathering even if I had been able to walk. It still can be a real problem if you're a grandmother and have never gotten yourself to the other side of the continent, into and out of cars and hotels, across states that you've never seen, to a vague destination in the mountains. Many women—such as my daughters—master such geographical feats in their teens. I didn't. This was my first solo trip.

I'm not a total travel novice: I've flown across the United States to our meditation ashram in New York by myself. A driver picked me up at the airport and delivered me to the front door. I have traveled around the globe a fair amount, always under the protective eye of some man: my father, my husband. A hired guard. My cousin Gloria and I went to Missouri and back by ourselves last summer, but I hadn't done the whole ball of wax alone. It's hard to believe that such cultural deprivation exists, but there I was: fifty-eight years old and traveling solo for the first time.

*Yah-hoo!* I immediately got the upside potential of this spiritual journey. I have the best travel agent in the universe: Dave used his magic, ultra-cheap program to book me into an awesome four-star hotel for the same price as the Down and Dirty Motel. This is how a *woman* travels alone.

Bill Miller would say something telling at the Gathering. He said that when he's performing, his employers often book him into charming, upscale bed-and-breakfasts with all the amenities.

"What do I need all that for? I'm a guy, by myself. Motel 6 is fine! If my wife's there, sure, all that's great. But alone?"

I say, "Hey, baby. I'm alone. I want décor out of *Architectural Digest*. A marble bathroom. French soap, a Jacuzzi, massage. A twenty-four-hour swimming pool. Gym. Turndown service. Multiple chocolates. Room service. A concierge. Valet parking. Everything. *More than everything!*"

The nice thing about being alone in Tennessee would be the absence of my husband, who would choke if he saw where I stayed. For him, Motel 6 is fine even when I'm along ... I will not get into that.

This would have been pure bliss, except for one small matter, which requires a bit of backpedaling.

When I was in college, I wanted to be a development economist. It was the sixties; we wanted to change the world. (Some of us still do.) I could see myself traveling all over the globe, helping developing nations decide whether to build roads, dams, or schools. Or mega airports for the dictator's jets. Unfortunately for these plans, I traveled a bit and discovered that I get near-terminal culture shock. Serious culture shock. It's the unfamiliar doorknobs and hardware that really upset me. Also the strange bathroom fixtures.

I can imagine my career as a development economist: I'm in Rockawallawoowoo, slated to present my plan. The conference room at the Imperial Palace/People's Reception Hall is jammed. I'm not there. They wait. Finally, a breathless emissary runs into the room:

"I'm sorry, Prime Minister, we can't start the presentation. The Project Economist is hiding under her bed."

What can happen in my own country is no different.

Flying into Nashville in the middle of the night, I faced the trickiest part of the trip: reaching my downtown hotel. This required me to unfold myself from my small, super-economy seat—a space large enough for a caged Chihuahua. Staggering out of the plane, several time zones from home, I had to find my rental car, figure out how to drive it, and aim it at my hotel—somewhere in the heart of "The Music (Country Music?) Capital of the World."

I did it. In a relatively short time, I arrived at my hotel in one piece, the only mishaps being turning the wrong way onto a one-way street and driving through a police crime scene.

You've been here twenty minutes and you've already broken the law twice, thought I. That didn't bode well.

While the hotel bore all the superficial accoutrements of a four-star hotel—palm trees, marble, and fountains—plus the parking valet I almost ran over—it had a few flaws. They put me on the twenty-first floor.

No self-respecting Californian stays on the twenty-first floor. Not if she's lived through the 7.1-on-the-Richter-scale Loma Prieta Earthquake in '89. The one that knocked down part of the Bay Bridge, and caused I-880 to collapse in Oakland and San Francisco to burn. You may have watched it on TV.

No, I didn't want any room on the twenty-first floor.

On the other hand, the view was great, and I wasn't aware of any recent earthquakes in Tennessee. Add "great view" to my list of things I want in a hotel.

<hr />

Awakening in my sumptuous room the next day, I moved slowly and carefully. The beautifully decorated space was a shell protecting a fragile embryo—me. All my writing, querying, wanting, and trying came to a dead stop the minute I got away from home. I was physically exhausted and not too far behind mentally—I hadn't a clue of my condition until that morning. I felt like that freeway in Oakland post-earthquake: rubble.

Everything was working, too. All the parts of me broadcast their distress: My many interior voices piped up like organs. My emotions and the physical sensations from every inch of my worn-out body felt like they'd been amplified. Every one played a painful tune. Having no idea how I would get through the day, much less to the other side of Tennessee, I could have come unglued.

Fortunately, the Voice took over: "You're exhausted. Rest. Use room service if you're hungry." Moment by moment, I was told what to do. This time, I did not resist. "Take a nap; you're tired." I went to bed.

No arguing, no: "But I had a full day planned. I came to Nashville because it's famous for music. I want to go to a show. And there's a roadhouse somewhere, it's in this book, where everyone goes to breakfast. And I need to see the downtown." I had books and articles, printouts from the Net—stuff from the hotel. A library of information about Nashville. I didn't even think about it, nor did I think, "I was going to work on *The Horse Book*. What if my agent calls and I haven't finished it?"

None of that came up: The Voice was in control. Thank God, because I bollocks it up so badly by myself. I called Room Service and went back to bed. Later, I put on a CD of sacred chants and read scriptures. The Voice took charge. I meditated for a long while.

I'm not a natural meditator. Just as some people have little inborn aptitude for skiing or singing, my initial meditation propensity was low. I've improved since I began meditating in 1975, but I'm no virtuoso.

*Never forget the power of grace.*

My mind is like a manic ground squirrel. Do you know what they are? We have them in California. They're little squirrel things with skimpy tails that spend their lives digging holes for your horse to step in and running in front of cars. That's my mind: It digs frantically and runs hard.

Over the years, my meditation practice has evolved: The power of grace intervenes as I struggle to calm my inner rodent and simply immobilizes it. Zap! I'm in deep meditation with a silent, tranquil mind.

Thinking about it, I realized that meditation, or any spiritual practice, doesn't have to look like pictures in books. Contemplating my lack of meditation prowess, I realized that something else has happened over the years. I started writing in 1995. I write many hours a day, and I'm in a trance state when I do. That's not a big trance, like you might associate with Houdini; it's a deeper level of consciousness than I've got the rest of the time. When I realized that, I realized that I'm in that deeper state most of the day. So in some sense, my meditation has become my life, but it doesn't look like the pictures of meditating people in books. Maybe I'm not such a bad meditator after all ...

People have said, "I belong to such and so religion, so I can't meditate." Well, I hate to break it to you: You already do. When was the last time you were looking out the kitchen window, gazing at the flowers swaying; and when you checked the clock, twenty minutes had gone by? That's meditation, otherwise known as spacing out.

That unconscious type of meditation got me through my M.A. in economics. I was a young woman in graduate school with a baby and house of my own; I got plenty frazzled. The only cure I knew of was what I called "Lizard Consciousness." My family had a boat. I'd drive the three hours to get to where we kept it, not to water-ski, but for lunch. At lunch, we'd beach the boat. I'd climb out on the bow and lie on my stomach, feeling the hot sun and the movement of the river. The reeds swayed, and I closed my eyes. I went to someplace inside—at that time, I had no idea that I had an inner life. The place was so still, so quiet. Absolutely peaceful. No thought at all. A couple of minutes like that, and poof! Econometrics no longer bothered me.

*Meditation is a natural state: Everyone does it, whether they know it or not.*

If I'd known I was meditating, I wouldn't have had to waste gas and do all that water-skiing. I could have stayed home and refreshed myself in my own living room. I might have gotten conscious enough to ask: "If you found getting your master's degree so difficult, why are you applying for the Ph.D. program?" This is the real benefit of spiritual practice: You wake up and ask the right questions. Maybe you even go in the direction you're meant to take.

I settled for Lizard Consciousness and long drives.

On that long and painful day I rested in my hotel room, thankful to God for meditation and Room Service and very thankful to the Voice, because I needed something to stop me. By mid-afternoon, I was patched together enough for the Voice to give directions:

"Go to the Country Music Hall of Fame and Museum."

I hate country music, loathing it almost as much as popular music. I like music from India and Nepal. Also I like chants, and a group called Dreamtime Continuum. And Bill Miller. A few others. I hate country music. It's about whining. I love to whine, but I don't like to hear other people singing about it.

Why was I directed to go there, when I was in a spiritual crisis?

I went.

The building housing the Country Music Hall of Fame and Museum (CMHF&M) is spectacular, a curved contemporary structure constructed of native materials. I felt better the minute I saw it. Beauty matters. Balance, proportion, rhythm, harmony, and scale: The five principles of design. Something beautiful and well-designed exhibits them. That includes music, as well as every other form of art. Beauty heals.

At the Hall & Museum, you take an elevator up to the third floor and cruise through the exhibits on your way down. Soothed by the time I got to the top, I still wondered why I'd been commanded to go there.

Took about two minutes to find out. I found myself on a very wide interior balcony. The floors are constructed so that one side—the right side as you enter—is open all the way down to the first floor. (There's a railing, of course.) The open space is very nice—a sense of volume and so on. They have video screens hanging from the ceiling, all the way down the huge room. When I was there, films of various contemporary country stars being interviewed ran simultaneously. They didn't interest me.

*On the spiritual path, everything is part of everything else.*

On the other side of the museum, exhibits lined the walls. You could push buttons and hear music. They had little comma-shaped wings sticking out that perhaps ten people could enter to experience exhibits, music, and photos.

The photos. Old photos of the origins of country music. The faces. The early sounds. Hardly anyone was at the Museum; no one noticed me crying.

Finding one's roots is part of the journey, an essential pilgrimage. Earlier on, I said that this book might have begun in the late 1930s, when my mother high-tailed it out of her family home in Seligman, Missouri, and headed for the bright lights of Los Angeles. She probably hit the mean streets, but she made a life for herself, and she married my father. I never knew why my mom left home; she was vague about it, and only went back a couple of times. She didn't say much about herself. I don't know how far she got in school: I don't know a lot about her life before I arrived. She had five brothers and sisters and they all had kids; until last July, I'd only met my aunt Bonnie and her two daughters. Bonnie left Missouri for L.A. a bit earlier than my mom, testing the California waters, so to speak, and creating a place for her younger sister to land.

Last July, three months before the Gathering, my cousin Gloria and I took a trip to Seligman. A pilgrimage. Neither of us had been there; our mothers had passed on, as had their brothers and sisters back home. All but one. Our aunt Nona was turning ninety. Both of us felt propelled: We had to go back immediately. It wasn't just us: When Gloria called Nona and asked if we could come, she said,

"Well, if you want to see me, you'd better hurry."

We hurried. Something moved us, and moved things out of our way. We aren't kids, but Gloria and I felt like it as we jumped into our brand-new Chrysler PT Cruiser, heading out of the Northwest Arkansas Airport as fast as she could read the directions to me.

Lost—we got lost everywhere. We were supposed to go to our cousin Roberta's house and she would take us to her mother's place, our aunt Nona's. We'd never met Roberta, but she had the sweetest voice on the phone. Her directions were clear; they just didn't match up with the countryside around us. Gloria and I drove over and through many leafy gullies and knolls before giving up. Roberta finally found us in a *holler*. A holler is a dry creek. Looked like that to me. Wouldn't want to be down there in winter: I expect it would be called a *flood zone* when it rained. She drove us to her mother's house, after the three of us jumped up and down and squealed and cried enough to alert all the hound dogs in the state.

My aunt's house is a pretty little white clapboard thing, immaculate. It's set in a wide lawn, with trees and plants all around. Flowers everywhere. Sun shining down. A vegetable garden out back that my husband would think was heaven. I felt kind of scared, walking in the back door to meet my aunt for the first time.

The kitchen was wood-paneled and warm, smelling of fried chicken and cornbread. My aunt came forward, taking my breath away. I don't know what I expected—didn't have a clear picture. I didn't expect *her*. Taller than I, even though she was a couple weeks short of ninety. Neither fat nor thin. Strong enough to last forever. *She's beautiful*, I thought, the realization coming too fast for words. Her smile was as welcoming as my mother's arms, and her eyes were like Mom's, full of the same brilliance. Good humor shining out. Playfulness. She used a cane. Her fingers were widened from hard work. White hair formed a bun on top of her head.

Her arms were around me and she held me so tight. Heart to heart, blood to blood. This was my aunt. I'd never met my aunt! And here she was, arms about to crush me, hugging me to her. And I loved her, this woman I'd just met.

Then my cousin Roberta hugged me the same way and I felt, *I am home.*

Finally, I was home. This was my home: these people, and this land. Nona took us all over. Where she'd lived, and where Gloria's mother, my aunt Bonnie, and her first husband had lived. Where my mother had walked and slept. Everywhere: green mountains, tree-covered and bountiful. Wild. The Ozarks. She took us out to Beaver Lake, which used to be called Indian Springs before the dam made the lake.

"We lived right up in there, over there," she pointed into the wild forest. "I had an old black mare, she used to sit down on her butt and slide down that hill. I don't know why she did that." Nona was insistent on showing us things; she wanted us to know, wanted us to get it right. All the time, my heart ballooned out of my chest. *Oh, my God. I am part of this*, I thought. *My cells came from here. My molecules. My soul. This is part of me.*

Roberta told me stories of her mother. "She was a midwife: She delivered all the babies around here, all of them, Indian or white. We go to the cemetery on Memorial Day and she walks through the headstones, pointing. 'I birthed that one; I birthed that one. That one ...' Seems like half the county, she's lived so long." My cousin's eyes watered. "She started delivering babies when she was eight or nine years old, apprenticed to an older woman." *Nine* years old and delivering babies, I thought. Good heavens. "The Indians call her Redbird Woman."

Redbirds: cardinals. I'd never seen them before staying at my aunt's. Brilliant scarlet forms swarmed like our California jays do at home. Swarmed over Nona's house, the lawn. Over the trees. Flew above her head. Flocked around her: Redbird Woman.

We were there four or five days. I felt like I'd always lived there. Do you ever feel that way about places? Have you found your physical roots, the soil from which your ancestors sprung? Do you feel the power inherent in the land that formed your ancestors' bones?

We visited Iceland long ago when my father was alive. His people were from there, dating back hundreds of years. What does living in a place for hundreds of years mean? What history? What ties? When I saw Iceland, smelled it, and stepped on it, I felt like I'd been extruded from that earth like the volcanic soil.

Missouri and Arkansas were the same. The other half of the physical me came from those states, from those Ozark Mountains.

And the spiritual part, too. Part of my soul feels right there. It wants to be there, and I shall surely go back.

We went to Roberta's house and met her husband, Cisco. Saw the vast houses where they raised chickens—impressive. Ashley and Sky went with us everywhere, Roberta's granddaughters. They took us to Eureka Springs, Arkansas, a Victorian town so cute I lusted after its real estate. Eureka Springs was old stonework and cast-iron railings, and a bandstand where my mother had danced so many years ago. Nona sat with her white hair and cane while we romped. Time kept flowing; it went too fast. So many thoughts and feelings. I have lots of American Indian blood in my family: I never knew that. What tribe? Cherokee. Do you think that's the reason I was attracted to the Gathering?

We visited Irma Westin, a gracious, older lady who lived in a house that had once belonged to Nona's family—my family. She took us inside: I couldn't believe that—we just dropped by; we weren't invited, and didn't call first. We sipped ice water and talked. Outside, a stone-clad staircase led to an underground cellar in which to hide when the tornados came. Nona told us where the house had once been.

"Over there, beyond the trees. I had to carry water every day, the spring was down here, so we moved the house." She pointed across a wide meadow ringed by trees. Beyond the trees was a long way to haul water. They moved the house.

I learned so much, some to my sorrow. My mother had tried to tell me about her childhood. She said,

"I had to walk six miles to school every day—in the snow."

With my excessive education, I scoffed. It sounded so stereotypical. I knew that the law required schools every so many sections or some such. She couldn't have walked that far: It was against the law. And it doesn't snow in Missouri, anyway. But Nona took us to where they lived, and I understood. It's far from anything *now*. That was sixty years ago. My mother walked *more* than six miles: I measured it on the car's odometer.

And it does snow in Missouri. Mother was trying to tell me of a reality I couldn't grasp. The life she lived was nobler than any made-up tale.

What do you do when someone's gone and you can't say, "Mom, I didn't understand. I had to see it to understand. I'm sorry." I guess you say it anyway and hope she hears.

One night, we'd come back from Roberta's and dinner. We parked under overhanging boughs with tiny green leaves. Still enough light to see, barely.

"Oh, look! Bunnies!" Gloria saw them first. Nine cottontail bunnies scampered about the lawn, between trees and plants. The Rose of Sharon bushes displayed their pale blossoms in a fan. The tidy white house stood like a fairy tale.

"Oh, look, Gloria!" They sparked and glittered, flitting, flashing. Filling the spaces between the blooms. "Fireflies!" I'd never seen them. Gloria and I jumped and giggled, girls home at last. Nona, her white hair piled on top of her head, laughed at us, waving her cane. We danced with the fireflies until they disappeared.

Old pictures in a museum. Pictures of working people with thickened hands. Pictures of old cars and packing labels. Guitars and lean bodies. People of the Depression and the South. Working people. Music from fiddles, not violins. Long-legged girls in cotton dresses leaning against old cars. Music that sang the song of this land and that life. Those were my mother's people in that museum. That music is part of me. Those people are part of me: my people. I come from working people. Both of my grandfathers were farmers and ranchers. My father started working when he was ten. At seventeen, he was a journeyman carpenter. He worked his way through Cal Berkeley swinging a hammer.

"The worst day of my life was when I had to take off my carpenter's belt and stay in the office," my father said. A child of the Depression, he never forgot how to pound nails, never stopped worrying about what would happen when the bad times came back. No matter how well he did, he never forgot that he was a workingman first. I still have his AFL-CIO Carpenter's Union Card somewhere. My father never forgot his roots, and neither did my mother, even though their paths took them far from where they started. That's what came back as I looked at those pictures and listened to my country sing. I spent hours in that museum, inhaling hard.

My feet planted on the hardwood floors, spread to hold me up because the emotion I felt was so ferocious, I cried. I have never felt so much an American as I did walking those decks, looking at those photos, and hearing that sound. That American sound.

I didn't feel American in the sense of "someone drew some lines on a map, so let's go to war." No. I felt like roots extended from my feet, mighty roots to hold up a mighty tree. Those roots went down through the earth to its red core, to the fiery blood-red core that is its heart. And those roots came up and fed me. Me. The daughter born of the woman from Missouri and the man from the icy North Sea. Me: hybrid, mixed-breed, full-blooded me.

I love this land, from the soul out.

## NONA REED
Redbird Woman

CHAPTER 8

# CROSS-COUNTRY

WELL, I GOT WHY I WAS supposed to go to that museum—now all I had to do was get to Coker Creek. I realized something: Mood swings are part of spiritual life, or at least my spiritual life. Usually, I begin getting agitated when I think about signing up for a retreat. It's the intention, the act of will, to expose my ego, mind, and nasty bits to the light of God's consciousness. The worldly self does not like the process of being stripped and remade. The worldly self has invented television, real-time TV, and many other stupid things, so that it never has to look at its scummy parts. Sign up for a retreat; the worldly part knows its control will be loosened, at least for a while.

It's a battle, you know, becoming free. Becoming the people we were meant to be.

Mood swings. Feeling like your soul was cast in cement: dense, dull, with no space to breathe or move. Feeling like it will never, ever get better—this is the way life is and always will be. And then it changes. Tears to hilarity. Sorrow and pain to exaltation. If you're doing your retreat with intention—so you mean it—you may go up and down. Feel things intensely. Good things, bad things. Things you don't want to talk about.

Or, life may not be so dark for you. One of my counseling professors said that every time he was about to have a breakthrough to a new level of understanding—which is what a retreat is about—he would have an almost overwhelming desire to teach in Europe. That's not too heavy: He was in good shape inside. But he'd want to flee the continent.

"That's the worst thing I could have done." He needed to stay where he was, feeling uncomfortable, bored and stuck, until the part of his soul forming beneath his conscious awareness was strong enough to burst out. "Parts of us are always being born, and parts are dying," he said.

This death-and-birth process is painful, but trying to avoid its pain can be ruinous, as evidenced by those who escape into drugs or addiction. Resistance to growth is behind the urge to run; we often don't know what's happening or why we feel so rotten. I've learned enough to know that when that opacity, that lack of light, takes over; something's trying to sprout. The mind fights a new reality; it fights going through doors. What's on the other side?

I saw something funny a while back: My husband was working a yearling filly. All you do to train yearlings is civilize them a bit—make sure they'll behave when the vet handles them. Make sure that you can pick up their feet and trim their hooves. Lead them around. Make sure you can tie them by a lead rope and not have them go nuts. It's horsy kindergarten.

Barry made up an exercise: leading the filly in and out of the empty stalls on both sides of the barn. He'd lead her through the stall door opening, turn around inside, and come out. Cross the aisle, go into the stall on the other side, and come out. Out, across, and so on, until she'd done the whole barn. Why? Because she balked at every single door. Doorways are scary for horses. If a lion were around, it would hide out of sight on the other side. Horses never forget that they're lunch for half the fauna on the earth; it's wired into their brains.

The filly acted like a person: "Oh, there's an opening. I can go through to an expanded place, a new place. Move in the direction I'm supposed to go to grow, or at least get out of the rain. Oh, it's so scary. I think I'll throw a fit."

Which is just what we do. Is it wired into our brains to resist when faced with the next level of our personal growth? So when people are moving into a larger reality, you can expect them to pitch hissy fits at every doorway? Life gets lively.

Also, life can get very funny. Do you know any members of religious orders, people who live cloistered or monastic lives? You may have seen them crack up with laughter at something that seems trivial or silly. You may join them; their mirth is contagious. You may feel intoxicated around people who have dedicated themselves to God.

That's the other thing about spiritual growth, enlightenment, and becoming what/who you're supposed to be: It's light. It sparkles. It's funny. I've known a few enlightened people. They're like living Prozac. Being around them is healing. They don't have to do anything, or even speak your language. They don't mince words and say what they must, but when they do it, they're funny and nurturing. Not abusive. Run from anyone abusive: God ain't behind that rage.

<hr />

Driving down the freeway from Nashville to Coker Creek brought on a four-hour hissy fit. Big-time culture shock. After the day before, I felt like a split log. I'd been solid, wooden, and one piece. Wham! Something hit me on the head and I was in two halves on the ground. One half wondered if it should bleed out; the other thought it would laugh to death. The process that hauled my cousin and me to Missouri in July had barely begun. As I drove, my mind flamed. I hated everything I saw.

You know what the mind is, don't you? It's that racket you hear inside your head. Not the *Voice*—the mind is the little voice that says you will die if the table isn't set properly. That your grandmother always wore gloves and a hat, and if people don't do that, or at least know they should, bad things will happen. It's your survival programming. You don't have to pay any attention to it, unless there really is a lion out there. Though it often raises false alarms, the mind does make things entertaining. Mine looked at the Tennessee landscape and shuddered.

"It's too green." The entire eastern half of the United States suffers from being too green. Probably, it's the result of that extremely disturbing summer rain. It never rains in California in the summer, unless you're over eight-thousand feet. Maybe ten. I drove, expecting the Foliage Police to bust the State of Tennessee for excessive greenness. Also, they'd planted the wrong kinds of trees, and too close together. Most unsettling.

The freeway signs were wrong. In California, we have lots of big signs. When you drive north through Silicon Valley, the signs say things like: Gilroy, San Jose, Palo Alto, and, eventually, San Francisco. We also have big signs giving the names of streets along the freeway. All are located so you have plenty of time to turn at the correct off-ramp.

But Tennessee's road signs—and sorry, Tennesseans, I like *you* a great deal—but your road signs? Too few, too late, and what do all those numbers mean?

Halfway to Tellico Plains, I realized that the exit numbers correlated with the numbers on the map, so I could simply remember my exit's number and then count down to where I should turn. This was easy—while mind-boggled, I still could count and remember a three-digit number.

Also—I finally figured out which gauge on the rental car was the fuel gage, so that I could stop trying to fill up my almost-empty car. (Oops. That was the *temperature* gauge that was so low. Gas was pouring out of the side of the car.)

Traveling is extremely trying. I attempted to argue with my annoyance:

"Sandy, you wanted to get away from home and see something different. You wanted a change ... This is a change."

"I don't care. It's too different. It should be like home."

That's like people who go to foreign countries and kvetch the whole time because they're *foreign*. Of course they are, that's the definition of the word: different from home.

Food was the area of most extreme culture shock. My shock rapidly turned to guilt as I lost control. To get an idea of how different Tennessee's food is from California's: I went to my local supermarket a few days ago. It's a not an uppity place, but I counted *thirty-one* types of pre-washed, packaged lettuce. That's regular lettuce. An additional eight types of *organic*, pre-washed lettuce existed, plus seven wash-it-yourself types, and six organic, you-wash-it varieties. I'm not making this up. That doesn't include spinach and other leafy things you could use in a salad.

For dinner, everyone in our family normally eats about one-third-pound of deep-water fish loaded with essential fatty acids. We have our fish broiled—no added oil. Accompanying the fish, we consume a gigantic mound of vegetable matter, either steamed or raw. Dessert? Wouldn't think of it.

In Tennessee, I found devouring platters of Fried Things thrilling but anxiety-producing. Would I go to hell? My father had nonfat yogurt and celery juice for lunch in the early 1960s. It's a good thing he's dead: Seeing what I ate would have killed him. I didn't know what chicken and dumplings were when I first saw them. What they are is delicious.

Enough food talk. I have to wash lettuce.

<hr />

In culture shock or not, I still had to get to the retreat site. It's hard to get lost when there's only one turn to make off the freeway, but I did. Wanting to get to Coker Creek (which is some distance past the metropolis of Tellico Plains) before nightfall, I left Nashville—early enough, I thought. No sense being compulsive. And I got to Coker Creek, eventually.

A rule of the universe: The narrower and more winding the road, the faster the jerk in the four-wheel-drive monster truck behind you goes, and the closer he gets to your bumper. He'll shove his hood so close that you can't see his headlights; you'll know he's there by the sound of his breathing. This is especially true if it's getting dark, you don't know where you are, and the road has no shoulders. Terror almost kept me from appreciating how beautiful the drive was. I must have gotten used to greenness: The countryside around Coker Creek is exquisite. Leafy forests. Fallen branches. Moss.

By watching street numbers, I was able to figure out that the retreat center was coming up. Hoping the guy in the truck wouldn't ram my car's rear, I veered left, bounding into the Coker Creek Retreat Center's parking lot. The main building was so big! I'd seen pictures of the meeting hall, but I was unprepared for just how beautiful the place is. The main lodge is a spectacular log building, exactly what you'd hope to see at the end of a drive like that.

I pulled into a parking place and jimmied my way out of the car. A few hours of terrified disorientation can stiffen muscles like you wouldn't believe. I looked around, trying not to seem like a displaced Californian. Some people unloaded their cars. Others sat on the front porch in rocking chairs. Do you believe it? Rocking chairs on the porch. How cute. How Southern. I felt like squealing the way my cousin and I did in Missouri, but figured I would look strange squealing alone. Next year, I'll bring Gloria.

My breathing expanded, my attitude soared: Look at this place. A stream ran through the property, meandering in front of the headquarters. That must be Coker Creek. Oh, gee—there's really a creek at Coker Creek. I wandered through a gate, across a bridge, onto the adorable front porch with the rocking chairs. Hello, hello. Lots of people.

I ran into Vicki Collins, the Gathering's Chair. In 2001, I was making up my mind about attending and emailed Vicki. I had some questions about the Gathering's content. Specifically, since it's sponsored by a church group, would we be proselytized or have a particular point of view rammed down our throats? The answers were: no and no. Vicki and I emailed a couple more times, when whammo! Something jelled. I felt like

I'd met my sister. Aspects of our lives were so similar that it was impossible that this woman live across the country and understand me so completely. She felt the same about me.

The shock of recognition. That's what it is, isn't it? You're cruising along and all of a sudden you run into someone, and it's as if he or she was planted there for your benefit. Recognition. We move forward through recognition of the truth, and of each other. Synchronicity: Carl Jung's term. The threads of our lives meet and intertwine in meaningful ways that can't be predicted by outer circumstances.

Many theories describe the phenomenon of recognition and synchronicity. Jung's in the West, and many schools of thought in the East. A Hindu text called the *Pratyabhijñā-hṛdayam*—a mouthful—presents the doctrine of recognition, or re-cognition, very clearly. In essence, it says that we have forgotten our real identity, our essential unity with God. Awakening to our true identity is the first step in reuniting with the larger God. We have to take baby steps at first, recognizing people and places that are bonded to us.

When I first started an email exchange with Vicki, I had no idea I'd offer to put up a web page for the Gathering, but I did. And I've kept putting it up. This never had happened before—but I was called to do the page, just as I'm called to do this book. Spirit calls. You answer, or end up diminished.

What was Vicki like in person? Would this be like those Internet romances where the person you've been corresponding with on-line turns out to have revolting personal traits that didn't come across the Net?

Vicki was exactly what I thought she'd be: strikingly attractive, intelligent, and diplomatic. She was gracious—and also very busy at that moment. I met her and her husband, who was also the wonderful man I expected.

I put my things in my cabin, then looked around the Coker Creek grounds. Overhead, the sky stretched high and wide, laced with wispy clouds. Pines rimmed the edges and lawns covered the rest. The air seemed alive; even the log cabins sparkled in the balmy dusk. The Gathering was already heaven.

## HOW TO SUCCEED ON RETREAT

We'll start our retreat tomorrow. Many of you may be wondering how to succeed at a retreat. It's the how-to age. If you go into a bookstore, it seems all you need for a best-seller is a list of ten things to do and a catchy title. *Ten Ways of Achieving Nirvana Today.* Everyone has a system and a plan to help you be you. I can never get past the first step. With retreats, only one step matters:

**Be there.**

To have a successful retreat, you have to be there. That means getting to the retreat site physically, which sometimes isn't that easy. And you have to be there, once you're there.

Sound easy? It's not. Everything within you will resist being there fully. Yes, I'm talking to you. The one with the nose stuck in the notebook, recording the lecture so you can regurgitate it later. That doesn't matter. If you're really there at the retreat and the speaker's inspired, you probably won't be able to remember the lecture or much else. The substance of what's being said will sink in if you listen, don't worry. If you take notes, you'll distance yourself from its essence. By all means, take notes in designated periods, write in your journal at the end of the day, and buy a tape of the lecture if it's available, but don't use a pen and paper to hide.

One great way of not being where you are is bundling up with your friends or family. Clumps of people walk around with their heads in a knot, inseparable, lost in chatter, lost in the drama they brought from home. Missing the drama all around them and inside.

Complaining to people who can't do anything about what's bothering you is a great way of not being there. So is gossiping about that juicy thing that you just heard. And retreats are such great places to hear the latest gossip, because everyone is there. "Did you hear about … ?" "And then he said … "

Another sort of distraction exists: "Oh, girlfriend, look at *him*. He is so *fine* … " And he's spiritual, too—he's at a retreat. Six hours of stalking later: "Why, hello. I don't believe we've met. Is this your first time at our retreat?" You can almost hear the eyelashes flapping and feel the heat.

What else? The technological age brings us new ways to escape. Laptops. Cell phones. You can be a thousand miles from the sanctuary grounds when your cell phone's stuck to your ear.

You're not even safe if you disengage the electronic equipment, because your mind cannot be turned off. Unless you take drugs or get loaded, and most retreat centers frown on that, you're stuck with the perpetual voice in your head. Watch that voice; listen to it. This is good. Watching that inner drama is one reason we go on retreat. Watching the inner and outer drama with detachment is why we're there.

Just watch and let the magic work. This book is about contemplation. It is a record of a contemplation I had for a year or so. A contemplation I'm having now. The knot that bound my thoughts and feelings, the events and desires, was a retreat called the Gathering, held in the green forest of Tennessee.

# THIS IS SOUL WORK.

CHAPTER 9

# BUSTED FLAT IN COKER CREEK

SUNLIGHT FILTERED THROUGH the mini-blinds. I opened my eyes: I was in bed in a log cabin. At Coker Creek. Fuzzily, I realized I was at the Gathering. The clock indicated plenty of time to eat breakfast and get to the opening ceremonies by 8:30. I tried to move. Couldn't. My back hurt as much as it ever has. Spasms gripped my spine, my muscles talking in fast pain barks. I knew what that meant. Oh, no. Not now. No.

I have a birth defect in the spinal nerves that has resulted in a couple of bad discs. My back has caused me endless hours of agony; it has made my life far different than it might have been. Most of the time I get along okay, except when I make a four-hour drive after a cross-country flight when I'm exhausted and in a period of personal stress. Riding in a car is the worst thing I can do to my back. It doesn't hurt when it goes out, but a few hours later I'm in agony. If you have back trouble, you know about this. Back pain is the worst.

I hadn't brought anything for it. Frantic, I thought of calling my husband and having him FedEx my pain meds and anti-spasm stuff, and my anti-inflammatories. But it would take twenty-four hours to arrive—the Gathering would be over by the time I got the medication, even if FedEx did make Sunday deliveries. I thought of telling Vicki or her husband of my plight, but they had their hands full. I was on my own—and I wanted to participate so badly.

I felt like a cracked egg: One slip and I'd be all over the floor. I got up gingerly and somehow got to breakfast. Every minute was its own universe. When I got to the dining hall, I was amazed at how much food they had, and how few people. Still, I was on time. I have a tendency to run late, which you will have noticed if you've been watching for the web report on the latest Gathering. That morning, I was on time.

Walking back to the main hall through the meadow, I was barely aware of the beauty around me. I don't know how many acres Coker Creek encompasses: It's big. Horse pastures and tall pine trees ring the green field. In the morning light, cobwebs and dew sparkled. I walked as if every vertebra were made of glass. In addition to pain, I felt anxious, the way the earth in the Santa Cruz Mountains must have felt before the Loma Prieta quake.

"Hey, man," said one boulder to another. "Somethin' feel weird to you?"

"Yeah. The last time I felt this way was 1906 ... " Uh-oh.

This reminds me of a Psalm. One of my favorites is Psalm 19. The language is stunning:

> *The heavens tell out the glory of God,*
> *The vault of heaven reveals his handiwork ...*

I love the entire Psalm, but for me, the most valuable part is at the end:

> *Who is aware of his unwitting sins?*
> *Cleanse me of any secret fault.*
> *Hold back thy servant also from sins of self-will,*

*Lest they get the better of me.*
*Then I shall be blameless*
*And innocent of any great transgression.*

Secret faults. The things we don't know about ourselves that may cause us to transgress—break God's rules—greatly. This Psalm holds enormous wisdom. What do we not know about ourselves? Usually things that are totally obvious to everyone around us, but are outside our awareness, secret to us. I was approaching a secret fault.

People from California know about faults. They're not just things like zits or a bad temper. Faults are cracks in the surface that reach down into the core. If pressure becomes too great, they can break open, causing fissures that pull you and all you love into the flaming depths. *That's* a fault. The only secret is: You don't know it exists until you run into it.

Something was happening inside me; what, I didn't know. Inching my way back to the main hall and the introductory program, I didn't know if I would make it. That whole morning, I didn't know if I would make it.

What got me through it? What gets me through when I approach the chasm? I think He was with me before I was born; certainly I know He was there when I was in my crib. At first I was only aware of Him sporadically, at my worst moments, when I thought of ending this time on earth. Now He comes to give me messages, to tell me to adjust my course, or look around. To see the truth and forgive. Always, He lives in my heart, or the air around me or the mountains or sky. The trees. I can feel Him with me.

Jesus Christ walked across that meadow with me, holding my hand.

I was born into a Christian family, though not your ordinary kind of Christians. My dad was very smart: He couldn't stand hearing a platitude uttered from the pulpit. He wanted philosophy; he wanted life's big issues addressed. If the minister didn't hold his interest, my father would sit in church doing his income taxes on the back of the bulletin, stirring himself to sing loudly and off-key. He wouldn't come back to any preacher who didn't hit as hard as he did. My mother was also a Christian. She didn't go to church often, but Jesus was in her heart. She did her best to see that He came to me, too, and would be delighted to know that the treatment worked. Given my openness to all forms of religious expression, some people are surprised when they discover that I love Jesus. I find that odd, because He's as real to me as my own body and with me as constantly.

I walked through that morning with Jesus, and a few Christian saints who are dear to me. Also my entire meditation lineage and some of their friends from the East. Plus another troop that started coming to me when I was researching my first book, still wondering why Indians were in it. Yes, a few departed historical Indians who've touched my heart joined the troop. A gang walked across that meadow with me, and through the next few hours. To paraphrase the Beatles, I got by with a little help from my friends.

The main hall was deserted when I entered it for the orientation. Just like the dining hall had been at breakfast. I had an ominous feeling I was late. I'm always late; at home, I usually blame it on someone in my family. Here, I was alone. Also, I was on retreat, one of the best places to perceive my defects. How could I be late? My watch said I was fine.

Vicki Collins found me and said, "There's a time zone change between here and Nashville. It's an hour later here." Was whoever drew the time zones conspiring against me?

Vicki showed me to my first workshop. The 2003 Gathering had workshops Saturday and Sunday mornings on various aspects of Native American culture. I had signed up for hoop dancing on Saturday. This is where the dancer takes a bunch of things that look like small hula hoops and dances while passing them around and through parts of his body. Starting off with just one or two hoops, the dancer adds more, and more, forming elaborate figures and designs, shimmying like a snake. He ends by creating a full-scale model of DNA out of a zillion hoops. I signed up for the workshop because I've seen hoop dancers and couldn't believe it.

Just the thing for my back. When I got to the class, Lowery Begay was giving a talk. Lowery is an award-winning hoop dancer and gave us an informative talk about hoop dancing and how to relate to Native Americans. "When you meet a Native American, don't barrage him with stories about your culture."

Jonathon Feather (Eastern Cherokee/Sioux) took over the class, telling us about his background as a champion hoop dancer and boxer. He gave a rousing demonstration, then invited the class participants to try. This was fun. People were amazingly good—some were able to dance with more than one hoop. The class was so entertaining that I found myself laughing and enjoying myself. Considering how I'd felt when I woke up, that was a miracle. I did not try the hoops.

The other classes were: "Rivercane Flutes" with Danny Bigay. Danny, a Cherokee/Choctaw craftsman, taught participants how flutes are constructed and gave some elements of beginning playing. Scott Crisp (of Cherokee descent) taught "Cherokee Hunting & Games," featuring principles of Cherokee stickball and use of the traditional Cherokee blowgun. "Questions You Always Wanted to Ask a Native American" gave participants the chance to inquire about Native culture. A group of expert teachers led this workshop: Lowery and Emerson Begay and their mother, Ida Begay, (all Navajo) taught the class along with Ben Sanchez (Navajo). Everyone at the Gathering was able to take two courses, on Saturday and Sunday mornings. This was a feast of American Indian culture.

After that, everyone walked across the meadow to the dining hall for lunch. The Gathering involved lots of food. Lots of nice people. One of the women at my table made an observation about something I said that blasted me into a new awareness. More on this in a minute.

Lunch consumed, we made another walk back to the main hall for Bill Miller's talk. I arrived late, as always, stumbling over people as I found a seat.

Clad in jeans, T-shirt, and a black leather vest, Bill set one of his paintings on a ledge at the rear of the stage. The image of traditional warrior leapt from the canvas. Bill looks like the photos on his CDs. A striking man, his loose, black hair fell below his shoulders, while his high cheekbones, aquiline nose, and sienna skin identified him as an American Indian. Moving to the front of the stage, Bill took over the room, speaking with easy intensity.

"At a certain point, things start coming to you by themselves. You follow that guidance, and things happen for you. Now, all I do is hang out and do my life." His guitar lay on the floor by his feet, a custom-made instrument bearing an inlaid eagle and other Native motifs. Behind him were a number of other guitars, to their right a rack of Native American flutes.

"A while back, I needed to raise some money fast; it was an emergency. I had a collection of Gibson guitars from the '60s, the real thing. A guy told me he'd buy them. What he'd give me was about a tenth of what they were worth, but I'd get the cash I needed right away. I told him I'd do it. My wife was mad at me. She said, 'Go to the bank! Don't give them away.'

"Even though it made no sense, I knew that I was supposed to do what I did. I heard a voice telling me to sell the guitars. It seemed crazy, because they were worth so much more than what I got, but I knew I was supposed to do it. After I sold them, I realized why: Those guitars were all bound up with things that happened to me in the '70s. They were holding me in the past, trapping me back there. I needed to cut loose from that, and getting rid of the guitars did it. I was free. That voice was right: I didn't know it until I did what it said.

"Then weird stuff started happening to me, all by itself. I didn't do anything but live my life, and stuff came to me." Big good stuff came: PBS called him to do a special. Bill filmed the special, *Songs of the Spirit*, in New Mexico with friends R. Carlos Nakai and Joanne Shenandoah and the New Mexico Symphony Orchestra. PBS plans to show the program nationwide for several years. *Major* good things came.

"My guitar company called me up and said they appreciated me using their new guitar line. They gave me all of those," he indicated the guitars behind him, "for free. And then this flute company called and said the same thing, and gave me their whole line of flutes. For nothing." He pointed to the wooden rack filled with instruments. "All I did was hang out and do my life."

As Bill spoke, I was jumping up and down in my seat going, "Yes! Yes! It's true." If you live your life, facing the challenges before you, things seem to come of their own accord. Several months before the Gathering, we got an email from a man in Australia who was interested in buying some of our horses. We'd never had a prospective customer from Australia.

At that time, we did not know that Jorge de Moya was a master horseman with very deep roots in the horse world. We didn't know about his innovative horse-breeding program on his Australian plantation.

We thought he was just some guy wanting to cross half the globe to see our horses.

Eventually, Jorge arrived. We immediately clicked. Jorge spent a very fast day with us, instructing us about our own horses. He left, buying our stallion and two of our best mares.

It seemed effortless, like the series of events Bill Miller described.

But was it? Do you think PBS would have called Bill if he didn't produce beautiful and meaningful music? If he wasn't reliable, so they knew he'd complete the concert recording sessions? Would they have called if he'd been singing to the birds in his backyard all his life, instead of tromping around the country on tours? No way.

Bill had spent his entire life preparing for that call. When it came, he was ready. It seemed effortless.

Ditto our experience. Did Jorge come to our ranch and see a bunch of rank horses we'd just pulled out of pasture? No. My husband and our trainer had worked them until they were fit enough to challenge Olympic athletes. And they were what they were intrinsically, bearing the blood of the foundation horses of our breed.

Not only that, Jorge said, "I started reading *Spurs Magazine* and couldn't stop. I spent the whole afternoon reading—I couldn't get up from the computer."

My words reached across the planet and found a kindred soul.

These incidents where good things happen so unexpectedly that they seem magical are really things we've trained for and are ready to receive. Richard Pascale, Ph.D., co-authored *The Art of Japanese Management* and speaks of this in describing the Japanese approach to negotiations. When the Japanese couldn't decide what to do, they'd decide to proceed, and assume that an answer would be there when they got to it. My church taught something similar: When you reach an impasse, go forward and do your homework—prepare—just like you knew the outcome you wanted was there.

And God will meet you.

Call it synchronicity, call it grace, call it an act of spirit: It happens. That mysterious, non-material force sometimes seems to disappear, but it doesn't.

Just as Bill gave up his guitars, only to get a national TV show, more guitars *and* flutes, God was not finished with us, either. One day in the months before the Gathering, an email came from a woman who'd just moved to Santa Barbara. She'd read my stuff about horses on the Net and wondered if she could board her horse with us. As I started to fire off a response—"Thank you for your interest, but we don't board horses"—I noticed the signature below her name.

She was a literary agent and publicist. At that time, I would have done pretty near anything to have a literary agent represent my writing and me. I checked out her web site. She'd worked for everyone from Michael Crichton to Magic Johnson. I looked her up in *Publishers' Marketplace*. She was there—a legitimate agent. This was another of those moments ...

I wrote back, "We don't board horses, but I have this book ... "

Next thing, she was at our house saying, "I don't do fiction, but I'll take your novel."

She left, bearing the first few hundred pages of my vast tome. I was too shocked to dance around the kitchen, screaming in ecstasy, for very long.

Had it really happened? Did I have an agent?

No, as it turned out. A while later, I received a very kind email saying, "I really don't do fiction. Your book is very good, but I don't know where or how I'd market it."

Being rejected by someone you know and like is worse than being rejected by strangers.

Was it over? No. Remember Bill's seemingly unconnected chance events? Good stuff coming from nowhere? A few days later, I was surprised to receive an email from John Friend. John is one of the top hatha yoga instructors in the country and founder of Anusara Yoga. When I decided to write *The Horse Book* after Mark Victor Hansen's MEGA Book Marketing University, I thought of John Friend immediately. That book is about horses, spirit, and physical posture. I'd written to him and forgotten about it.

So now, by perfect coincidence, John emailed, saying he was handing my request for information to some of his teachers who rode horses.

An idea hit! I fired another email off to the agent who'd just rejected my novel.

"Wanna do a horse book?"

She fired back:

"Yes! Yes! Yes! Do it! Write it!"

How many writers ever get to hear that from an agent? By perfect coincidence, she'd seen the movie *Seabiscuit* the night before and cried all the way through it. She was a spiritually inclined horse lover and knew the moment for my book had arrived.

She said the magic words, "Write a couple of chapters and I can sell it!"

Nice, huh? That moment took fifty-eight years to arrive.

Right away, I started the new book. I wrote about horses. Wrote some good stuff; stuff never seen in any horse book. Lined up some great people to interview.

And froze solid. I kept writing, but it felt like blue jell toothpaste came out of my fingers into the computer. Strange foreign symbols emerged, meaning nothing. The work didn't feel coherent—and finally, I couldn't write at all.

Frozen. Turgid. Opaque. Contracted. Without room to move. That was my inner state when I left for the Gathering. The opposite of effortless. That's why I was such a wreck heading into Tennessee, obsessing about *The Horse Book*—I had the best possibility of real publication I'd had to date. All I had to do was write it—which is when I choked.

At the Gathering, I told this story at lunch, and the woman across from me said, "Fear of success."

She nailed it exactly. I'm wired to work and try and produce great stuff—and never succeed. The minute success was in sight, I froze.

At a retreat, you don't just learn from the presenters, the key speaker, or the entertainment. You learn from everyone, especially the other people who attend.

"Fear of success," she said. The truth is a great gift. My life has been about success—proving I'm worthy and adequate. I've succeeded, but not at something that felt truly mine. Even though my writing feels like it's dictated, it comes through me. Whatever that voice is, it chose me to broadcast the message. The smaller parts of me were afraid to step through the door to something larger.

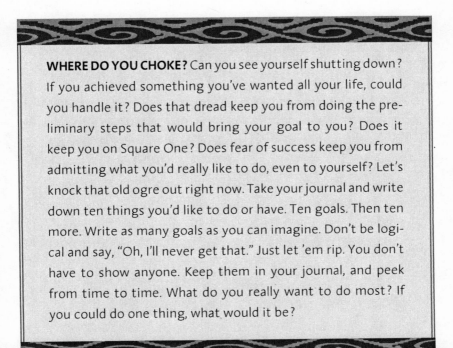

**WHERE DO YOU CHOKE?** Can you see yourself shutting down? If you achieved something you've wanted all your life, could you handle it? Does that dread keep you from doing the preliminary steps that would bring your goal to you? Does it keep you on Square One? Does fear of success keep you from admitting what you'd really like to do, even to yourself? Let's knock that old ogre out right now. Take your journal and write down ten things you'd like to do or have. Ten goals. Then ten more. Write as many goals as you can imagine. Don't be logical and say, "Oh, I'll never get that." Just let 'em rip. You don't have to show anyone. Keep them in your journal, and peek from time to time. What do you really want to do most? If you could do one thing, what would it be?

Meanwhile, Bill was still talking. My brain had been swallowed by the "Wow, this is so powerful, I think I'll zone out" syndrome. Something happens when a spiritually elevated person's speech profoundly impacts me: The message goes straight into my heart, bypassing my brain. Hopefully, the relevant stuff will surface when I need it, like now.

Also, I was busy. Remember our *subpersonalities?* Mine were baying like a pack of hounds.

Shuddering with embarrassment, one part of me heard Bill's talk, thinking, Oh, wow. That's the real Bill up there. The one I wrote that letter to.

The physical part went, Will I live through this? Will my back disintegrate totally, so that I die in that cabin tonight, or maybe right now?

Spiritual parts and the Voice: Oh, wow. Is this groovy.

Other parts listened: The words went in and disappeared. I don't think this is Alzheimer's. Other people have reported the same phenomena at spiritual events.

My Inner Writer, which has been to far too many book-writing-and-marketing seminars, was freaking out: Oh, wow! Listen to that! What he's saying is a book outline. Oh, my God! Does he know what he has? I mean, Bill, just tape-record it! Get somebody to transcribe the tape—*staple* your talks together and it's done. You have a *book*, Bill! Why didn't someone tell him?

I told him after his talk, "Bill, you have a book. Why don't you write it?"

"Several major publishers have told me they'd publish my book," Bill replied.

At that, my Inner Writer clawed her hair and *screamed!* Does he know what all those people in seminars would give to hear those words? What did you do, Bill? What is your Great Secret Tip to getting published? Market it and you can make millions—in addition to publishing your book. That's *two* books.

I've already talked about what he did to get publishers to line up for his book: He did his life. He handled what was in front of him, one step at a time for however many years he's been around. So now, he's just living, and it's coming to him effortlessly.

That's just a little too easy. Nothing's that easy.

Yes, it is. If you do what's in front of you, you're also training yourself. This self-training is called behaviorism. The theory has such a bad rap among "spiritual" types, who tend to regard behaviorists as soulless people who experiment on lab rats and go around chanting, "Training and environment. Training and environment." This isn't a true picture: I've known behaviorists who were kindhearted and godly souls. Behaviorists simply consider how one acts and what one does as keys to personal change.

While Bill talked, he gave a demonstration of behaviorism. He talked about doing gigs for money early in his career. I forget what the musical term is, but it means, "When you go to a venue and play music that someone else wrote, smiling, until they pay you and you get to go home." This is not pleasant for an artist. At talks elsewhere, I've heard him speak of playing over the racket of drunken bikers, handling hecklers, loudmouths, and other obnoxious folk. He's played in terrible places. Now he's getting better places and really wonderful places. He just keeps going. He gave a bunch of tips about what he does when he performs, in addition to giving a demo—knocking us flat with his presentation. I'll let him tell you about his tips in the book I hope he's writing.

What I got was: He didn't quit. He kept going, training himself to deal with whatever happens. So that now, he can go anywhere and take over not just the stage, but also the whole building. Blow people away. He's used his daily life to hone himself finer, so that when he gets to play in the really big places—his personal-goal-type places—it's just another job. You must do this, because if you skip steps, when you finally get what you want—you'll freak out.

Bill was still talking; I was getting lots of insight and inspiration. The warring voices in my head kept firing at each other. The absolute worst of the bunch picked away behind them, as it had been the entire time I'd been in Tennessee:

*Why aren't you working?* it whispered, even though I was at a retreat, the purpose of which is not to do what you always do, even though I could barely walk, and had been commanded by the big honcho Voice *not* to work. This weasel kept chipping away, saying the scariest things:

*If your agent finds out you haven't completed your two chapters, she'll drop you. Terror. You'll be back at the beginning again. You'd better get to work.* More terror.

I'm a compulsive worker, a workaholic. Addictions are not just to substances, but also behaviors. Gambling, shopping, spending, exercise. Working. Only the Voice, the Supreme Commander of Grandma Sandy's Inner Army, kept that viper under control.

Do you experience this kind of inner mutiny? Can you identify the parts that push you to do self-destructive things? Can you feel how hard they are to fight? I knew what I needed: a hospital and traction, or at least to be flat on my back.

This cacophony of interior idiots was trying to destroy me. Even worse—they *were* me. Only the Voice kept them in check. All the while, I sat in the main hall, trying to look like a harmless Californian.

. Is it any wonder that terrorists could strike anywhere on the planet? If all this lives in my head, the head of a mostly nonviolent grandmother, what about the rest of humanity?

Bill finished his talk. Everyone milled around the stage. Vicki came up to me and said, "Bill said he'd be glad to have you interview him."

I was delighted, having asked Vicki if she'd see if Bill would let me interview him for *Spurs Magazine*. I've written a great deal about him over the years, but these have been my impressions, not interviews with him. Wow. Bill and I arranged a time the next day. The crowd dispersed to get ready for the powwow.

I held back, thinking, *How exciting. I get to do the interview.* Only one problem: I'd completely forgotten that I'd asked Vicki if she could arrange an interview. I had no questions, no tape recorder. No nada. My back was worse. I felt a fog closing in.

⋙⊰◉⊱⋘

How can one rest when a powwow's going on? The drums do it: that BOOM Boom, BOOM Boom, BOOM Boom—like a heartbeat. The singers' voices rise and fall like a piercing tide. Powwows put me in a trance state in thirty seconds, maximum. Instant primal experience. The voices and drum cut through the logical mind and let something else shine through. This was only my fourth powwow—being powwow-deprived—and it was marvelous. Powwows are an addiction for which treatment is not necessary.

The Gathering's powwow was fun and involving. The entry ceremony was moving, as a number of dancers, all veterans, presented the United States and Cherokee flags. Jonathon Feather was the Master of Ceremonies. The Head Man Dancer was Scott Crisp, while the Head Woman was Vickie Standingdeer (Cherokee). Hear 2 Sing was the host drum; Ben Sanchez and Lowery Begay were Lead Singers. The visiting drum was Big Red.

My previous powwow experience has been at our local Chumash Band of Mission Indians' Annual Powwow near Santa Barbara. My daughter and I attended our first some years ago. The visual and aural spectacle threw us into rapture; the display of regalia was breathtaking. My daughter Lily and I walked around the powwow circle, which had several drums. The announcer called a group of dancers into the center.

"It's like a horse show," Lily whispered as the dancers moved around the circle.

They're very similar: Horse shows have an assortment of classes, and shows of the various equine breeds have different rules and requirements. In our breed, Peruvian Pasos, one class may require a Western saddle and bridle, while another might require Peruvian tack. What the horse has to do varies in each class, or the class may require a different kind of rider (male or female, amateur or professional).

Powwows seemed like that: different types of dance, each with a required regalia and dance mode, some for men, others for women. We watched, and found we could pick the winners pretty easily—the fruit of watching thousands of horse show classes. You learn to watch for a thread, and for a quality of movement and expression: The winner is obvious, much of the time.

The Gathering's powwow seemed a kinder, gentler powwow than the bigger ones I've attended. The dancers were more approachable. The rules seemed to be looser, too. I was taking pictures and someone told me, "That's okay here, but I probably wouldn't do that somewhere else."

Yipes. I hadn't even thought about etiquette. It was a nice place to learn, and some very good dancers were present. I even danced! Or shuffled rhythmically, sort of. The wonderful woman who named my "fear of success" phobia convinced me to take a spin around the grass.

"I can't go out there, I'm not dressed." No matter, she got me out.

A potato dance was being organized when my back said, "That's it. Put me to bed or you'll be screaming." As the dancers divvied up potatoes and each couple held one between their foreheads, I headed for my cabin. I could hear laughter behind me, as the dancers moved to the music while trying to keep the potato from falling. Last one in is the winner. I didn't see that, or the rest of the powwow. Lowery did his hoop dance—what else did I miss?

Was I crying when I lay down in my cabin? If not physically, certainly in my heart. How could this happen? I came all this way to be laid low by a scrap of tissue? My back had been getting worse ever since I learned I could interview Bill. When I left the powwow, my back felt like a bit of an electric drill had bored into my spine.

I put on a meditation tape that always knocks me out and lay there, hoping I'd recover enough to go to Bill's concert that evening.

"Busted flat in Baton Rouge ... " I could recall Janis Joplin's voice. I'd hit bottom in Coker Creek.

# CHAPTER 10

# SECRETS & FAULTS

LYING ON MY BED, THE STRAINS of my chant tape around me, I felt so vulnerable I could shatter. I lay quietly, waiting to see if rest and meditation would help me. It happened almost immediately.

A voice spoke, one of those internal voices, but it seemed to hover a few feet above me and to my left. It was a young girl's voice, part of me. She was upset about the upcoming interview with Bill. I listened to her concerns and assured her that everything would be all right. She believed me, because she disappeared—taking my back pain with her. Poof! The stabbing pain disappeared, as if it hadn't been there.

Shocked and amazed, I nevertheless knew that I needed to rest and drift into meditation. My mind was very excited, wanting to rush out and announce my miracle:

"The pain is gone! It disappeared, just like that! What a powerful demonstration of the connection between the mind and body. Wow."

No, I was supposed to wait. I relaxed into a state between sleep and wakefulness, just floating, but aware. More was coming: I could feel it.

My chest felt like it split in half—a crack as wide as the universe ripped my heart. Something leapt from my core, a shard-like clear crystal, composed of energy.

That energy hovered over me, sparking. I felt piercing terror for perhaps two seconds, then drifted back into meditation. I knew what that shard was, and how it got there.

Several years ago, my doctor said something that really frightened me:

"You have cancer."

In the surgery and the rest that followed, I thought I handled my fear. I talked to my friends, and wrote powerful poetry. I took care of myself. My internist said, "I can't believe how well you're handling this."

Everyone said that. I thought it, too: "I'm tough. Don't mess with me, cancer ... " I was not going to be intimidated by disease or death. I was a Yogini—a female spiritual warrior. I had triumphed.

Except that I'd spent the previous two years driving myself to the edge—and beyond.

That gemstone bursting from my heart was fear of death. Its sliver had penetrated my hub, where it was encapsulated. That shred of fear drove me to work like a maniac.

Death is a funny animal. You can think this and that about it; you can believe that you're ready to die and not attached to your body or this physical world. As death's face turns to you, all that dissolves. I shook with terror.

When my doctor said, "You have cancer," I heard, "You are going to die." Facing death was the hardest thing I've done. I thought I'd faced all my fear, but I hadn't; a tiny splinter lurked inside, goading me.

As it hovered overhead, I understood what had happened. Something similar occurred when my father was killed: I didn't grieve for him. Maybe I was too shocked, maybe too much in the grip of my sophisticated culture. Unexpressed grief ran me for twenty years. I became Wonder Woman—doing everything I could to get him back. It didn't work: He didn't come back. The only thing that worked was feeling my grief.

## DO YOU KNOW HOW TO CONTROL YOUR FEELINGS?

Say you have a big meeting to attend, and people will be there that make you see red. You don't want to start screaming at them and blow it. Do you know how to handle those feelings? This also works for fear of death and grief—it's what I did as that splinter of primordial fear released above me.

To control your feelings, feel them. Try this exercise: Sit down in a chair someplace where you're alone and have some privacy. Imagine the meeting—or whatever it is that you're facing. Imagine what the room will look like, who will be there. What they'll look like and say. Imagine the words, and what you'll feel. Let the feelings come up—and feel them. Feel them beforehand, if you're preparing for something, or privately if you're grieving. (I've included some materials on grieving in the Resources section.) See how the event goes after this preparation. I was taught this technique in graduate school and use it all the time. It works for me, sometimes fully, sometimes just enough.

No technique could work in the face of cancer: That fear was off the scale. Death is a primal fear. A very smart guy named Ernest Becker wrote a book entitled *Denial of Death*, which later won the Pulitzer Prize. Writing as he was dying, Becker stated that almost everything we do is an attempt to block out the fact that we will die. Everything from capitalists amassing fortunes to the ancient Egyptian Pharaohs building the pyramids is the result of our inability to deal with the fact that this life will end. (I'm not talking about religious interpretations of the afterlife, just the physical fact of death.)

My fear was not so much of death but of not finishing my work. I was afraid that I'd die incomplete, not having gotten out the message that I was born to deliver.

Lying on my bed at Coker Creek, I watched all this. I felt so delicate, almost newly born. Something was unfolding, more was revealed every minute. The Voice was in control. I was supposed to do something.

My meditation tape lasts exactly thirty-six minutes. At the end of that time, I leapt up, grabbed a clipboard and pen and went outside. Sitting on the porch, I knocked out some questions for my interview with Bill. They flowed from me as if I were taking dictation. Next, an outline of *The Horse Book* emerged from my pen: chapter names, subheadings, content. Whom I should contact for input. This piece was far more complete than what I had previously written. It took forty minutes to disgorge: My pen was practically smoking. I hoped I'd be able to read my handwriting later.

When it was complete, the Voice said, "Put it away. Do not look at it until I tell you."

I did and went to dinner.

Not bad for an afternoon's work.


What had happened to me? I had a spiritual experience, and a psychological one. A biggie. I've thought about what happened a great deal. What a perfect example of the Psalmist's wisdom:

*Who is aware of his unwitting sins?*
*Cleanse me of any secret fault.*
*Hold back thy servant also from sins of self-will,*
*Lest they get the better of me.*

A secret fault. My secret was the splinter of fear lodged in my heart. I didn't know that was there: It was completely hidden from me. The fault? As I've said, Californians know about faults. My chest felt as if it cracked open—a metaphor and a literal experience. The fault, the crack in my hard, protective crust, opened to reveal the secret in my core.

"Cleanse me of any secret fault," the Psalmist says. Need I say more? It popped out and disappeared. I felt that encapsulated pain full-strength for about two seconds. Having dumped its load, the feeling disappeared. That's what God does. It's also what a healthy psyche does. Did I have that experience because I was at the Gathering? Would it have come on its own someplace else?

What difference does it make? The Gathering provided the exact circumstances necessary for my fault to burst open and unload.

Am I ever glad. Do you know what that little depth charge was doing? Pushing me to get published—that's where my frantic drive originated. I had to be published right away because deep inside, I thought I was going to die. Not someday: very soon.

The truth is any of us can die at any time. The Buddhists say there are two things in this life of which we can be certain: (1) We will die. (2) We don't know when.

That makes daily life more intense, doesn't it? We will die and we don't know when. Any minute could be our last. Those realizations are the beginning of conscious life. I'd gotten them, but hadn't realized one little thing.

We've talked about a fault, a metaphorical crack opening in me. What was my true fault?

My fault, my sin, was that I didn't trust God to give me the time I needed to realize my purpose. I didn't trust God to control my life.

I belong to God. God determines what my life will be. I didn't trust God to do the job. If I'm supposed to be some big-time author with a huge audience, God will arrange it. It's not my problem. All I'm supposed to do is what's in front of me. If I'm supposed to write for my husband and pen articles for my web site, great! That's the plan! God's plan.

I didn't trust God to give me what was mine.

There lies the unwitting sin: *Who is aware of his unwitting sins?* I sure wasn't. All that was unconscious. Unknown to me. There's more: The 19th Psalm is so rich!

> *Hold back thy servant also from sins of self-will,*
> *Lest they get the better of me.*

A sin is simply missing the mark; it's a mess-up. Self-will was behind all this frantic get-published stuff: *I* wanted it done. *Maybe* God wants to reupholster the universe or hang out in the Milky Way this year, not get me published. I didn't know what was driving me, and I was pushy in trying to get my way. This drive definitely got the better of me. That's a sin of self-will.

*Ferret out your secret faults. Be kind and gentle to yourself, but look at everything inside and out with unflinching eyes.*

Do I know what's best for me? No. What I want so ferociously may be absolutely wrong. A friend, an ordained minister, told me about a famous author whose work offended some nutcase. "I read his books, and had no problem with them, but apparently they rubbed some crazy guy the wrong way." The nut began stalking the author, harassing his kids, and terrorizing the family. They had to move and go into hiding.

"How do you know God isn't protecting you from that, Sandy?" my friend said.

I don't. The only thing I know to do is follow that Voice. That works.

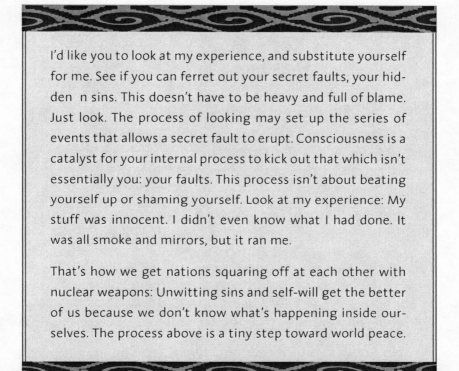

I'd like you to look at my experience, and substitute yourself for me. See if you can ferret out your secret faults, your hidden n sins. This doesn't have to be heavy and full of blame. Just look. The process of looking may set up the series of events that allows a secret fault to erupt. Consciousness is a catalyst for your internal process to kick out that which isn't essentially you: your faults. This process isn't about beating yourself up or shaming yourself. Look at my experience: My stuff was innocent. I didn't even know what I had done. It was all smoke and mirrors, but it ran me.

That's how we get nations squaring off at each other with nuclear weapons: Unwitting sins and self-will get the better of us because we don't know what's happening inside ourselves. The process above is a tiny step toward world peace.

"Sure, Barry, if you want me to go back to my writing just for you, that's fine. Those were wonderful years. You're my most truthful critic and ardent fan."

ANGELS DON'T LEAVE
Bill Miller playing at the Gathering

# CHAPTER 11

# SINGING THEIR HEARTS OUT

HAVING EXPERIENCED A COUPLE OF MIRACLES and outlined a book that afternoon, I threw on my purple-and-green velvet, mirror-trimmed, goddess suit. Time to party. By purest happenstance, Bill's concert was the next event.

Entering the main lodge, I felt awed. The soft lights and wood created an intimacy unexpected in such an open building. The ceiling seemed higher than its two stories. Metal staircases spiraled up on both sides and columns fashioned of tree trunks still bearing their bark held the roof aloft. Looking around, I wanted to take the lodge home: It's a beautiful place to spend time. Or party. Everyone had gathered, smiles sparkling as conversation rose and fell around the room.

Jonathon Feather served as MC, doing the great job he'd done all day. Mona Juckett opened, singing bluegrass and gospel in her distinctive style. Brothers Emerson and Lowery Begay along with Danny Bigay performed original music on traditional flutes and instruments, making an impressive display.

Bill began his show, creating the magic for which we'd come. How to write about music? They're non-overlapping art forms, music and prose. I've got Bill's web site listed later in the book. Best thing to do is listen to some and see for yourself. I own all his CDs, finding his music spiritually powerful, beautiful, and innovative and sophisticated in its composition.

Bill's rack of Native American flutes sat on one side of the stage, with the guitars behind him. As he performed, the painting of the old-time warrior he'd put up that afternoon took special significance. After that: pure rapture. Mona Juckett, who sang during the opening act, joined him onstage. I had heard that Mona was an amazing, passionate musician; she was that and more. She could play her harmonica anywhere on the planet, with any group, and keep pace. She and Bill made foot-stomping, soul-stirring music that had the audience on its feet, dancing in front of the stage.

How to write about a musician? How to evaluate his work? One way would be in terms of aesthetic criteria of design: rhythm, harmony, balance, proportion, and scale. Bill's music easily measures up in terms of those. What about more personal criteria: Where does he take his audience? Some performers take them to wild, abandoned behavior: drugs, sex, and rock 'n' roll. To the mosh pit, where the revelers may or may not catch people jumping from the stage. Some music is a frenzied hymn to addiction and violence, pulling the listener to a lower state, a state easier to enter than escape. Musicians take their fans to their own inner state: Their music mirrors their hearts' inner sound.

Where does Bill Miller take his listeners? Can't speak for everyone, only myself. When my mood is elevated, I want to ride my horse. I get body memories: Every inch of me remembers my finest ride. I've spent thousands of hours on horseback, starting when I was a tot. Riding produces transcendent mental and spiritual states, much like meditation. Ecstatic states. When my mood starts to rise, when I'm having a good time, I can feel the reins in my hands, and my horse's soul coming back to me. I recall the glory of moving with a finely trained, sensitive creature that gives me its power and will.

This happens in the strangest places: in grocery stores, or walking down the central aisle of a shopping mall. I can imagine myself, *feel* myself, riding a horse. Being in a mall would trigger every survival instinct my horse has. *He would hate it.* Yet there I am, reliving my best ride, my greatest thrill, walking past the fountains and fast-food shops. We humans are all of a piece—bodies and souls, memories and present moment.

After going through the "I'm riding, and it is fine" stage, if I rise higher in consciousness, I find myself in the meditation hall. I've spent a very long time there, and have had most of my deepest and most profound experiences in a number of halls and temples. My life seems a series of interludes, times that I must pass through before I can return to the welcoming arms of the meditation hall and nirvana. Swami Durgananda dissects the state of meditation almost like a scientist dismembering an invertebrate in her book, *The Heart of Meditation*. For me, it's like this:

I sit quietly with closed eyes, the screen of my inner vision blank. I feel pulled inward and my attention moves inside. Something opens up in the blank field before me. That field is almost like a movie screen. When that something opens, it's like the fabric of reality tearing. The Sanskrit name for this is *madya*, or the central still point. From this still point, this opening, I can go across to the other side.

The "other side" is a different place, which I typically experience as darkened at first, motionless and tranquil. I'm aware of my body and the world around me. Sometimes my mind chatters and I can't go any deeper. I get just a sip of the inner bounty. Sometimes, I dive so deeply that the outer world disappears, my body's sensations with it, and all that remains is the inner world and what I'm shown. I'm very clear that I'm not alone in this place.

It's like finding the Voice within, but this time it's multisensory, appearing in words and images, sensations, sounds: all more wondrous than the outer world. Over the years, I've had prayers answered, enigmas resolved, and experienced visions and miracles as I sat in meditation. I've thought: I never want to leave this place. Nothing is as good as this.

Inevitably, the meditation dissipates and I find myself back in my seat in the meditation hall, which I never really left, with enough to occupy my mind until the next time, or perhaps, for the rest of my life.

On that night in Tennessee while Bill sang and Mona played the harmonica, I found myself mentally on my horse. I felt myself riding wild and strong, the way I did when I was a young woman. The music played on. My spirit rose higher; I found myself in my private meditation hall. This wasn't what I had in mind: I usually only meditate with people of my tradition, who know what meditation is and how a meditating person looks and acts.

Like it or not, there I was, aware of the concert and the people around me, pulled to depths of vision. Deeper and deeper, I was *somewhere*, a place I'd never been. Meditation visions are like waking dreams: I was wide awake, in an altered state, experiencing something that wasn't real but which felt more real than the people around me.

I was somewhere bathed in clear light; I felt like I was in a chamber of my own heart, but it was huge. As big as the night sky, bigger than that. A sphere came to me, filling my inner vision. A glowing, opalescent globe filled two-thirds of my inner screen. It hovered there, slowly rotating. It was still, yet the soul of movement. It seemed to be covered with a glistening, oily film that made its pearly luster more exquisite. The majestic orb floated above me and to my right. It didn't do anything, or say anything: It just filled the heavens, entrancing me. It seemed good, and protective. A gift. Mesmerized, I would have been happy to watch it forever.

Other things happened. A bath in an ocean of grace, God's river and gift to the world. Touching and lying in grace, visited by the old ones and the holy ones. More, and always more, without end, without measure.

When you're in the middle of something like that, it's hard to look cool. I kept bouncing out of the meditation, as my body would move or quiver with oceanic energy roaring through it.

Glancing around, I thought, Do I look okay? Did anyone notice?

Oh, how we rob ourselves for social approval.

I still see that sphere, years later. I feel its sheen and oily touch. It's added a hum. It hangs there, softly humming. I hope it stays forever.

What was that? It was a cookie, like my dog trainer gives my little Cocker when he's done what she wants.

"Oh, g'boy, Raj! Such a good dog. You get a treat." Then she gives him something his heart desires above all else: broiled chicken skin. The reward has to fit the value system of the creature receiving it.

I'd done what the Great One, the Great Mystery, wanted. So I got a cookie: a vision of the world on the other side.

God's reward system. God's a behaviorist, too.

When I have experiences like that, I know I've done my job. I've jumped through hoops, crossed continents, and said what I needed to say, moment by moment. My heart yearns for experiences like that. Like a good dog, I will do what's required to earn the reward.

Thank you, Bill, Mona, Emerson, Lowery, Danny, and Jonathon, for providing the trigger to set it free.

THE DRUM

# HITTING
# THE TRAIL

SO FAR, THE GATHERING WAS A resounding success. After Bill's closing remarks Sunday morning, I would interview him. Then I'd go to my last workshop, the Closing Ceremonies, and that would be it. If I hadn't been so happy, I could have bawled. I loved everything about Coker Creek and Tennessee, including all that green. I loved the people. I wanted to stay with them and eat cake and bacon unashamed. Another powwow would be nice.

We sat in the main hall Sunday morning. Bill gave a talk. I don't remember a single word. He picked up his painting from where he'd left it the night before and started to leave. He and his group were departing for a nationwide tour.

I ran up to him as he was heading down the central aisle. "Do you have time for our interview?"

He shook his head. "No, I'm sorry, we have to leave. We're late."

I joined a crowd following him to the parking lot. A number of people, mostly Indians, stood around his car. The rear hatch was up and Bill carefully stowed his painting on top.

"I've been eyeing that painting for two days," I said to him. I couldn't believe my bantering tone; I was almost swaggering. "I've been wondering what I could trade you for it. All I've got is a horse."

Bill had been climbing into the front seat. He turned and faced me, smiling.

"But I wouldn't trade you a horse for that painting," I continued. "You're so busy, you wouldn't have time to ride it." The way we sell horses is like marriage brokering; we look for long-term compatibility where everybody will be happy, especially the horse. I made a gesture of acquiescence toward the painting. "I'll have to let it go."

"I ride," Bill said, getting out of the car and walking toward me. "I've been riding since I was ten. When we're done with the tour, the real reason we're going to Las Vegas is that I'm taking a bunch of kids out in the desert for a ride for a few days. I can do more with them out there with horses ... "

"These are youth at risk?"

"Yeah. I do what I call a 'Spirit Ride.'" I could feel his love for troubled young people.

"I'd really like to talk to you about that. I'd like to hear about your experiences," I said. Kids and healing with horses? Oh, yeah. That was my territory.

"We'll talk later." He got back into his car and the whole gang of them pulled out, disappearing down that terrifying country road.

I walked away, smiling and thinking about our conversation. Bill Miller is a horse person. I had no idea.

Maybe an hour later it dawned on me that I hadn't gotten the interview. I didn't care.

This is the difference between satisfaction and contentment: Satisfaction is a pig that has stuffed itself until sated. If the pig heard "No, we have to leave," it would have belched and rolled over, too bloated to react. Once the gorge wore off, the reaction would be different.

Contentment, the spiritual version of satisfaction, is poles apart. When disappointed, it says, "Oh, that's too bad," and lets go.

Contentment is busy looking at the shining opal sphere; nothing could be that rewarding. "Well, next time ... " The interview falling through wasn't a problem.

The Gathering was screaming to a close. I went to my second workshop, taught by the powwow's Head Man, Scott Crisp. Scott, of Cherokee descent, taught us about stickball and how Native American blowguns are made and used to hunt small game. Scott impressed me with his knowledge and easygoing way of presenting it. What I didn't know about Native American culture was beginning to impress me. I had never heard of either stickball or blowguns made of rivercane or anything else.

Stickball seemed like a cross between rugby and field hockey with fewer rules. Scott told us stories and gave demonstrations as to how to use the sticks. Apparently Indians were forbidden to play stickball for many years, as it was considered too rough. Hmmm. I wonder what the people who made those rules would think of ice hockey.

The blowgun demonstration was a hoot! Rivercane looks like bamboo: It's a reed with hollow segments. Scott told how the Indians broke through the segments using hot coals and formed formidable darts with natural materials. Best, we were able to shoot targets, with Scott providing motivation.

"Pretend you haven't eaten for three days. Hit that squirrel!"

Some of us hit the "squirrel"—a Styrofoam cup—quite handily. Our group could have stayed well-fed if squirrels were plastic cups. As fast as it began, the workshop was over. I'm left with memories of Scott and my fellow Gatherees: kind, smart people with perceptive comments. If the rest of the workshops were as good as the two I attended, I might go to the Gathering just to attend them.

During the Opening Ceremony, people made sage bundles, wrapping small amounts of sage in cloth and tying them. Each bundle represented a prayer. I missed this, being on Nashville time at that point.

At the Closing Ceremony, everyone gathered around a fire. Vicki Collins held a prayer feather and led the group in prayer. People formed a line and took one of the sage bundles, tossing it into the fire with a prayer, and releasing the prayer of the person who made the bundle. Holding the feather, Vicki spoke about what the Gathering had meant to her. She passed the feather to the next person. Whoever held the feather had the stage: No one interrupted him or her. The feather made its way around the circle.

A woman stood tall, a single feather erect at the back of her head, a blanket wrapped around her, tears in her eyes. "This has meant so much to me. Last year ... " She said what she needed to say and passed the feather. I recall so many hands holding the feather. The speaker might be wrapped in a traditional blanket or wear a stylish jacket. Some people were thoughtful and profound; others struggled to put a fear or pain into words, or express an ineffable experience. Some just wanted to thank the group and the Gathering's organizers for providing a safe time, a safe place for a little while. Everyone spoke.

The closing circle reminded me of a Friends Meeting. The few Quaker meetings I've attended had a similar feel. The practice of democracy and letting everyone have his or her say, of respect for the individual and the group, was very apparent.

Months later I found myself remembering the Closing Ceremony, reflecting on words said by a participant. Some were fighting fierce battles, battles that people everywhere face. Coping with trauma. Drug- and alcohol-related issues. Relationship problems. Loneliness. Loss. Betrayal. The Gathering was where they came to sustain themselves. I heard and saw people dealing with issues that I face or have faced. Being human is not easy. We seem to have periods when disaster is held at bay, and then it strikes massively, making us pay for our moments of happiness.

Other things blasted into my consciousness. This was a Native American retreat, but I've written little about Native culture or Native Americans. The Native presence was strong at the Gathering. However, this is not a strictly Indian spiritual event such as might be held by the American Indian Church. The Gathering isn't a Sun Dance, Sweat, or other traditional ceremony. Plenty of opportunity existed to be around and interact with American Indians. After personal interaction, the major thing I learned about Native Americans is:

I don't know a thing about Native Americans.

This was a sobering realization for someone who has spent nine years writing two series of novels that feature many Native characters. Experiencing Indians directly was very different from reading about them in books. What I got was: I don't know nuthin'.

Well, that's not entirely true. I know slightly more than nothing, enough to avoid major pitfalls. For instance, a reader might think, "She went to a Native retreat, when is she going to discuss *Native American spirituality*? What happened at the *ceremonies*?"

Oh, dear. Major red flags.

Have you ever heard someone ask, "Would you please tell me about your Caucasian spirituality?" Or Polish spirituality? Or South Floridian spirituality? Like there was one spirituality for an entire population of very different types of people?

People talk about *Native American spirituality* like it was a giant loaf of mass-produced bread hovering over the continent, the spongy kind that's the same from end to end and inside out. Images of buffalo and feathers may accompany the stereotype. Maybe tipis and painted horses, too. Be aware that these are cultural accoutrements of *Plains* Indians. (Except for the loaf of bread—that's a simile.)

Native Americans were present at the Gathering; it was definitely an American Indian retreat. When you see the presenters and speakers on the Gathering web site (www.thegathering.us), you will notice that their tribal roots are always mentioned. The indigenous People of this continent traditionally identify themselves with their tribal (Sovereign Nation) affiliations. Forget the homogenized bread analogy—the reality of "Native America" is that it is a diverse, highly individualized population with many ways of experiencing and expressing spirit. As many as there are people.

"Native American spirituality" trivializes and diminishes the individuals involved and their cultures.

Years ago, I was researching a novel. I contacted Vicki Collins, the Gathering's Chair. "What should I call Indians?" I asked. "What's kosher, Vicki?"

Vicki gave me some ideas and said she needed to talk to some friends about it. In due course, she responded, "My friends said you can call us American Indians, Indians, Natives, the People, First Nations People, or indigenous people." I could feel her laughter as I read her words on the email. "No one seemed to know where 'Native American' came from. Someone said, 'I think white people made it up so they wouldn't feel so guilty.' But you can call us that, too."

Even the term "Native American," then, may be inauthentic.

What is *Native American* spirituality?

What about spirituality in general? In talking about spirituality, we're referring to the most intimate part of ourselves, the place where we touch God. Spirituality is our link to the Divine. We're talking about the flow of sacred energy as it inhabits each of us and makes us who and what we are. Can anything be more personal? More indescribable? More hallowed? Can anything be more particular to an individual?

How can *spirituality* be common to a whole people? *Any* people?

Spirituality is like a jeweled tapestry covering and including the earth. We are that tapestry, each of us being a distinct, glowing jewel transmitting the Divine. Separate but interrelated. Not contained by words, or even describable by them.

*Native American ceremonies.* Ceremonies are particular to a given Nation and culture. Many are closed to outsiders or open only to specifically invited individuals from outside the culture. My understanding is that many traditions forbid participants from talking about ceremonies. The same prohibition applies to speaking about one's individual spiritual experiences.

I will not talk about Native American spirituality or ceremonies any more than I have. The last thing this planet needs is another interpretation of Native anything by a non-Native.

If this is true, how does one learn about American Indian culture and religions? My learning started when all those novels were injected into my brain, beginning with spiritual experience and moving into study afterward. The books I wrote were crammed into me by an irresistible force. If I'd tried to stop writing, or changed what I was given, I felt like I would have died. So I wrote and then I researched what I'd written.

On the spiritual side, investigation showed I'd written words almost identical to American Indian mystics—people I hadn't heard of when I was writing. When I read Black Elk and other Indian holy men, I was shocked by that recognition I spoke of earlier. I found this synchronicity, and the force behind my writing, very frightening.

On the cultural side, I needed to do research. When I started, I was blown away. Wow, I thought as I plowed through books. This is big. I need a lifetime's study and experience to do this justice. I kept reading: I have shelves of books on Native Americans/American Indians. Having completed masses of research, I realized that I knew very little compared to all there is to know and nothing from direct experience. I solved the problem by writing my characters as human beings; I know about them. I left the culture alone.

Being at the Gathering was a privilege. Finding out that I don't know much is a pretty good result. But I learned more than that. I met people for whom I felt great affinity. I saw the modern representatives of ancient peoples who have gone through genocide, rape, the destruction of their cultures, and theft of their lands. I hope to know more. I hope to learn more. I hope that the gracious hands of the Creator will bring us together and hold us tight.

Some words I heard in the Closing Circle caught me like anchors, yanking me to a halt and hauling me back. Looking conflicted, several people asked, "Can I be a Christian and an Indian?"

Others nodded emphatically, "Yes!" But some continued to look pained. I stood by, puzzled, having stumbled into another issue about which I knew nothing.

The Gathering occurred under the auspices of the Native American Ministries of the Holston Conference of the United Methodist Church. I do not know the religious preferences of those who attended: Everyone was welcome. I discovered that being an Indian and a Christian has been exceptionally difficult for many. Because of the way that history turned out—or was bungled—Indians who feel Christ in their hearts can be rejected both by Indians and Christians alike. This is an agonizingly difficult problem.

Bill Miller told me of the abuse he received from Christians when he sang hymns in his own language at a conference where he was an invited performer. "They held up their hands like this to me." He made crosses of his index fingers, the sign associated with warding off the devil. He also told me of abuse he has taken from fellow Indians because he talked about his relationship with Christ.

Why do we humans think we have the right to tell others what form their experience of our Creator should take? We do this all the time. Right now, people think nothing of ignoring national and personal boundaries and killing each other over personal beliefs.

They call it justifiable. Why is it that all wars are just wars to those who foment them?

I think all the religious groups are guilty of telling others how they should experience God. Not only is this deadly, it is the opposite of the truth of every form of worship I know. Everyone does it, too. I've done it in the past, to my embarrassment and chagrin when it was pointed out to me.

What's a person devoted to God and spirit to do?

What I do in this book is talk about my own experience. That's all anyone can legitimately do.

In my experience, God goes wherever God wants, without regard to what we have been taught. The most fun examples occur when people who don't believe in a supreme being get walloped. I heard the story of an atheist who attended a meditation retreat. He ended up not just a believer, but wild-eyed and dancing, sobbing as divine love poured from his heart. God didn't care that the guy didn't believe.

If my inner experience doesn't meet someone's ideas, am I not a Christian? Whose words can invalidate Jesus in my heart?

People used to be burned at the stake for incorrect thought, or experience outside the norm. The need to destroy anyone who doesn't toe the doctrinal line runs deep in our tatty little species. We love to do other things, too.

My younger daughter recently took a Black Studies course. As a result of the course, she realized the extent of the crimes perpetrated upon people of color. It was a horrifying thing for a young person to discover, even if she knew the outlines. My daughter and I discussed her feelings, speaking about the abuse of one group by another, abuse that can escalate to the murder of entire peoples.

I told my daughter that genocide is happening right now, just like slavery. *The National Geographic* ran a feature story in its September 2003 issue demonstrating that, worldwide, the level of slavery is higher today than when Lincoln signed the Emancipation Proclamation. The world isn't nice; it never has been.

My daughter said something telling. "The teacher asked people in the room to raise their hands if they had been the victim of discrimination." Most of the class members were people of color, and most raised their hands. "But there were other people in the class," my daughter observed, "who are victims of discrimination every day, and who couldn't raise their hands."

People who look like solid members of the majority culture carry burdens that make their lives miserable, or end them. But they can't say a word because of the shame that society puts on who they are. People who are gay come to mind immediately. Other groups: people with diseases like AIDS and hepatitis C. Alcoholism and drug addiction. Who feels sorry for them, especially if they aren't in recovery? When someone you love suffers from such a disease, how they got it becomes secondary to their pain.

People who have been abused emotionally, physically, or sexually often live in shame, afraid to tell what happened, and haunted by fears and flashbacks. Can they tell passersby what's going on if they have an episode? Can a survivor say, "Oh, don't mind me. I'm just having a flashback from when I was raped," to the guy who bumps into her in the grocery store, triggering a panic attack? Can he or she speak to his or her abuser about what happened and get an admission of guilt and an apology?

The survivor can confront the abuser, but it's likely to make things worse. I spoke to an eminent psychotherapist, a specialist in the treatment of trauma. She told me that studies have shown that ninety percent of the time, an abuse survivor who confronts his or her abuser about what happened is clinically *worse* off after the confrontation than before. Why? Most often, an abuser won't admit what he did. His self-image won't permit it. Typically, an abuser will attack his or her victim's credibility or deny the abuse happened. Then the survivor has to deal with that, in addition to other symptoms.

Can survivors talk to their families about what happened to them? Certainly, though people often lose their families if they talk about what happened.

"Uncle Jimmy would *never* do something like that! He's a *nice* man."

The abused person becomes the family nutcase and outcast. That's the power of denial and how diseased family systems work.

What about other diseases? Everyone empathizes with John Nash of *A Beautiful Mind*. He won a Nobel Prize and had a movie made out of his life. What about ordinary mentally ill people? Would you raise your hand in that class if you were schizophrenic?

Our compassion goes to those with socially acceptable, non-disturbing conditions. If a kid gets run over by a truck, the entire community rallies behind him. Feeling very righteous and kind, they offer every type of support to the victim and his family, for as long as it takes him to get well.

What if another boy runs into a different kind of truck? What if his brain has a flaw that makes it see dinosaurs and hear voices that no one else can? What support does he get? Can his family tell people how much it hurts to see their son like that, day after day? Does the PTA hold a bake sale to help them because their medical insurance doesn't cover mental illness?

Can you imagine trying to reintegrate into society if you've been in jail? If anyone finds out, he or she will immediately assume you're bad. How can you be good if everyone sees you as bad? Or if you see yourself as bad? What if the enemy's on the inside, too? Talk about something you have to hide. Who would admit that in class?

Where's the love? Where's the social evolution?

When my mother died, a grief counselor gave me a tape of meditations for the grieving by Stephen Levine. Levine and his wife, Ondrea, are widely thought to be the most effective grief counselors in the country. The tape was wondrous; Levine didn't dodge the pain.

Stephen Levine points out that all of us live in an ocean of sorrow—not just those with enormous losses or afflictions. Grief is part of the human condition. It can be experienced as fear, anxiety, pain, sadness, and a host of other feelings. We've all lost loved ones, been passed up for jobs, suffered indignities, and been abandoned. We've had to deal with illness in ourselves or those we love. Everyone grieves.

Healing is accomplished by embracing the grief and pain, feeling it, and then allowing it to be held in the even larger ocean of the heart. These are difficult words to realize in this world, but Stephen's meditation tape took me to a place where that could happen.

But what about our daily lives? What about at the Gathering? Some people alluded to such conditions during the proceedings. I expected that many others might have been afflicted. Bill Miller makes no bones about his past.

How do we more than survive our afflictions? How do we triumph over them? That's a personal question that has to be answered by each of us. The solution is a matter of how one perceives the experience and what one does for relief. Disastrously, some become lost in drugs and addictions. I say: Look up. Raise your consciousness to a higher realm and cling to it.

The things we're asked to bear can be very difficult, seemingly without purpose or sense. Infinitely painful—resulting in the cry of a wounded heart. And somehow, such trials help us. The person I am now does not compare with the girl I was. What I look for in my friends, what I value—all are different than they would have been had my life taken the direction it seemed headed in at the start. Absolutely everything about me has been tempered and strengthened by the hardships in my life.

Grace got me through. Love got me through. My own toughness got me through. Your spiritual connection will get you through, too.

Some people at the Gathering shared their hard times. We all have hard times.

May the arms of the Creator hold us tight.

CHAPTER 13

# THE EVIL
# THAT WE DO

*"Here's to evil, it keeps things humming!"*

– A toast by the devil from *Deconstructing Harry*
by WOODY ALLEN

I COULDN'T FORGET THE CLOSING CEREMONY.
The slender shape of the prayer feather moving from hand to hand
hovered in my mind. When they held it, people could stand and state
their truths. For some, the bright morning, lush pines, and green lawn
formed a crucible for pain.

One person's face and words, and the way he doubled over when
his feelings struck, haunted me. He spoke of being slandered. People
close to him had spread lies. The lies proliferated, damaging his career,
poisoning what others thought of him, and devastating him when he
discovered what had been said and by whom.

His words ripped into my heart. I, too, have been slandered.
People who don't know me as well as you do have said I did and said
things that I not only didn't do or say, I never even *thought* of doing or

saying. Anyone who knew me would know I'm not like that. But these people didn't know me; they knew their idea of me, concocted from half-truths to satisfy their needs. Like wasps, their words went out into the world, stinging me wherever I ran into them.

When I read Leonard Peltier's book, *Prison Writings: My Life Is My Sun Dance*, I was struck by Peltier's statement that he worked hard to keep from wishing harm on those who wished it on him. If we don't stop it, he notes, the circle of hatred and desire for revenge will never end. I felt Leonard's words, because I knew the pain that comes from being defamed, and the powerful hatred that arose in response. Evil begets evil.

Evil is everywhere: I spoke of an ocean of grief earlier. The sea of evil surrounding us may be larger. It's outside of us in terms of what others do, and inside of us as our own dark passions and uncontrolled acts. As I contemplated the image of the prayer feather and that morning in Tennessee, I realized that any soul wanting to survive this world must triumph over evil.

I began to outline strategies for dealing with it. I wrote about psychopathology and forensic science; set out various definitions of evil, revisited pieces I'd written earlier. I wrote and wrote and wrote. Unsatisfied, I scrapped all that, and wrote some more. None of it was right. Nothing captured exactly what I wanted to say. I felt like I was in a clothes dryer, spinning madly while being roasted alive.

Just before losing it entirely, I found something my first meditation master had said about evil. Swami Muktananda didn't talk about evil very much; this passage was all that I could find: two paragraphs that set out the problem and solution perfectly. As an enlightened master, Muktananda condensed a great deal of meaning into a few words. In my experience, his words illuminate the core of an issue, imparting lasting inspiration and value.

Swami Muktananda was asked, "What is evil? What can people do about it?"[3]

He answered, "Hurting other people. There is no worse evil. People talk about heaven and hell, but there is no hell worse than hurting others. Even to think of harming or torturing other people is hell.

"... The worst sinner is one who does not understand his own Self, one who insults his own Self, one who does not attain his own Self. It is because we do not understand our own Self that we do not understand another's inner Self. Because of this ignorance, evil is created. So when one perceives his own inner Self through meditation and knowledge, he finds the divinity that lies within. Then he will not see anything bad in others; he will not find anything evil."

I cried when I read this, because Muktananda captured not only the essence of evil, but also the essence of goodness.

For those who are not used to the terminology, I'm going to add a few words. Swami Muktananda was an enlightened being. Because I'm neither enlightened nor Swami Muktananda, I can't explain exactly what he means by the *Self* or *That*. I have had my own experiences of these concepts, which *I am the screen upon which the events of life play.* hopefully glimmer through this text. I'll use those experiences and the work of other thinkers to create a framework.

In the earlier discussion of the work of psychiatrist Roberto Assagioli and his theory, psychosynthesis, personal identity boils down to pure awareness without content.

Once we have the experience of contentless consciousness, we may become aware of what Assagioli calls the Higher Self. The Higher Self is like a lens that focuses divine knowledge and energy through us. The Higher Self is so profoundly who we are that we may not know it exists. The Higher Self works under the content of our ordinary activities and concerns and the structure of the mind. It may surface in times of great need, appearing as visions or words of guidance. The

Higher Self may be out of conscious awareness for most people, yet it's there, the highest and best part of us working for the soul's flowering.

I understand Muktananda's Self as similar to or the same as Assagioli's Higher Self.

*Finding that center, and experiencing our oneness with each other and with God, is the spiritual path.*

Assagioli and Muktananda are not the only people aware of the Self or Higher Self.[4] Assagioli mentions a number of theorists, including Jung and a variety of yogis. People living the Transcendent level of Maslow's Needs Hierarchy have a similar experience. This knowledge of a divine spark that exists within everyone is found around the world. For instance, the great Oglala Lakota mystic, Black Elk, said:[5]

> *Peace ... comes within the souls of men*
> *When they realize their relationship, their oneness,*
> *With the universe and all its powers,*
> *And when they realize that at the*
> *Center of the universe dwells wakan-tanka,*
> *And that this center is everywhere,*
> *It is within each of us.*

Having found our inner goodness, we see it everywhere. When our inner divinity is shooting out of our eyes and ears, illuminating all we touch, we don't have to fear evil. We realize that this same Self exists in everyone else. How could you possibly hurt anyone else, if all you see is God? If all you see is your own Self?

I would end this chapter now, except that a nagging inner voice keeps saying, "Uh, what about the one or two of us who haven't gotten to that state? What about people who have to face really nasty guys, maybe very soon? Could you add a bit more?"

Well, yes. Here's my take on the subject, based on my experiences of evil and my psychological training. To master evil, pick a spiritual path that takes you to an experience of the Self and practice it as hard as you can. Choose the path that calls to your heart, but get moving. If you're in a situation loaded with evil, you need spiritual ammunition pronto. When I have been able to see my devils as the same as myself, as possessing hearts and souls like mine, I have turned enmity into understanding. If I did it, you can do it, too.

The other thing to realize is all those bozos who have been making you miserable are there for a reason: your growth. Do you know how many people end up with advanced degrees in psychology because of the people who gave them trouble? The evil in your life can be extremely beneficial to your soul, not to mention your career.

> *Your life is your spiritual path.*

Evil is *motivating*. I have had much more contact with evil and psychopathology than I wanted in this life. The first lesson I learned is: Mastering evil is on-the-job training. You learn by doing. When you're belly deep in alligators, it helps if you know their first names. So we're going to study evil, describe its anatomy, and maybe take it out for dinner.

The first step in combating evil is knowing what it is. Evil is not just something bad happening, like being struck by lightning or killed in an epidemic. Calling something *evil* implies that it was inflicted with intent to cause harm. It also implies breaking of moral principles. A lion killing its prey is not evil; a corporate officer raiding the company treasury is. Human beings do evil.

Some of you might be thinking, "How can people do things like that—ruining other peoples' lives for greed?" Or, just having been discharged from the hospital after your boyfriend beat you again, your thoughts may be focused on your particular situation. "Why did Ricky do it? I tried as hard as I could to do what he wanted and he still hurt me. What do I do now?"

Some people haven't a clue as to the divinity within, theirs or yours, and will destroy you any way they can. Evil is evil. It exists to spread pain, fear, death, and destruction.

How to deal with this? What I did was suffer for a few decades and then have a glimmering of intelligence that changed everything. In the middle of some 1970s human potential movement workshop, I realized: "Life doesn't have to be the way it is!" As the trainer worked with someone, I could see the woman acting out behavioral patterns similar to those favored by people in my life. In the context of the workshop, I could see what she was doing was an act, rather than hard-and-fast reality. What bothered me was an illusion: Things could change. And from there, it was a snappy thirty-four years of harder work than I possibly could have imagined to become "serviceably sound."

*All we need to be in life is serviceably sound.*

*Serviceably sound* is a great concept, coming from the world of horses. So often, we demand perfection from ourselves, condemning ourselves for any deviation from the ideal.

We need to consider *purpose*. When the veterinarian examines old Dobbin before you buy him, he or she will ask, "What do you want to do with this horse?"

"He's going to be a lawn ornament."

Dobbin will be termed "serviceably sound" if he can stand up and chew: Serviceability is defined in terms of intended function. If you can do what you're intended to do, you're fine. You don't have to be perfect.

On the other hand, I think that human beings are intended to fly with angels. I guess we should just pick the target we want to hit and go for it without beating ourselves up.

How does evil develop? I'm going to outline some psychological concepts. The better theoretical grounding you have, the more likely you'll be able to use it in one of those sure-to-arise, evil-laden situations. In just such a circumstance, you'll go, "Aha! I see what she meant. This isn't real. This person is acting out patterns." You'll find a new way of dealing with that situation fast—including leaving it.

Essentially, the psychological underpinnings of evil are about dirty glasses—the kind you look through to see the world. Let me explain this. Minds can divide themselves up in various ways. A while ago, we talked about subpersonalities, those useful parts of us that perform various roles: Me at Work, Me at Home, and Me the Spiritual Goddess. The subpersonalities develop early, as parts of our psyches discover they are good at things. They become troublesome when they take over the entire personality.

Let's look at another way a personality can be segmented. Say a child was born—*Wah! Here I am!*—into a family with lots of rules and judgments. "This is good; that is bad. Stop that! I saw you do that! Stupid! Bad boy!" He quickly learned that he was good when he smiled, laughed, and behaved the way the Big People wanted him to. He wasn't good if he was angry, vengeful, malicious, or if he struck back.

As he grew older, he learned that his was a *good* family. They thought the right thoughts, loved their country, and had a great mission. Everyone who thought like them was also good. Good people thought, looked, worshipped, and believed like his family. Because he was a good boy, he didn't have bad thoughts or feelings. So he really didn't have them. He was totally unaware of his anger or rage, or how much he wanted to bash in his parents' heads. His mind split so that he couldn't see large portions of himself that others might see clearly; for instance, when he had temper tantrums or tortured animals. He knew he was morally perfect. If he felt angry, who could be responsible?

What could he do with the feelings that rattled around inside of him, feelings he couldn't admit existed?

Blame them on other people, who weren't *good*. People of a different color, religion, nationality, or sexual preference were perfect targets. Totally unaware of his inner split, or the feelings that he had but couldn't feel, the young man saw these *bad* people as the representation of every evil. They were bad; he was good. In a nutshell, that's how the defense mechanism projection develops. In *projection*, unconscious material is projected onto—seen as belonging to—others rather than felt as one's own.

Whether we're talking about the development of Adolph Hitler or a borderline personality, the process is the same: The individual learns that big hunks of his or her emotional contents are not okay and dissociates from them. He/she doesn't feel the troublesome emotions, but does see them in other groups.

This is not something that just a few, really messed-up people do. We all do it. Until we can acknowledge that every human state is potentially ours, we project what we don't like about ourselves onto those different from us. The more we live in a partitioned-off world of good people and bad people, the more we'll project, being totally unaware of it.

The truth is, each of us carries the potential of feeling every human state and emotion. If we didn't, how could we feel moved watching a movie from a foreign culture? When we see an African mother whose child has just died grieving, we cry along with her. We know how losing a child feels. Why does the film about a serial killer horrify us, if not because we can feel how alienated the killer is from his basic humanity? Why do we go back to see the movie ten times, if not because some part of us is thrilled by his electrifying bloodlust? We all contain all the parts.

Projection is only one psychological defense mechanism. They're called "defenses" because when reality gets too real, when we can't handle data about ourselves that conflicts with our self-concepts, we defend our false worlds with them. We do it automatically, without even knowing we did it. The guy who believes, "I'm a nice guy," would never slaughter innocent people living on land that he wanted just because he had the power to do it. But he could kill them and take their land if he felt they were the scum of the earth, which is how the early settlers of the American West viewed the Indians. In his book *Killing the White Man's Indian*, Fergus Bordewich gives numerous examples of statements by European settlers that are projection pure and simple.

When I was in graduate school, we had to memorize pages of different types of defense mechanisms. If you've ever been in marriage counseling, either as counselor or participant, you may listen to what's said and think, Are these people in the same marriage? Are they from the same planet? That's because our perceptions are so different. We see the world through perceptual lenses, which are colored by our experiences, heredity, and our *little mental peculiarities*. These can make us killers, so we should know about them. A few other defense mechanisms that lead to evil include:

*Denial* is like *projection* in that the individual with the problem doesn't see it. Denial neatly sweeps all evidence of a problem into mental oblivion. It's common in people and families impacted by alcoholism and drug addiction, but other people use it, too. I experienced the power of denial before I had my knee replaced. Although I couldn't straighten my leg or walk, and was experiencing excruciating pain, I didn't think the operation was necessary. Afterward, I asked my doctor if I really needed it. "Your knee was just bloody bones rubbing together," he said. I was in denial about my condition for several years.

*Generalization* is another popular defense: "You *always* do that ... " Always? Even in the shower? When taking out the garbage? Generalization takes a behavior and sees it happening everywhere. "They always do that ... " Those members of another race, religion, or sexual preference don't *always* do that, but they can be killed for it anyway if generalization is operating.

*Distortion* is another winner: "She said it was all right," when in fact she said it wasn't all right at all. Some people call this lying, but it's not exactly that. The person doing the distorting doesn't know he's done it. This is the truth, as seen through glasses with a warped prescription.

*Deletion*, another favorite. Don't like what someone said? Eliminate the parts that don't fit your point of view. "He said he hated his mother." When, in fact, he said that he hated his mother when she was drinking, but loved her dearly and was agonized to see what she was doing to herself. A very different message.

That's why I said that faulty glasses cause evil. With the wrong family and social conditioning, our lenses of perception eventually will look like the bottom of soda bottles: warped, distorted, and almost impossible to see through at all.

This doesn't take into account biological and genetic issues in perception. Problematic behavior used to be laid at the feet of bad parenting or social learning. Researchers are finding that many mental diseases are due to faulty biochemistry or even incomplete hook-ups in the brain. In a study released by the University of Southern California, individuals with APD (Antisocial Personality Disorder, formerly known as sociopaths and psychopaths) have been found to have a missing connection between parts of the brain.[6] This puts a new spin on evil. Is something evil if it's due to a physical abnormality?

This simplified anatomy of evil hinges on splitting the world into *us* vs. *them*. Kids begin a separation process around age two, differentiating themselves from their mothers and environment. This is healthy and allows us to function as individuals. I'm talking about more than that, a syndrome where people live as though life were a team sport: "They lose, we win! Yay!" "My religion scored a goal! Theirs lost!" "My country won that battle! They lost." Enemies and friends. Bad and good. Death and life. Division and strife.

After all this, who does evil? Where does evil live? In all of us. In addition to our greatness, our divine spark, we all have an inner smallness, a nasty bit that wants to hurt others and stir up trouble. Part of us wants to cheat, lie, and get something for nothing. Part of each of us will distort the truth to make ourselves look better. Part of us revels in making others small. Until we reach enlightenment, all of us are capable of great wrongdoing.

**MAN, I'VE HAD IT WITH EVIL.** Let's do something else. How about something good? Pick something good to do, and do it. Can be small, or can be large. Help someone. Make a contribution. Wash the dog. Write some possibilities in your journal. And then do one of them. If you can't do it now, write down a time and date by which you will do it. Let's do something good!

After that, let's sit quietly for a few moments in a peaceful place. Rest your feet on the floor with your hands on your thighs. Breathe fully, taking a few deep breaths to start. Filling and emptying the lungs. Relax, and relax some more. Think about who you really are, beyond good and evil. Scan your body with your awareness. Do you feel a pleasurable sensation anywhere? See any lights? Allow your attention to rest on those spots. Follow the light with your mind. Linger with it. Feel your breath moving in and out. If thoughts come, let them. Don't hold on to them. Watch the place from which thoughts arise. Watch the place where breath arises while you restore yourself. Know that you glisten with

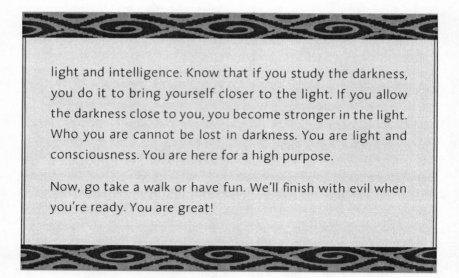

light and intelligence. Know that if you study the darkness, you do it to bring yourself closer to the light. If you allow the darkness close to you, you become stronger in the light. Who you are cannot be lost in darkness. You are light and consciousness. You are here for a high purpose.

Now, go take a walk or have fun. We'll finish with evil when you're ready. You are great!

So far, I've been talking about regular, day-to-day evil. On top of this is horrific evil: the kind that kills and cripples, starts wars, and destroys the planet. In my experience, those who have done truly heinous things have been:

1. **Addicted to drugs or alcohol.** I have seen people under the influence of drugs and alcohol behave like demons from the lowest reaches of hell. In terms of destructive impact and malevolent intent, these people had ceased to be human. The problem is bigger than the addict's destructiveness while using—it warps everyone in his or her social system. In addicted/alcoholic families, family members assume roles that allow the addict to survive and let everyone else pretend everything's all right. The roles of enabler, fixer, hero, and scapegoat cripple those who live them. Often, healing the affected family system is harder than healing the addict.

2. **Mentally ill.** Historically, mentally ill people have been treated cruelly. Their symptoms have been considered signs

of demonic possession or moral weakness. While I don't want to perpetuate myths, certain diagnoses do impact others negatively. Many mentally ill people are never diagnosed and treated. One reason is their sheer numbers—around *thirty million* people in the United States may be affected by personality disorders according to the best available survey.[7] Our medical system would be hard-pressed to treat an additional thirty million patients. Many sufferers don't get help for another reason: Denial prevents them from admitting they're ill. While they are suffering, those around them may suffer just as much. Children and others who can't escape are most impacted.

3. **Good people.** The people who slandered that fellow at the Gathering and me were good, churchgoing folks. They considered themselves pillars of society. They acted out every "good person" role faultlessly. Their families and friends were equally upright. If they talked about others, it was only from the pain of seeing what their shortcomings caused and a desire to make things right. This kind of good person uses church attendance to demonstrate moral superiority. Fine clothing, a lovely house, attractive children, memberships in clubs, etiquette and manners, and even the cleanliness of the family dog (not to mention all four bathrooms) are indications of moral superiority. Unaware of any personal fault, such good people can create bad people everywhere they look.

Curious: We have bad people—sociopaths—doing evil, and good people—churchgoers—doing evil. What's the difference? None essentially, though the latter group may use subtler means to destroy. We've run into a feature of the world: the pairs of opposites. Good and bad, up and down, heavenly and demonic, black and white, hot and cold. Almost everything on the planet can be described in terms of its opposite. Good and evil in particular. What does this have to do with morality? Here's a story:

After finishing my master's degree in Marriage, Family, and Child Counseling, I did an internship in a treatment center for runaway adolescents. Ninety percent of the kids in the house could be labeled "bad." They did everything that we associate with bad kids: drugs, sex, and rock 'n' roll, plus some interesting activities involving selling things, including themselves. They also disobeyed their parents and ran away from home, which landed them with us. The place was lively: One of the counselors brought her guard dog when she had to be on duty overnight.

One day, a situation got out of hand. We had to call the cops to restore order. Everyone felt bad about what had happened. None of us wanted it to turn out the way it did. We counselors sat around afterwards, trying to figure out what went wrong. "If only Lenny was here," my supervisor said. We nodded and groaned. Lenny would have known what to do. He could have gotten control; the incident would have passed leaving everyone feeling good.

Who was Lenny? A Super Counselor?

No, he was one of the patients, probably the baddest of the bad in terms of what he'd done. Certainly, he was the showiest wrongdoer in the house. But he was charismatic and a natural leader. The other kids respected him and paid attention to what he said. He'd made it in his world. He would have been able to defuse the explosion.

Unfortunately, Lenny ran away the night before.

"Never overlook the good in bad people," my supervisor said. "Bad people do many good things. They help each other; they're loyal to each other. They do lots of good in places where good people would never go."

Her words fractured my habitual vision. "Look for the good that bad people do, and the bad done by the good." I've never forgotten those words.

We must become aware of both our light and darkness. We must become aware of our hidden faults. Dark and light are different sides of the same coin. Have you heard that Snow White and the Wicked Witch are the same person? The person who thinks she is totally good, wondrously pure, completely innocent—Snow White—sees none of her darkness. Snow White becomes the Wicked Witch if she's crossed. After all, she's totally good, so anyone in her way must be totally bad. You can do whatever you want to a bad person, right?

The more cut off Snowy becomes from her darkness, the darker witch she is when aroused.

The good people I was talking about above weren't really good. They had no inkling of their own faults, did no self-examination, and had no idea of their impact on others. They did nothing to become more conscious. They acted out roles like mindless puppets and congratulated themselves for it.

Really good people aren't like that. Can you imagine Mother Teresa putting on airs? She wouldn't even let the Nobel Prize people give her a party, insisting the money be given to the poor. Do you think she went to Mass to look good in the eyes of the community? Did she dress to make a fashion statement? No. She went about her business, doing good works.

True goodness exists outside the pairs of opposites. It's not in opposition to evil; it doesn't need to create bad guys or inferior people to lord it over. True goodness is about following the orders of your deepest soul and God. I think that's what my meditation teacher was talking about when he said we should know our true Self. Becoming one's Self is the way out of the evil that surrounds us.

**AN EXERCISE ABOUT EVIL.** Take out your journal and write about the following questions. Have you suffered evil at the hands of others? What happened—take some time to write about it. How did you feel? What did you do? Were you able to resolve it so that you felt better about yourself? Do you still have lingering feelings? What would it take to resolve these, ideally? Do you recognize the characters I've outlined? Can you think of any more types of people that habitually hurt others? A harder question: Have you ever done evil to others, even if what you did was justified or the result of what they did? What did you do? How did you feel doing it? Did it resolve the bad feelings? How do you feel about it now? What is the worst thing you've ever done? No beating yourself up about this, just report behaviors and your feelings.

How about a Q & A session? What you've always wanted to know about evil, and probably already do. First, what's evil about evil? What's wrong with taking what you want and doing as you please? Why should people curb their addictions or control their behavior? Shouldn't the strong prevail? Why not subscribe to racist and supremacist doctrines that preach superior races and genocide?

*Each of us carries a divine spark, which is the gift of God and our true identity.*

The primary reason is one that's been presented repeatedly here, with examples from a number of philosophical schools: We are intrinsically valuable sparks of the Divine.

Evil nullifies this spark, either by killing or damaging us physically, or by attempting to destroy our holiness. Our souls rebel at this, whether we look at the world according to the "divine spark" theory or some other. We know we're supremely valuable.

Looking at my own experiences of evil, the worst part was the attempted murder of my sacredness. However vaguely, we know that we are valuable; we know that we are children of God. The slurs and slanders, the vicious things that people do to each other, hurt because we know who we are. The pain of an attempt to destroy the soul is immeasurable. It will drive people to do all sorts of things. Coupled with the mental and spiritual pain is fear. An abusive environment is loaded with fear. People who behave violently and inconsistently, who can't be counted on or trusted, who cause pain of all types, are terrifying. Uncertainty is terrifying.

Being expected to stay in an abusive system and do and say things we don't feel produces great pain and anger, fruit of invalidating our soul's essential freedom and absolute truthfulness. Evil is evil because it is an affront to our deepest nature and a perversion of what we're meant to be. *We* includes those giving abuse as well as those receiving it.

Another question: Why do people do evil? It's just as easy to do good as it is to do evil. Why not do good? Well, many scriptural references exist as to why we pick the bad road. I'll let you choose your favorites. I had a professor who said people fought because of boredom. "They do it for excitement." True, interpersonal drama is engaging. War is engrossing.

Why do we do evil? Someone explained it convincingly:

"I DO IT BECAUSE I *WANT* TO." His malevolence filled the room. I cowered when he moved closer. Face jammed into mine, he bellowed, "I *drink* because I want to. No one makes me: I *want* to. I WANT TO." He hadn't been drinking, but his rage mirrored his drunken state. My mouth opened and closed, but I couldn't say a thing. He screamed, "I don't want to hear about how it makes you feel. I don't *care* how you feel. I drink because I *like* it."

A terrifying exchange, but it settled something for me. Why do we do evil? The same reason we do anything: We want to. We do what we do because we want to. Choice is fundamental to human behavior. Everything we do, we do because we have chosen it. Maybe we're in a situation where we hate every single option we face. Nevertheless, whichever road we take, we've chosen it.

People choose evil. Maybe we're not developed enough to know that slandering another human being or spending all our social time in bars isn't going to get us anywhere. Maybe the lenses clouding our perception are thicker than manhole covers, but we still choose what we do. Maybe we know that we'll cause another person excruciating pain, and we do it with relish.

We do what we do because we want to.

Not a comfortable thing to acknowledge, but a useful one. We stop being victims and become human beings who can choose something else. The trick is to make better choices and avoid situations that we know will lead to disaster.

When that man who drives you wild shows up at the party alone, the time to remember your marriage vows is before the first kiss, not when you're putting the key in the motel room's door. Then, it's too late.

Afterward, saying, "I did it because I wanted to," is much more accurate and constructive than, "He seduced me." Or, "I drank too much." Or, "*He's* my soul mate, not dumpy old George." Or, "With all the rotten things George has done to me the last twenty years, I deserved *some* happiness."

All of the excuses are cop-outs. You knew where things were headed the instant you saw *him*. You knew before that—why were you so happy when George got sick and couldn't go to the party?

Why do we do evil, whether it's ending up in a motel somewhere or wiping out our civilization? Because we want to.

We put the pretty face on it to lie about it.

"Ye shall know the truth and the truth shall make you free." (John 8:32) It starts with knowing what's going on in your own head.

Which brings us to our last question: Do we need the Devil? I don't dispute scriptural references to the existence of the Devil. I merely ask: Couldn't we get the same result without an evil entity bent on destroying us? Is the Devil another cop-out, something to blame for what we do ourselves?

A serious question. In regard to this, someone told me the following story:

"I never thought anything about taking it. My doctor prescribed it; I thought it would be fine. I've taken all sorts of medicines with no problem. The first night I had a terrible dream. It was like something was waking up inside of me. Something evil. I could hear its breathing, heavy breathing, like a monster. It filled my mind. The dream was creepier than any horror movie I've ever seen. It pulled me into some world, some horrible place. And this thing, moving and breathing, was behind it. It filled everything. It seemed to be sniffing the air, searching for something. Thinking thoughts that are so bad ... I can't talk about them ... " He shook from head to foot and wouldn't look at me.

"I woke up feeling really lousy. Disturbed, you know. That nightmare, and that breathing. I could still hear it. During the day it was like something super sharp looked out from my eyes. I meditate, so I thought, I don't have to pay any attention to this. These are just thoughts. But they were very powerful. I took the medication again that night—I didn't realize it was doing it.

"The dreams were worse the second night. The thing was more awake. It was really like the Devil—the Devil was inside me, waking up. I had this disgusting feeling; it was so sickening. The dreams went on all night. The next day was worse. The sense of the thing looking out of me was stronger. A couple of times, I wanted to hurt people I loved. My child. My wife. I wanted to take the baby by the feet and smash her against the wall. I didn't care. Or that thing didn't care. The only thing that stopped me was my meditation practice: I knew I could control my thoughts, and I had to control them. It was the hardest thing I've ever done—not giving in.

"The next night was when it happened. I still didn't connect the medication with the dreams. But the third night, Oh, my God!" He trembled. Licking his lips, he whispered, "It woke up all the way. I felt like I was drawn into a spiral, deeper and deeper. I couldn't stop. The thing was at the bottom, and it was *me*. It was awake, the monster. And it was me. The Devil was in me—and it *was* me. *I was the Devil!*

"I clawed myself out of the dream. It was the most horrible experience of my life. Dirty, filthy. Sickening." He wiped his forearms with his hands, trying to wipe something off. "I never thought I'd feel clean again. *I was the Devil.* All day, I wanted to hurt people, just hurt them. Mostly the baby and my wife. I finally put two and two together: It was those pills. I'd never had a dream like that before, and I haven't since. The dreams started the day I first took the pill, and stopped the last day. I never took that medication again. I wouldn't."

"Did you tell anyone?"

"You're the first person I've told; I couldn't tell anyone before, it was so bad. I did tell my doctor. I told him he should never prescribe those pills. He didn't seem to understand how awful it was. He said, 'I've never had anyone else have that reaction.' I found out the pills worked in your brain, in the pituitary gland. I never forgot what happened. In some ways, it was a good lesson. I've seen the worst in myself. I don't ever want to let that out."

I've heard another similar story since, where a medication acted on the brain and opened this center of ultimate evil. The stories reminded me of what I had seen of people on drugs and alcohol: Creatures from hell couldn't be any worse.

Some parts of the human brain should not be accessed. Certain drugs and alcohol go straight to parts of the brain that should be left alone.

"Don't go there ... " is a hip saying. *Really* don't go there if it takes you to the devil within. Fear is a very useful emotion. We should fear parts of ourselves as if they were Satan. They may be. Maybe we don't need to fear the corruption of something outside ourselves; maybe we need to fear what's inside.

"To understand the purest ... we must accept holding hands with things that are not so pure ... "[8] a Native American musician, Robert Mirabal, wrote. "Give [darkness] to me so that I can become stronger in the light." What makes us stronger in the light than experiencing darkness? Sometimes we great beings, beacons of light for and of the universe, get a little closer to the flame than we might like. We end up singed and blackened, but purified.

Here, I'm speaking to those of you who are from alcoholic or addicted families, or who have succumbed to your own Addict and fought free, and to those who have suffered at the hands of those with untreated mental illnesses. I'm speaking to those who have been trapped in abusive situations. I'm talking to survivors of sexual, emotional, and physical abuse; those who have been raped or degraded. I'm talking to survivors of war and torture. If you fall in these groups, you know a different reality than others. I've written the following set of tips for you.

If you aren't in the above groups, the tips also work. When facing challenges, my experience is that those who have been abused feel the same things as those who haven't. Those who have been abused just feel more. Sometimes, much more. Darkness comes to all of us. How do we find the light?

## THINGS TO REMEMBER WHEN FACING THE DEVIL: A GUIDE FOR SURVIVORS

Mastering evil requires reaching to the deepest levels of reality. It's an extremely useful meditation and personal growth tool. Here are a few of my ideas for your journey. In some cases, if the item fits, you'll get just a glimmer of awareness that the item applies to you. That's all you'll get; none of this ever appears on billboards for your edification.

1. **Something vast and intelligent runs the universe.** This being, which I call God, has all the power. Evil will puff itself up and pretend to be all-powerful to frighten you. It's not. If you've survived great evil, you know this: You wouldn't be here without the Supreme Power's protection.

2. **Love is the answer.** Love is prior to good and evil. Love exists as an infinite, boiling ocean, the foundation of the created world. Everyone and everything springs from it. Discovering and experiencing our source, and becoming its conduit, is our reason for existence. Holding on to the experience of love in the presence of evil is the key to mastering darkness. Finding your personal purpose and living it is the greatest protection against evil. What are you supposed to be doing during this lifetime?

3. **When you are living correctly, God will appear as protection, insight, or whatever you need.** Supremely free, bowing to nothing, grace is God's operating arm. It goes where it will. Grace will save you from evil. Do everything you can to call it to you.

4. **Suicide is a permanent solution to a temporary problem.** Sometimes, when you are overwhelmed by evil or dealing with its residue from the past—depression, flashbacks, and memories—you may feel that good and joy have deserted you. You may feel that God has turned from you forever. Know that God cannot leave you, and your negative state will pass. Find a safe place to be when such feelings strike; find good and reliable people to help you. One thing that will

prevent happiness from returning is an irrevocable act made in a desperate state.

5. **God eats evil.** Someone told me, "When you take God into your heart, evil's still there. They fight." He used his hands to indicate eternal warfare. Not in my experience. God eats evil, simply removes it from a heart that's ready. Poof. Gone. That doesn't mean that you won't go deeper into yourself and dig up more, or the situation won't unfold so a different aspect of darkness shows. Evil is plentiful, but God holds the cards.

6. **Find your anchor.** If you are facing evil, either in the present or in the form of flashbacks and memories, you need an image to hold on to. Something to keep the fact that God is in control in your mind. Find a mental image (through meditation, journaling, prayer, whatever) that represents God to you. Call that image to you as many times as you need. You can draw it and hang it on the wall, put it on your computer screen. Hold on to it. When evil hits, with its accompanying terror and pain, you'll need that image. Whatever takes you to God, anything from the image of a saint to a photo of a tree: hold on to that. If all you can do is turn to the light and pray, do that. If all you can do is hold on to the feet of what you find sacred, do that. Go into training now.

7. **Embrace everything—including evil.** Evil is part of the whole, Snow White's inescapable twin. Don't try to run from it; simply be aware that its purpose is to destroy you in any way possible. Respect it. Protect yourself from it. Stay safe. Remember that it's very useful: Nasty things can have a positive payoff. Abused people have used their anger at their abusers to grow and heal. The desire for revenge has resulted in many classics of literature. If you are an artist or writer, evil produces terrific material. Embrace evil, use it, and dump its hold on

you when it's outlived its usefulness. Abused people who stay angry are the next generation of abusers. At best, they're no fun to be around.

8. **Become a spirit warrior.** Stalk evil as your enemy. Watch, observe, study, and learn with extreme intention. I outlined a few psychological mechanisms that produce evil—*learn them all*. Take communication skills courses, assertiveness training, negotiation training. Martial arts or other practices that increase your self-esteem are great. Get into therapy, talk to your minister or rabbi about your situation. Study the negative system in which you find yourself. Be able to outline the players, the stakes, and the process that evil uses when manifesting in your life. Know your triggers, your danger points—and everyone else's in your "game." Learn and use a warrior's skills.

9. **Do your homework.** To support everything I've said, you have to involve your entire life. Pick a spiritual path that works for you and stick to it. Live a lifestyle that makes you strong, personally and physically.

   Give up addictions. Keep good company: Hang out with people who strengthen you and support your growth. Seek the company of holy and true teachers, either in actuality or in books. Living a life of spirit requires enormous discipline. And—it gets easier the more you practice. Just as bad habits stick, so do good ones.

10. **Vote with your feet.** Unlike trees, we are not rooted in the ground. If you find that some people are poisonous for you and they aren't interested in changing—leave. I'm not saying walk out on your wife or family when the going gets rough. I'm saying that if, after one-hundred-percent application of your skills and doing everything I outlined above, you find that some people are damaging to your health and they refuse to change,

why hang around? If you are in an abusive situation and leaving is dangerous, prepare carefully. Get help from local agencies and make sure you're safe. If you are dependent, financially or any other way, upon the people making you sick, make sure you break free of the dependency before leaving. Otherwise, you may end up going back with egg on your face. Reading this, you may be horrified, saying, "How can I leave? It's my *family. My aunts and uncles. My mom and dad ...* " You may fear that your extended family will say terrible things about you if you leave. Know this: Your family *will* say terrible things about you if you leave. You'll also *think* terrible things about yourself. This is the glue that keeps the poisonous system going. Your guilt will go away in a few months. You can always go back for major holidays. Most likely, your family will continue to hate you, but that's why you left. You didn't just walk out: It took years of being poisoned. The way they act when you leave is a symptom of why you left. Another piece of the puzzle: When you leave, you must find something worthwhile to do with yourself. If you don't, you'll find yourself in an identical psychological system somewhere else. *You're* part of the problem.

**11. Use everything.** If you are confronted by evil personally or as a group, you must use every resource you have available to combat it. Work together as a community, strategize, and learn. Evil has destroyed civilizations. Could a groundswell of good people have stopped the Holocaust? Could the genocide that appears all over the globe, all the time, be halted if we chose to halt it? We won't know until we back moral issues as strongly as we do our favorite professional ball teams.

**12. When you feel like you're on a mission from God, you may be dangerous.** Sociopaths, marauders, and conquerors often grab on to a higher authority, God, as justification for doing what they want. Anytime you have overwhelming negative feelings toward some person or group, know that you are dangerous. Anytime you feel they're totally bad and you're good, be aware that Adolph Hitler, Joseph Stalin, and the folks who put on the Spanish Inquisition felt the same way about their targets.

**13. Evil as conflicting editing and punctuation:** Did you know that feuds, wars, and marital disputes can be seen as editorial conflicts? In the ongoing stream of experience, who started it—whatever *it* is—is a matter of perception. His defense mechanisms conveniently editing out contradictory data, the first Prime Minister shouts, "You did *it* to us. So we did *what we did* back." "No! That's not true!" shouts the other Prime Minister, outraged. "You did *what you did* to us, so we did *it* back. It was *your* fault!" "No, it was *your* fault!" Neither side knows whose fault it was: Neither has the elevated point of view to be able to see what is going on. In this limited system, fault is a function of where the periods and commas go and what's deleted. It's an editorial function. The parties involved can spend centuries wrangling about whose fault it was and who started it. The truth is: Who started it doesn't matter. It has to stop!

**14. Have a list of "things I will never do" and follow it.** Since we human beings have so much trouble telling right from wrong, we need a list of prohibitions to keep us from erring. I use the Ten Commandments. Other traditions have their lists. Adopt a set of behavioral rules and never break them.

# AFTER THE JOURNEY

# CHAPTER 14

# AFTERSHOCKS

AS FAST AT IT HAD CONVENED, the Gathering dispersed. I found my way to Nashville, across the country, and home with minimal fuss. Mission accomplished. Was that the end of it? Oh, no. The residual tremors that follow an earthquake can be as powerful as the earthquake itself. The Gathering in Tennessee was over; the one in California hadn't begun.

Spiritual life is a continuum. The end of one event marks the beginning of a new way of being. Doors open to a larger life—expanded opportunities requiring innovative spiritual approaches. As we complete one task, fresh trials and blessings appear. If your life is like mine, the trials will be bizarre and unforeseeable. So will the blessings.

While I was at the Gathering, I felt a compulsion to write. I *needed* to begin this book and to work on *The Horse Book*. Clouds of words banged inside my skull like wasps. Every time I wanted to pick up paper and pen and let a few out, the Voice said,

"NO!"

No taking notes, no writing at all. I had sat through Bill's lectures, aware that I was to sit and listen. I wasn't to be half in the room, half in my paper and clipboard, recording the present for later consumption.

Insights stacked up. I was sure they'd disappear before I got the okay to set them down. Some may have skedaddled, but enough stayed—they seem to be filling these pages just fine.

When I got home, the Voice boomed louder. It gave clear directives, promulgated absolute laws. It was a dictator, pure and simple, running every aspect of my life.

The Voice said I could write, but only about the new book, this one. Absolutely no working on *The Horse Book*, despite the snazzy outline delivered to me that afternoon in Tennessee. The outline would remain parked on my clipboard until I was given the order to work on it.

More rules: I could write on this piece for one hour a day. You can feel me gasp: I usually stay on the computer until my shoulders won't move. I was to use a timer to measure my writing hour, and when the timer beeped, I had to get up and follow orders. The orders came from inside me, with all the authority in the universe:

"Walk the dogs."

"Go for a swim."

"Ride your horse."

Have fun, in other words. It almost killed me.

Some things I'd done for entire days before the Gathering were OUT: no surfing the Net. No eBay. One half-hour per day to answer emails, absolute maximum.

This was a complete break with how I'd lived. It also was the end of my eBay addiction. I went to the Gathering, participated as hard as I could, had the experiences I did, and followed the Voice's commands afterward. Two years later, my eBay addiction remains *dead*. Kaput. Gone. That's what can happen when the psyche and God are in the right relationship. I experienced an almost instant recovery that most rehab programs couldn't effect in years. God is that powerful. It's also the easy way to kick the habit, I couldn't even log on to eBay: Something would yank me out of my chair and the next thing I knew, I'd be walking my dogs.

Speaking of dogs: My compulsive dog-search also stopped. I discovered that we already have four real dogs, all of which crave my company and attention. No more seeking canine love on-line; now I love the pups I've got. My real estate compulsion also vanished. Previously, I combed the Net looking for nirvana with horse facilities: Ranches in improbable places where we would never move, but I had to spend hours investigating. All that unproductive activity disappeared.

I call it God's One-Step program. All Twelve Steps delivered at once via unforgettable experiences that enlighten and terrify.

Shorn of electronic vices, I was left with reality. And myself.

I'm not used to living in the real world, I'm from Silicon Valley. I spent the first fifty years of my life in what became Silicon Valley, except for leaving for a few weeks to travel. Travel is one of the few excused absences from work allowed in my culture. It's permissible because it's educational. The San Francisco Bay Area has always been the way it is: The home of achievement-obsessed, MEGA performers. Between 1945 and the early 2000s, the major change in the Bay Area was the number of zeros after the dollar signs for which its entrepreneurs played.

The subject of my culture comes up here because it's all that's left. After going to the Gathering and following the Voice, my more manageable addictions were knocked out. When you peel away the top layer, you get down to the real addictions. Work addiction. Where did I get that one? My culture, among other things. Are we products of nature or environment? Heredity or training? This was a raging topic of dinner table conversation in my childhood. I think it's a both/and: our genes, parents, and more shape us.

By way of illustration, consider this slightly butchered economic and psychological history of the post-WWII San Francisco Bay Area.

Why did Silicon Valley arise where it did? First off, I blame the Great Depression. The Great Depression created a generation that would do *anything* not to go through the Great Depression again. Remember Maslow's Needs Hierarchy? Many of those who survived the Depression were stuck at the basic security level: Their lives were about Getting Enough. No matter what they attained, that sense that it could all be yanked away ran them. They covered this anxiety with those goofy fifties haircuts and poodle skirts, calling each other nicknames like "Buzzy" and "Toots." Is this nature or nurture? Seems like an economic calamity did it to me.

The GI Bill allowed these people to go to college, and eventually get good jobs, buy houses, and raise kids who would become computer geniuses (hereditary or environment?). The GI Bill happened because of World War II, another under-acknowledged cause of Silicon Valley. Also because of WWII, many Buzzes and Tippies ended up moving to the San Francisco environs. They liked the area when they were shipped through it during the War. Why not go back and settle down there? Since they were Depression-spawned workaholics, many of these newcomers became unconscionably successful. They couldn't help it. Deciphering the causes of anything is tricky. Nature or nurture is a gross simplification.

Which brings us to my family. My father's family was in San Francisco before Silicon Valley and the GI Bill were glimmers anywhere: true natives, almost. They had been in the City since the 1920s. Hard times drove them down from Canada just in time for the Great Depression. My father started work when he was ten, sweeping out his uncles' construction jobs after school. Before school, he delivered two paper routes on the bike he made from junkyard scrap. They raised rabbits for food. He had to kill them, and hated it, never eating rabbit later in his life.

My aunt Elma, who is a very nice person, said, "Well, you know, Sandy, that's just how it was back then. No one had any money. We all worked together to survive."

Some were less accepting of the hardship. Some fought back ferociously. My father came home from WWII, where he'd distinguished himself as a member of the first Underwater Demolition Team. He leapt into the housing boom that would change San Francisco forever. With $500 my mother saved from her wartime job, he started—aided by my mother, aunt, and a few others—what was to be the largest residential construction company in Northern California by a long shot. He operated at one-hundred-percent output every moment he was awake. You have to see someone like that to know what it means..

When I was a teenager, I snuck out to our garage to watch my dad work out one night. Every night after work, he either went to a business meeting, lifted weights, or swam a mile at home, or went to the Olympic Club in San Francisco to wrestle. The garage doubled as my father's gym and workshop. I could hear his convulsive breathing as I stood in the breezeway. His weights were two feet across, four inches wide at the rim. Like wheels from trains. He put so many of them on a bar that it bowed in the middle. He had dozens of barbells, all sizes, stacked on racks around the gym. Lying on his back on a bench, my father hoisted the long barbell off a stand and raised it above his chest. Groaning and panting explosively, he lowered it almost to his body, and then hoisted it aloft. He repeated the process: Almost touched, pushed it back up, and lowered it to his chest, back up. Forever. Lungs working like bellows, flesh screaming, sweat flying. I watched until I couldn't stand it anymore.

"Everything I've done, I've done because I felt inferior," he told me several times. He was the least inferior person I've ever seen, sporting a bodybuilder's physique, in *Who's Who in America*, winner of *everything*. Football player, war hero, captain of industry. Champion amateur wrestler. *"I felt inferior."* He had once been a bucktoothed, one-hundred-forty-pound weakling whom no one expected to amount to much. Rage fueled him.

He pulled in the driveway at night, head shoved back so rigidly that his spinal column could have been one of his barbell rods. He tucked his chin to create perfect posture. Out of sight behind the car door, his non-driving hand squeezed something that looked like a nutcracker but was really a barbell for the hand. He held his chest out and inflated. He'd have worked his jaws, too, if they sold an appliance for it. He worked every minute.

What produces that drive? Why the need for perfection?

The Great Depression. Economic deprivation and a low position in the social strata made the man. That and World War II. The Last Great War. Veterans of more recent wars talk about their traumas and what being a hero cost them. Guys from WWII didn't. My father only talked about the war to his father. No stories of gore, no gratuitous self-inflation. How many landings on occupied shores did he make? The Underwater Demolition Teams cleared the way for the Marines. He didn't talk about it, just couldn't stop working. He was cheerful, too.

"How are you, Andy?" men would ask on jobs all over the Bay Area.

*"Oh, never better."* Off he'd go to bang out another subdivision.

At its peak, Oddstad Homes finished six houses a day. Movement, machines, sweating men. Work. No lack of work, ever again. My father was out the starting gate like a Triple Crown winner, and expected the same of everyone else. He worked, and you worked. Seeing a human being operating at one hundred percent is an inspiring and terrifying thing. Psychologists say most of us operate at about ten percent.

What about my culture? I can't generalize from my family to an entire geographic area without employing more statistical analysis than I intend to put here. But say you took several million people, all with stories similar to mine and stuck them on a peninsula, or between mountains and a bay. What if you threw in some of the world's greatest universities and a population that breathed innovation? That would be the San Francisco Bay Area.

When I was growing up, it seemed like everyone shared my father's ambition, willingness to work, and intelligence. In my grammar school in the 1950s, a kid made a *color* TV for his science project. They didn't exist in the '50s, but I saw the thing. A monstrous cathode ray tube focused colored dots on its screen. We couldn't watch it, because no color programs existed. The dots were fascinating enough. Of course, his father made the thing, but what does this say about a society? A kid had better be smart. A learning-handicapped kid was dead meat.

Along came the computer revolution in the 1970s, ushering in the Second Gold Rush. The brightest, best-educated, most motivated people *in the world* stampeded to my home turf. They remade the Valley from silicon, not gold. We natives were ready, pressed from the same mold. Making the mold, in some cases. That the computer industry developed where it did was no accident.

Nature or nurture? Who cares?

Some addictions aren't recognized as a problem: compulsive *achievement* being one. That's what technological society's about: We measure people by how much they make and what awards they've won. "He who dies with the most toys wins" is a popular bumper sticker in Silicon Valley. People become resumés with bodies; life is a war of credentials and financial statements. I know about this: I used to see people as collections of *achievements*. I saw myself the same way.[9]

Where did this leave me? After the Gathering, with the Voice controlling my behavior, my addictions were cut off cold turkey. In less than a day, my Addict was screaming. I am a compulsive worker, a workaholic. When I work, I do not feel fear, sorrow, pain, sadness, or lack of purpose. My only negative feeling might be frustration if the work doesn't go as fast as I think it should. When I hop into my professional persona, I'm on top of the world.

Prevented from working by the Voice, my Addict choked and reeled, sure of death.

"Don't you think I'd better get to work on *The Horse Book?*" the Addict gasped.

The Voice was immobile: "No. You can only write about the Gathering. Your hour of work is up; take a nap."

Day after day, more commands:

"Call Mary and make a lunch date."

"Call Cindy—go to that spa."

"Look at that piece of property. I know you won't buy it, but look anyway, just for fun."

Can you imagine being commanded by God to have *fun?* I knew exactly what this was: getting me where it hurt. I thought of Jesus, who in Mark 10:21 told that rich guy to give all his money to the poor and follow Him. My minister explained that passage, saying it wasn't money that was so bad, but the man's attachment to it. He needed to give up his attachment to attain heaven. Everyone has his or her attachment to break.

I'm told to have fun—while writing this book, getting it published, and helping the Gathering with some of its profits. I've never published anything before and have no idea whether the book's sales will cover my costs. The project seems crazy to me. This goes straight to the heart of my attachment.

When I was a kid, my father told me many times, "Never work for nothing. No matter what you want to do, you can always figure out a way to get paid for it. Never do anything for free."

The standard of success in my life has been money. This process is knocking the legs out from under it. I'm doing what I'm told and enjoying it. I also don't have any choice: It's a command.

Some writers say, "Grow spiritually! You'll have so much more choice."

Nope: no choice on the spiritual path. You do what you're told and learn, or fall off the path. The trick is to make sure you're listening to the right inner voice.

I plea-bargained, "Don't you think I should look at the outline you gave me at the Gathering? I mean what if ... ?" It had been written in disappearing ink? Stark terror hid beneath this: What if my new agent, whom I barely knew and who barely knew me, discovered that I wasn't working on a book that she could sell, merely writing about the Gathering and things I've learned from life? What if she found out a mysterious inner Voice commanded it? What if she dumped me? I'd be back at the beginning, leafing through books about finding an agent. Terror shot through me.

The Voice felt my fear and responded, "Email her a copy of what you've written." I almost choked. She'd know I've been loafing. She'd drop me. The command was repeated, "Email her what you've done."

Knowing I was destroying my future, I booted up my computer and checked my email.

A message from my agent was in my inbox. She had to leave town because of a personal emergency. She would not be answering clients' calls or emails until further notice.

She did not care what I did; she had her own problems. No one in the universe cared what I did. I could do whatever I wanted.

Realizing I was free almost killed me.


Since I no longer spent hours on the Net, I felt rested. I enjoyed my friends. I wrote, laughing like the old days. Pages piled up.

"It's way too long, don't you think?" the Success Addict whined. "Remember, *The First Five Pages* ... ? No one will read it ... "

"Who cares? Make it longer."

"It should be edited down to six hundred words, like a magazine article," said She Who Would Be Published.

"No. Do what I say."

"No one will read this ... It's too looonnngggg ... " The anguished Addict wailed.

"It doesn't matter."

"What do you mean, it *doesn't matter* if anyone reads it?" Almost hysterical.

"It doesn't matter."

The Voice doesn't care about winning. It doesn't care about pleasing bosses, what they say in magazines or being published. It cares about being obeyed and communicating what matters spiritually. Beneath the commands, the Voice sang to me:

"You are great. You are good. Let the love inside you out. Let the world inside you out. Write what I say—that's all you have to do."

After a few days of hideous distress, the Addict gave up and faded away. I began to feel good. Still no word about when I could start *The Horse Book*, but I knew that I'd be told. At times, the Voice became less intense than it had been after the Gathering. This scared me, because my life was working.

"Don't go away ... "

In graduate school, one of my counseling professors said he'd had clients worry about getting into therapy.

"If my devils leave, maybe my angels will leave, too."

"Angels don't leave," he said.

I think he was referring to the fact that the positive aspects of our psyches tend to emerge in therapy, while the complexes, phobias, and painful parts are processed into oblivion. Or are polished down so that the sharp parts don't hurt so badly. Bliss and visions emerge; terrors and limitations vanish.

After eons of spiritual work, I can tell you that's a nice thought. My angels definitely show themselves more consistently. I'm more aware of the presence and support of God. The demons have left. Sometimes, along with the angels. And my experience of God, leaving me standing, waving my arms. "Hey, guys! I'm still here ... " Which is when the demons come back. They're *changed* demons, though, not the ones I fought at first. More like second cousins once removed: The family resemblance is there, but they don't bite so hard. Or the same way. The demons change and grow, just like the problems, so you don't really know if you're going forward or back.

And then the angels and God return, just like they'd never pulled their disappearing stunt. Ha! Ha! Gotcha.

Spiritual development cannot be summed up in mottos for refrigerator magnets. It's complicated, and deep.

◄◄◄◄HΟΙ►►►►

The Process, God's Process, is like a corkscrew. It punctures the surface, and spirals inward until it can go no farther. At that point, the cork is yanked, and whatever's inside comes out. Sometimes, inner turbulence warns the individual that something's up. Sometimes, it's like our good old California quakes: no warning.

Blissfully thinking that I'd put in a few good months' work philosophizing and growing, I piled into the car. I didn't feel *significant* or in *process*. I was kind of pooped and wheezy, the way I usually feel driving through Los Angeles. Which is where I was—Barry and I were heading for the USC/Norris Comprehensive Cancer Hospital to take care of a trifling problem. No big deal. Maybe some unconscious nervousness about what might occur allowed my soul to open, or the residual of what had happened at the Gathering chucked it out. Perhaps the corkscrew just hit bottom on that drive. I was lounging in the front seat, lazily pondering writing and publication. Why was it so important that my name appear in print?

Hatred and visceral anger exploded inside me. All my life, stated or unstated, achievement has been the source of human value. Yes, warmth and love existed in my family, but behind everything was the need to win. I was the family hero, the high-flying superstar who brought home the honors.

Do you know what it's like to have to be the best in a world where everyone is the best? To be Secretariat in a field of Secretariats? Put the spurs to any horse on that track: It will run to win. Who will create the next New Thing? The next Yahoo!, or Netscape, or technical revolution? I've heard that in some Silicon Valley circles, asking, "What's your net worth?" is acceptable party chat. A screw grinds human beings into the ground in my culture, a different kind of screw than the one that liberates. How many feel its personal costs?

My culture doesn't change people; it devours them.

More, people are similar everywhere. That person at the Gathering talked about how much slander hurts. It hurt enough to prod me into working my waking hours so I could say,

"See! I'm not the bum you think I am! I've amounted to something!"

My name on a best-seller would do the job.

Gasping, I realized that the rage I had experienced was a gem as valuable as the one at the Gathering. It had been wrenched from the depths of the fault in my soul, the gaping fissure just below my seamless surface.

Why did this come up? Maybe from fear of where I was going. Certainly because my addictions had been trimmed by weeks of abstinence. Addiction hides the pain of knowing the truth. When the addict lets go of the drug, no matter what it is, the fault opens, and the gem of understanding is able to pop out.

I wanted to write *The Horse Book* so that people who have slandered me—or their shadows in my brain—would be forced to admit that I am a valuable human being.

But they would never do that; they were incapable of it. I was fighting a losing battle.

Seething, I sat with my rage. My proposed book wasn't a kindhearted look at life with horses—I wanted revenge in print.

Anguish and despair fought, but something else won. Something inside me spoke, a small voice, *my* voice:

"No. No. I want to write a book about horses because I love them, and because I have things to say that others aren't saying. I want to write a song of horses and people, showing all the sides. The light and glory. How we say we love them while we destroy them. I want to write a book that shows what horses are, and where they can take us. A book about God and horses and life. A book that matters ... "

Tearful, I felt my book's true heart. It's about love.

"Now you may write the book about horses ... " The Voice was soft and gentle. I'd been given permission to write something worth writing.

We reached our destination in L.A. We parked the car and entered the hospital.

⋘⋘HO H⋙⋙

The most important spiritual event of the book just occurred. Did you get it?

I was given permission to write. After all that I'd done to assure my writing success—the seminars and workshops, nine years of writing, the querying and trying—I'd reached a level of purity where I could write something worth reading.

Everything we do is a product of our state of being. We aren't aware of that state, except in extraordinary circumstances, but it's obvious to everyone we meet. Our state of being. The platform from which we perform our lives. Our personal philosophy as embodied by us.

"It's so obvious," I explained to a friend. "One of my philosophy professors said, 'Everyone knows about everyone else. We can see someone new and know all about him or her in *seconds*. We know who's good for us, who we should stay away from. And then we ignore what we know, and marry the person, and are miserable. But we *know*.' He was right, too. Like look at you ... " And I proceeded to describe my friend. "You have a kind expression, your body is relaxed, you're really smart—anyone can see that. You wish people well ... " He blushed. "It's obvious. The same for everyone else. I can tell if someone's trying to con me, or be something he isn't. I can tell who's angry or in pain. Who's really happy. It's obvious."

We do know about others, and after some work, can get glimpses of ourselves. I didn't know the explosion of anger was inside me, but I could feel myself working and chugging and *trying* to succeed. That's why nothing had happened: I wasn't in any state to do more than realize something was wrong. And there, on that L.A. freeway, something broke loose and I got it.

Whether you're a writer or a car wash attendant, a computer geek or a doctor, everything you do and say, every interaction you have, is branded with your personal essence.

*Your soul's development and state communicates every instant. It colors your life.*

You can take all the workshops you want and earn as many degrees as exist. You can learn all the techniques, have personal coaching and therapy, establish goals and schedules and plans. You can be the CEO and founder of a giant corporation with every symbol of success. Not one bit of it will matter if your inner state isn't clean. You and everyone else will still feel your inner lack. You can will your way across the universe, and you will not attain what you really want until your Self/soul/spirit is pleased with you. Until you have cleaned out enough to be worthy of your Self. That's what happened to me on that drive.

I've never had the experience of being given permission by God to do what I wanted to do. What was its impact? It's hard to describe straight-on. Let me tell you a story about something that happened long ago.

My family had a boat. It was my dad's really, the *Daddy-O*. The name was a hipster pun, the O standing for Oddstad, our last name, and the

*Daddy*, for my father, our daddy. As I recall, the *Daddy-O* was about twenty feet long with a white fiberglass hull. Riding low on the water, it was upholstered with white and pearlized teal Naugahyde. Pleated and rolled, padded and puffed, with a jaunty windshield, it didn't look like what it was.

I would steal down to the dock early in the morning. We kept the boat at Russo's Harbor, a pleasant family resort on the sloughs of the Sacramento/San Joaquin River Delta, a thousand miles of waterways ripe for what I was going to do. The delta's sloughs were empty at dawn, especially then. This was the 1960s, before they became watery freeways. Glassy and slick, the water reflected the cloudless sky. Reeds marked the boundary of the channel on my left. On the right, rows of piers and beaches littered with floats and pails marked civilization. A levee arose beyond the shore, keeping the delta's water in place most of the time. Roofs poked up over the embankment. Vacation houses stood on the other side, nothing much, but posh for then. The world was silent. Only the water birds and I evidenced life. I'd pull off the boat's canvas cover and slide into the front seat, hard-muscled and lean as the machine. Immortal in my youth, I knew exactly what I would do.

The key fit perfectly into the ignition. When I turned it, a spark erupted in the engine behind me, the engine hidden under the crème puff cover. The *Daddy-O's* pleats and rolls were camouflage. They were my father's trick: mother wouldn't ride in his boat unless it was cushy. You'd never guess what the boat was, just seeing it.

The spark ignited and something awakened. The noise the *Daddy-O's* engine made wasn't a growl or a whine, no sputter or purr. It was a promise. I felt the promise in my gut, in my butt and thighs and feet. In every muscle that I would have to use to keep myself from flying out. We pulled away from the dock, aquatic predators. The thing moved through the water, its low rumble speaking of its secret.

The *Daddy-O* had a three-hundred-thirty-two-cubic-inch Chrysler Marine engine under that teal blue hood. We never were able to measure how fast it went on open water. Around seventy, we figured. "It's completely uninsurable," my agent said, years later. This was in the old days when niceties weren't so nice. It rumbled down the channel like a chained dragon. Rumbled through the no-wake waters, waiting. Summerhouses and tame lives stood on the right, and the wild reeds on the other side opened every once in a while so we could see where we were going.

Limitless possibility. There, right there, was the break in the reeds. On the other side of the reed-covered embankment that separated the wild and docile was Frank's Tract. Created by a dam, Frank's Tract was square miles of open water. Treacherous and deceptive water: The unwary boater could impale his craft on long-drowned orchards, or break his hull on hills that hadn't disappeared just because water flowed where air once moved. If you found the right stretch, Frank's Tract was made for speed.

I turned left, into the open water, my world a sky and its softly rippling reflection. We'd prowl until I found a straightaway that seemed unlikely to destroy us. I'd line us up, taking my time. When everything was ready, I'd push my foot to the floor.

The thing hesitated, like a bucking horse in a rodeo chute. And then it reared up, front end out of the water, propeller biting deep. It screamed. The boat leapt forward, soaring, roaring, screaming, holding more energy in that glass hull than it should have been able to contain. We'd fly like that, me standing up and leaning forward, using my weight to keep the prow down enough so a gust didn't flip us. So I could see the water ahead. Eventually, the boat would catch up to itself and level out. It would drop down onto the water, and then we'd really move.

Fly. In the morning, with no chop, it was easy. Later, in the afternoon, when the wind came up, the Tract was an ocean, boiling with waves and white water. Then, the *Daddy-O* would ram its way across, striking the waves, belting the waves, ramming the waves, but passing over them. Nothing could stop it. Nothing could stop the power or the speed; nothing could stop the thrill of its engine behind me. It was my servant, doing what I wanted. All I had to be was strong enough and bold enough to hold my foot down that hard, for so long. Nothing could stop that machine.

Two things could stop it. A bomb—something blowing it out of the water. Or something breaking its connection to the spark. The igniting spark, the *Yes!* that set everything in motion. A tiny spark awakened the giant and set it free. Take the spark away, and all you had was a floating lawn chair.

When my Self told me I could begin to write, it did what putting the key in the ignition did for the *Daddy-O*, set the world of inner power in motion. I could feel spheres turning, powers moving, aligning my purpose and me. *Drive?* Do you want inner drive? Try all the power in the universe behind you. Within you, streaming out your hands into a machine. That's power.

That is why we seek permission from the higher world, from God: Because as much of God's power as we can handle goes with it. The world of power lives on the other side.

Oh, look—Barry and I have just walked out of the hospital. Let's go back to our story.

Driving home, I was so stunned that I didn't feel anything. I was too shocked for tears. And yet, I'd known before we arrived.

I needed more surgery. It wasn't the cancer.

I thought of Tennessee and the South. We had something in common: We survived the war, but were almost done in by reconstruction.

Why *now?* I'd just gotten the go-ahead to start writing. Why now? How could I plan interviews when I was scared stiff? I knew what was coming; I'd been down that road. I wanted to scream, but was too frozen.

Life is such a roller coaster: good, bad. Terrific, horrible. Pleasure, pain. Wham! Wham! Body blows. What had I done? I work my fanny off to do right, and this happens. Where's the mercy? Why would a loving God do this to me? Where was justice? Where was love?

CHAPTER 15

# TIME AND
# TIME AGAIN

THE SUN BURST OVER THE HILL, making its daily, exuberant comeback. I was propelled from my warm bed by thoughts that I must get the presents wrapped and sent that day. What kind of grandmother was late with her grandchildren's Christmas gifts? But first, I needed to finish this story.

The sun climbed, a yellow orb burning through gray clouds. I sat, feeling and remembering, my soul drawing me deep. It was December 22. In a few days, we'd celebrate the birth of the divine child on this earth of rock and clay, of flesh and will. We'd celebrate the sacred spark that lives in each of us, and a birth whose wonder stopped the heavens.

Around me, a sacred pause. The vast opal sphere rotated, the universe pulled by its motion. Stillness. The earth was blessed, will be blessed, and has always been blessed.

Circles of seasons, circles of dawning, circles of darkness.

My life has changed; what was in motion has born fruit. After that trip to L.A. when my inner fault disgorged its rage, I spoke with my literary agent about my personal issues and weaknesses. The conversation turned out as I knew it would: She understood. We developed the clearest and most supportive business relationship I had ever had. A cottage industry grew at the ranch, an industry promoting me. My husband's been tuning up my short pieces for the magazines. I knocked out this book. We're blasting away on half a dozen projects ... with no end in sight.

I put off that surgery ... indefinitely.

Yes! Yes! Yes! Joy can be expressed! Light happens!

Light and dark, a moving pattern, never still. Joy and sadness. Life and death. Good and evil. The pairs of opposites that mark this earth.

Two days ago, December 20th, I sat writing. I'm allowed to write quite a bit now, as long as I take care of myself. No beeper had to tell me that I'd had enough: I was stiff. Hauling myself out of my computer chair, I wiggled and lurched into standing position. It was past time for a walk.

"Here, Raj! Here, Sammy! *Outside!*" My little dogs danced around my feet, wiggling with joy. They know what "outside" means. When I put on my jacket and approached the door, the dogs' ecstasy grew. "Wait, you guys! Let me get the door open."

Walking through the garage, I stopped dead, staring at the view. The valley erupts into a vault of space and light. The hills, dusted with green blades by the December rains, piled in mounds across from our ranch. The Sierra Madre Mountains formed a pale backdrop. Distance, space, room to move. Sage tumbled from the hilltops. Old oaks, hairy and barren, slumbered through this winter season, sinking their toes deep into rocky shale. The sky amazes every day, no matter the time, no matter the season. Even when tinted orange by the Southern California fires not too long ago, the sky's exotic hue simply reminded us that nature is first. We humans don't hold all the cards.

I stood in our driveway, arms spread, trying to touch the mountains, and shouted, "Good job, God! You do good work!"

Sick of my lollygagging, the dogs ran ahead, protecting the property from gophers and our cats. Their legs moved faster than my eyes could track. I began the walk that would loosen me up enough to write again. There's an oval trail between the house and the upper pasture, down through the barn, between the lower fields and back up. Five laps is a good workout. Arms swinging, striding out: I felt great. The searing back pain I'd felt at the Gathering had not returned. I was able to ride my horse a few times a week. My horse waited for me down below, awaiting my carrots and me. (I suspect he's a carrot addict.) Everything sparkled—leafless shrubs, a big pepper tree. An ancient oak. Past the oak, I looked into the pasture up the hill.

I jerked to a stop and stared, mouth open.

She had her left rear hoof cocked up, just the point touching the ground, like she had an abscess. A horse can get one of those in a couple of hours; they're nothing, same as an infected toenail in a person. The horse goes dead lame because they hurt like crazy, but most of the time they're not even worth a vet call. Barry could put a poultice on it when he got home. But she also had her right rear leg drawn forward almost to her right front foot. She stood akimbo, back twisted strangely. Wild-eyed, the mare turned her head to look at her sweat-covered sides. Colic? Founder?

Oh, Twiggy, I thought. Oh, Twiggy. You're really in trouble. Oh, sweetheart. My horse—she was the horse I rode, until my body fell apart and I couldn't handle such a wild one. Oh, my Twiggy.

Sprinting to the barn, I called the vet. Fortunately, Greg was at the Clinic: An appointment hadn't showed. He and his assistant were on the way.

Time stops: It stops. Reality swung wildly, from absolutely normal to totally unhinged. While I waited, I stayed away from her, not wanting to spook her into painful movement. Just stay there, Twiggy. Don't move; that's a good girl. We've had her for so long; she was barely three when we got her. Is she sixteen now? Twiggy. She got her name because she was painfully thin when she came to us, a supermodel in a breed where voluptuous form was the mode.

During her first year with us, Twiggy filled out. Her lifeless, almost black coat turned glossy and bright. Dapples appeared all over her hide, signaling health. Her mane and tail grew thick and long, moving in the wind, swaying as she walked. When she went under saddle, she became what she was. A swan. A centurion. A schooner at full sail. A magnificent creature showing the world what a horse should be.

Oh, my Twiggy. What happened to you? She stood, tortured, while images spanning years spun around me. So many memories: Benni Barto riding her in her first show. I tried to tell her, "Benni, Twiggy's been bucking with me."

"Twiggy *bucking?*" The trainer couldn't believe it: She knew the animal well. She had been trained at Benni's ranch, under her supervision. "Twiggy *never* bucks!"

Benni tossed a saddle over her and piled on. She was riding the mare at a very prestigious show. To give the youngster a chance to get used to the strange environment, Benni wanted to school her in the main arena before the show started.

"She's been *bucking* ... " She didn't listen to me.

Twiggy bucked from the minute Benni hit her back. Eddie Guitierrez ran alongside, holding the mare on a lead line. Benny sat the horse, taking a deep seat in the saddle. She bucked out of Benni's stable area, into and across one arena, across the other warm-up area, and into the main arena. There, she bucked for forty-five minutes, Eddie running alongside for ballast.

She bucked that day, and the next, and the next—Twiggy never was one to hold back her feelings.

When she finally went into her class on the show's last day, the preparation had worked; she knew the arena and could work comfortably there. She won her huge and important class. The unknown mare catapulted us into the top ranks.

Oh, sweet song, moving swan. A creature of strength and valor, legs like iron, tendons of steel. So strong she was bulletproof, our old vet said. Moving across a thousand grassy seas and show arenas. Head up, neck arched, driving from those magnificent rear legs: horse a connoisseur could love. She stood before me, sweating, looking at her sides.

The vet arrived with an assistant. I stayed back, not wanting to interfere. No problem catching her: She wasn't going anywhere. Greg looked at her, mystified. Shaking his head, he said that they had a poultice made up for her abscess in the truck. This wasn't an abscess. Working carefully, he picked up her left rear foot and used the hoof testers. Those are like big pliers, with a large circle at the end instead of a pointed nose. If you gently squeeze the hoof in different places, the horse will show you where it hurts. No reaction at all, anywhere. It wasn't her foot.

"She's got sweat dripping off her hocks," Greg said. Stress: Something horrible had happened to her. But how? In her safe pasture? How could anything happen to her since breakfast? She was fine that morning.

When he lifted her hoof to test it, she lost her balance, weaving, and scrambling to stay on her feet. She fell hard, struggling to rise. My beautiful horse, so strong, proud, and regal. She couldn't get up. Greg did everything to find out what was the matter. He moved her hind legs in every possible way, looking for a reaction that would tell him what it was. No sign of pain in the legs. He palpated her, trying to see if it was a fractured pelvis.

"You can usually feel a displacement inside." He felt inside her. "I can't tell with her lying like this. When they're standing, usually you can feel an edge ... "

Life streamed past me: This was impossible. She struggled to rise again and again. A horse on the ground is in trouble; any predator could get it. A horse will stand if it can.

She fell three times before Greg left; she couldn't stand, much less walk.

We stood by her and discussed what it could be.

"It's like our Great Dane; her back end just fell apart. It was neurological," I said.

"It didn't fall apart in four hours," Greg responded.

No, not since breakfast. It could be so many things: a fractured hip. Nerve damage, that's what it seemed like to me. There's a disease horses get from possum excrement: It's awful. Friends have lost horses from it. Maybe that. But this was too quick. Greg mentioned a few other possibilities. He wanted to save her; you could see that in his face.

"If we get the ambulance out ... " He looked toward the driveway where the ambulance would have to park. Greg didn't have to tell me: They'd have to drag her down the hill; she couldn't walk. The gate wasn't wide enough, so they'd have to pull the fences down. They'd have to drag her. No.

Only in Hollywood do horses scream in pain. Real horses bear agony almost silently. A foaling mare may release a deep groan more horrible than a scream. The pain of the universe, without words. Twiggy's groans when she tried to get up were worse. No, no ambulance.

She lay quietly, fine, dark head outlined against the taupe soil. Glossy winter coat ruffling in the wind. Her eyes rimmed with red. Her lips parted, exposing long, yellowed teeth.

When did the beauty grow old?

Greg filled her with anti-inflammatories and painkillers, and carefully bedded her so she'd have a soft place to lie. He took some blood. I don't know what he did. That was my horse, so proud. So arrogant. Lying on the ground. She couldn't get up. She'd raise her head, her sculptured Spanish head with its long neck. Twiggy was beautiful and graceful, even when helpless on the ground.

My mother's face came to me, bound with Twiggy's prostrate form. Bound in a night from a dream, many years ago. When we lived in Woodside, my mother stopped by one night. It was unusual, as she was getting older and didn't drive much at night. I was glad to see her, except that Twiggy looked like she was going to foal soon. We're always on edge when a mare is due. I greeted mom and walked with her into the living room.

"Oh, my God!" The closed-circuit TV monitor to the barn showed the mare down in her stall: She was having it! My husband charged out the back door, while mom and I followed more slowly. My mother had trouble walking, even in those days, and it was dark. I held her arm.

When we reached the barn, the wide outer doors were thrown open, and moonlight streamed in. Twiggy lay on her side, black against the silver gilt straw. The baby lay behind her, rear legs still inside her mother. Twiggy raised her head, straw in her mane, an elegant lady caught in her boudoir. She raised her head and turned to see the black form moving behind her. Twiggy nickered to her child and the baby responded. Moonlight froze the scene.

My mother and I watched Twiggy and her baby bond. The foal made a tiny noise; the mare turned her head and shoulders to reach her baby. As time passed, she licked the little one, cleaning and stimulating her to stand. I stood next to my mother in that hallowed place, sharing a sacred moment. Twiggy, that little filly, my mother, and I remain locked in my soul.

She lay on the ground now, pride stripped, strength stripped. My mother's face flashed before me. My mother's gone now, but her presence was there. A whirlwind of memories, years of shared life. Greg was saying,

"We'll have to wait and see. Maybe the anti-inflammatories will do something. We'll let them work. Call me first thing in the morning." The vets left.

Did I know when I saw her fall that she would never rise?

When I woke up, I looked out the bedroom window. I could see her dark form lying flat and still. She died last night, I thought, running outside. She hadn't; she was much worse than dead. I won't describe it. I called the vet, knowing what had to happen.

"It's her pelvis," Lisa said. She was the vet on duty when I called, rushing over to help us. She pushed the mare's hip and you could see it move. "She *can't* get up; it's unstable." There was nothing else to do.

Twiggy's eyes were rimmed with blood red. She raised her head, looking at us. I ran and got some carrots and stroked her while she ate them. Oh, beautiful one. Queen of horses. Beautiful in pain and weakness. A cry rose inside me.

I'm glad my husband is a tenderhearted man. He held Twiggy's head while the vet did what she had to do. His tears fell on the mare's face.

When it was over, she lay still, the wind ruffling her shiny winter coat. The foundling who won the big show. The mother of the horse I ride now. The beautiful one. Still and gone.

She comes to me even now. She and my mother and that night from heaven with moonlight streaming in the stable doors. Two sets of mothers and daughters in a holy time.

Every living thing dies.

We come into this earth, and we leave it. It's a wheel of birth and death and becoming. Who would have thought the dark mare, glistening with health, the strong mare, never sick or lame, would break her pelvis and die?

Who among us knows how much time he or she has left?

⋘◄HΩH►⋙

The wheel moves me today, the cycle of light and love, of coming and going. Of the deathless spirit that binds us, human and animal. The Great One. I look out my window at the immortal hills and the eternal oaks, knowing they would yield like putty to bulldozer or bomb. Nothing is permanent, everything moves.

A dear friend lost, an aunt found. A fortune come and gone. Youth, health. Earthly love. All ripped away, impermanent. Images flutter around me, settling like leaves on the forest floor. My mother. Father. Horses. Places. Faces. Relatives. Friends. My family, husband, children. The little ones. Dogs who have left and live with me still.

When is an ending sad? When is it happy?

The opal sphere has been with me since that Saturday concert when Bill sang. Opal universe, moving magnificence. Grander than that. Its tone deepens, becoming so powerful my bowels shake hearing it. A canon of angels, a roar of joy. The universe is moving, catapulting toward the opening, the place where the outer world cracks so that we may feel the truth. The inner world that many never see.

This world of beauty and pain, ugliness and loss, gain and excess is not the whole of it.

The opal sphere moves closer, rolling over continents and centuries. Something is coming. Can you feel it? Will you feel its bright lance?

However it appears to you, whatever form it takes, God reaches for you, offering his Holy Child, offering Himself, offering the One, giving you your Self. However they appear, the world of the opal one exists. Its roar fills me, takes me.

Prophet, teacher, Savior, sage. In days, we will celebrate His birth. And go on living as we do. Touched, untouched. Who will be touched?

Substance, flowing like water, rich, rewarding, flows under the world of sticks and things. A rising tide fills those who would drink. Life's source.

One day, I will lie somewhere. My lips will draw back from yellowed teeth. Rasping breath will pass in and out. Grayed flesh, sallow skin. Time will slow. I will watch my body from far above, connected to my earthly form by a slender thread. Floating above my flesh in a world fading to white. Saying goodbye to a dear old friend. A foolish friend who tried and lost. Who tried and won.

What matters now?

The thread connecting me to that form, this world, lengthens, stretches, snaps.

An explosion flashes from that break; light bursts from the severance point, traveling to the edge of the universe.

Leaving, I will say, "Thank You. Thank You. Thank You. My Lord and my love. For letting me touch Your earth, for letting me see the fraction of Your glory. For giving me a body and will to serve You. Thank You for every instant, every pain, every just injustice. And thank You especially for that lovely time on your great earth, with singing folk, with mighty dancers, with movers and lovers of God.

"Please, Lord, accept this soul, all I call my own."

I leave you love.

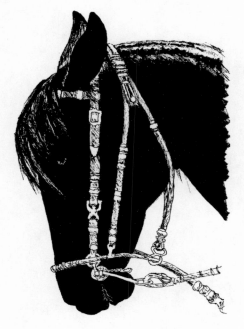

TWIGGY

# CHAPTER 16

# SCARY

THIS CHAPTER WAS NOT SUPPOSED TO EXIST: The previous chapter was supposed to end the text. Something happened, one of those terrifying things. As I wrote about Twiggy's death and the birth of the Divine, I was in an ecstatic state. I felt connected to the heaven that creates music and song, prose and poem. Words came to me, exactly the right words to express my thoughts and feelings. I felt both inside myself as I typed, and in the grand universal realm I'd love to inhabit always. So much energy was pumping through my body, I'm surprised I didn't ignite. At the peak of this deluge of creative insight, the battery attached to my computer began beeping. (This is the battery that keeps it from frying if the power goes out.) Beep! Beep! Beep! At first, it was a low roll, but the motion kept building.

We had an earthquake.

A 6.5 on the Richter scale—not as bad as the 7.1 Loma Prieta quake in 1989, but bad enough. I sat at my computer, lamps jiggling, trees outside shaking, chandeliers swinging. An earthquake, delivered at the moment I was pushing out this book's climax.

"This is too much." Really too much.

The earthquake theme of this book wasn't planned. It evolved as

I wrote: I love Psalm 19. It's only natural for a Californian, or anyone who's been through as many quakes as I have, to read it and think, "Secret *fault* … Oh, yeah, fault. Like the one behind the house." An earthquake metaphor works to describe the crack and disgorge nature of depth psychology and spiritual growth.

And then Twiggy died, birth and death, the images. My mom's face. Christmas coming.

But a real earthquake? And right then? That was overly dramatic.

I sat at my computer, composed and unafraid, thinking, Is this The Big One? We still haven't had The Big One. I wonder if this is it? Will I die? Didn't think so: Wood-frame buildings are what you want to be in if a quake strikes. They move with the ground. This house is wood-framed.

The quake just kept going. On and on. Aftershocks. I prayed, "Is this part of the book?"

"Yes."

"Do you want me to write about this?"

"Yes."

"What?"

"I'll tell you."

Oh, God, God. Why does God have to be so scary? I sat next to an undulating glass sliding door; it moved like a sheet of Jell-o.

"Should I do anything?"

"Yes, move away from the door."

I sat on my bed, looking around and listening to the computer's shrieking battery and things falling downstairs. I felt weird.

When it was over—they do stop—I went to see if I still had a family. I did. Everyone had his or her story. No damage. Back to work.

Later, my daughter and I walked around the property. We got to the barn and looked at the hills on the other side of the road. The biggest bird you've ever seen hovered over them, its trajectory indicating it had come from our ranch: It had to fly over our ranch to get to where it was. We watched, speechless, as it disappeared.

"Mom, that was an eagle."

Yeah. An eagle.

It's not like they appear out of space: Eagles live a hard twenty-minute drive from here, by Lake Cachuma. No sensible eagle would ever come here: At Cachuma, they're surrounded by National Forest. Protected, sort of. The oil companies want to start drilling out there, but the eagles are still more protected in the Forest than here. I'm sure their hunting is better by the lake. No reason for an eagle to come here, ever.

They show up whenever I'm in a pure state. When I came back from the Gathering, two were flying over this property. Eagles. No mistake: not turkey vultures or hawks. They aren't that big. I saw eagles.

Every time I go on retreat, they come. Sometimes, more than one comes. Once, they had a party across the street, a bunch of them soaring and swooping. Another time, a bald eagle—I saw the white head and tail—and some brown friends (juveniles?) landed in the pasture next door. They waddled around. Eagles are not as showy on the ground as in the air. They come when I'm doing what I'm supposed to, when I'm in a pure state. When I'm following orders.

"Mom. That's an eagle."

Okay. You may think this is some California, New Age, hippy, woo-woo baloney. Maybe it's anthropomorphic, I'm projecting, or just nutty. Maybe so. Maybe it's pure chance. Okay. Maybe it is.

I find it terribly upsetting. I reach my depths and this stuff starts. Am I responsible? People were killed, died in the quake, was that necessary?

The Voice answered:

"It's part of my plan." Then, "I have everything planned."

Now I have to figure out how to get this book published. I have to figure out how to do all the dozens of tasks required to make it a success. Contacting people, speaking, negotiating. Things I don't want to do. I want to stay small ...

When I embarked on my spiritual journey, I wasn't looking for a total revolution. I did not want to change my entire life. I'm a recluse. I like to sit on my hill with my family and ride my horse. I like writing about what really matters. I didn't anticipate being required to do hard, scary things like being judged by strangers. Talking to people I don't know. Or do know. I just wanted to ...

"You were born for this. Do it."

We are born for our lives. And our lives are born for us. We need only do them, one step at a time. We also know this.

# EPILOGUE

IT TURNED OUT THIS WAS THE BOOK I was supposed to write, not *The Horse Book*. Other projects clamored inside me, proclaiming their right to emerge. Nope. This was the only writing I could do. I carried it to the end, doing what was required to put this book into your hands.

The process should have been easy: This book was born amid eagles and earthquakes with a divine mandate. Did I float on a pink cloud all year, dispensing grace?

No. It was a rotten year. My back went out so badly that even my doctor and his magic syringe of cortisone couldn't fix it. Recurring disasters struck my loved ones. I suffered from writer's block, verbal diarrhea, and, finally, total paralysis. The publication process resembled the eternal phoenix: going up in flames, arising from the ashes, burning, transforming. Depressing. This was not fun. This is a book about spirituality. Where were the blue lights? The gems of wisdom? (Scattered in the text, a wise-ass inner voice says.)

What did God do to rescue me? Send another eagle?

No, a disaster arrived that was so bad it transcended all previous experience. In that disaster I found my reason to finish this book.

I sat counseling someone. Words flowed out of me, lots of words.

Some were comforting and supportive; some were confronting and direct. Words kept coming. I had to say them; something inside would not hold them back.

As this was happening, I was aware of a point of consciousness behind and above my head. It was watching, recording, and putting

*My words heal.*

what was happening into a larger perspective. Something came to me: My words touched the people who needed my help. My words found a place in their hearts, the exact place needed to heal their wounds.

This was a shock: I've always considered myself an ineffectual shmuck, residue of third grade. The insights kept coming: Someone needs this book. Maybe lots of someones. Life isn't about, "Oh, poor me, I've got so many hang-ups. It's too much work. I can't do it ... " *People need this book.* I don't know who you are, or what will be meaningful to you, but this book was supposed to be published.

That insight turned me around. Spiritual life is not about having fun. It's not about showy visions and manifestations. It's about putting into the world what needs to be there. It's about serving others and leading them to their highest potential, without being motivated by personal gain.

I kept going instead of piling up at the finish line. Many of us fail, when all we need to do is push a little harder to get over the line and win. I don't like to call these people *victims*, because I've been close enough to quitting myself.

*The reward of being human is being who you're supposed to be.*

The reward comes when you realize that what happened in third grade is over and you're not that person anymore. It's crossing the finish line in whatever way you must. Do you cross in a wheelchair? Fantastic! Finish last? Fabulous! Life isn't a race. It's a symphony: A dark, turgid, ugly symphony shot with brilliance and love and rewards beyond measure.

This book came through my fingers and brain, but what really wrote it was my daily spiritual practice and following the Voice. Those kept me going when I wanted to quit.

If we're lucky, we'll become aware that what we've always done isn't working. It may be that moment when we awaken on the railroad tracks, having been run over by a train, again.

The instant we resolve to stay away from those tracks forever is a spiritual awakening. We set forth on a new path, as far away from the tracks as possible. This lasts a couple of weeks, or a month, at which time we discover that the tracks have moved: They're right in front of us.

*Whatever your beliefs, they need to fit your soul. When your soul is pleased, you will know it.*

We *can't* get away from those tracks: We bring them with us. This is a shattering realization.

At that point, each of us can be saved. What saves us is God, however experienced, and the changes we make. What keeps us from sliding back after reaching the turning point is daily spiritual practice. One of the most powerful practices is helping others out of love, without thought of reward.

The trick is to find the practices that work for *you*. Mechanically acting out rules that someone hands you will not cause eagles to fly over your head.

We're like seeds: God plants us. With sufficient water, nourishment, and time, we sprout. After that, we're both gardener and plant, pruning ourselves so we grow properly. Or not. All the time, God keeps shoving conscious life force through us, hoping we'll take it and use it. It's always there, no matter how many times we cut off our own growth or end up a bramble. God keeps sending that life force, that energy, that light, as long as we're here.

Spiritual practice is learning how to be a good gardener.

*You are the garden.*

www.steppingofftheedge.com

# THE GATHERING

Dear Readers,

I was so moved by my experience of the Gathering that I wanted to share my enthusiasm with you. I set up this Section so that the retreat's leaders, Bill Miller and Vicki Collins, can introduce it to you personally. I think you'll feel their spirits shining through their words. In addition, Bill Miller gave me an extended interview, which offers words of healing and solace to everyone. Should you want more information about the Gathering, it is available after Bill's interview.

It's my great pleasure to introduce my special guests, Bill and Vicki. Their friendship means a great deal to me; I hope they will become your friends, too.

Sincerely,
Sandy Nathan

# WHAT THE
# GATHERING
# MEANS TO ME

*Bill Miller*

OVER THE YEARS, THE GATHERING has become a homecoming for me. I've developed immense, dear, deep relationships from it. I see the Gathering not so much about soul saving, as it is about soul *awakening*. The Gathering is a place where I can share my art from my heart and soul; I can share my art, music, and life stories in a way that teaches. I feel safe opening up in the retreat's atmosphere. I'm grateful for the Gathering, because, unlike other places I've been, it allows me to be who I am in Christ, and still be a Native American all the way.

The Gathering is about reconciliation: reconciling those who have been abused, who have been alcoholics or addicts, and who have been through other hardships with peace and contentment. Everyone can come together and heal those old scars, make peace with those old feelings. I can share my faith with my brothers and sisters from the world's cultures and religions in a free and open way. God has blessed me in order to help those who have suffered reconcile themselves to what happened—and they do. That's why I consider this conference a *soul awakening*.

In inviting people to come to the Gathering, I want them to know that the area around Coker Creek is special. I believe that power spots exist in the world, and in the United States particularly, because it is part of the land of the First Nations' People. The area around Coker Creek is a very powerful spot for the Cherokee People. It's the traditional land of the Cherokee; the land has something special. The Cherokee National Forest borders Coker Creek, as does the Cherokee Reservation. (These are the eastern Cherokee, who stayed when the others were removed to Oklahoma.) When you're at Coker Creek, you're very close to a living, breathing Native American community. That has its own power to it, as does the land itself. I suggest that people who come to the Gathering go beyond Coker Creek and go to Cherokee, the Reservation's main town. Visitors should go past the main area of the town, the tourist part, and check out the museum. They will find beautiful things inside.

I invite people to come to the Gathering not just for the scenery, but to get together with the Native Americans who are hosting it. It's a very intimate conference compared to some of the huge ones I've attended. The people who lead it are just normal people sharing their gifts and skills, and their spirits. It's not a clinical thing, with experts sounding off.

I hope to meet you at the Gathering in September. It is a homecoming to me; I hope it will become one for you.

— BILL MILLER

Mohican-German Musician, Speaker, and Artist
Winner of the 2005 Grammy Award for Best Native American Music Album;
other awards including multiple NAMMY Awards;
Spiritual Leader of the Gathering

# AN INVITATION
# TO THE
# GATHERING

WHEN THE HOLSTON CONFERENCE of Native American Ministries Committee first had the vision for the Gathering back in 1997, it was intended to be a cultural, educational, and spiritual event in which both Native and non-Native people of all faiths could come together in an atmosphere of mutual respect and understanding. It is that ... but it has become so much more.

In order to understand what the Gathering is, you must first understand what it is not. It is not an event designed to cure writer's block. In fact, the event has nothing to do with writing or writers. It has to do with *people* and their *spirits* ... and helping those spirits to regain their proper balance. When this balance is achieved, we find ourselves better able to use our talents (which in Sandy's case is writing) and live happier, more productive lives.

Will the Gathering magically fix all your problems? Heal an illness or a broken relationship? Solve financial difficulties? Cause you to "live happily ever after"? No. Sandy went home from the Gathering free of her eBay addiction. Will your addiction be cured if you attend? I would certainly make no such claim. But I do believe that you will return home spiritually renewed and better able to face the difficulties that life hands you. If you come in the right spirit, you will be blessed. This I promise you.

Although the Holston Conference is one of the geographical divisions of the United Methodist Church, we have carefully avoided the teaching of any particular doctrine in order to make the event welcoming to people of all faiths as well as to those not professing any religion. I once read, *"Religion* is for people afraid of going to hell. *Spirituality* is for those who have been there." The Gathering seems to draw "those who have been there." Some choose to discuss their trials in the Closing Circle as part of their healing process, while others of us may keep them to ourselves, but we all find healing and peace. Maybe not answers, but renewed strength and understanding ... and healing of our troubled spirits.

I will be eternally grateful for the countless ways I have been blessed through both the Gathering itself and the many, many wonderful people who have passed through my life because of it. Most of all, I thank Creator for allowing it all to happen. May His richest blessings flow to you all as gentle rain, and may our paths come together again. My love to you all.

—VICKI COLLINS
Director of the Gathering, 2005
Holston Conference of Native American Ministries Committee, 1999-2005
Committee Chair, 2001-2005

Please see the Gathering's web site for more
information on the Gatherings.

# www.thegathering.us

We hope to see you there.

# AN INTERVIEW
# WITH BILL MILLER

AT THE GATHERING, I WROTE QUESTIONS for an interview with Bill Miller. One of the things I admire most about Bill is that he is a person who has done it. One of twelve children raised on a Wisconsin reservation, he has overcome almost every obstacle one can imagine: an alcoholic, abusive father; poverty; racial discrimination; and his own alcoholism and depression. Bill has emerged not only spiritually and emotionally healthy, but is dedicated to using his talents to help others. Many of Bill's fans are working through the difficulties he has conquered. I knew that they would like a more intimate view of how Bill triumphed and some tips on how they might apply his success to their own lives. If you aren't a fan of Bill Miller, it's my pleasure to introduce you to a human being who has transformed his trials to song.

I found myself talking with Bill on the phone during the preparation of this book. I realized, "This is an interview."

It wasn't the interview for which I'd prepared questions: It was better. Realer. I'm writing the initial conversation the way I recall it, without much tidying up, because it illustrates life so well. Life is a whole lot of ordinary, boring stuff, and then: wham! Something interesting happens.

I needed to talk to Bill about what became "What the Gathering Means to Me," which appears above. We played phone tag. Back and forth, back and forth. Finally, I called the number he'd left on my answering machine.

"Hello?" a male voice said.

"Is this Bill Miller?" Part of me hoped it wasn't: If it were, I'd have to talk to him. Did I tell you about my fear of celebrities?

"Yeah."

Oh, no. Now I'd have to say something. Fortunately, I have a lifetime of sophistication on which to draw. "Uh, I'd like to talk to you about doing an Introduction, or something, for the book … you know, the one about the Gathering … ? Vicki talked to you about it … " Starstruck, I barely choked it out.

"Uh, well, yeah. I'm really busy." And he proceeded to spool off about a dozen things he was doing, such as getting ready to go on tour, doing the artwork for a friend's CD cover, and a bunch of other things that left me feeling old and slow. He ended with, "And I have to take my daughter to the hospital right now."

I was ready to hang up.

Bill kept talking. "She's okay. She has spinal bifida, but she's fine. She has to have all these tests every so often."

Spinal bifida is a disorder resulting from unfinished development of the brain, spinal cord, and/or their protective coverings. It's caused by the child's spine failing to close during the first month of gestation. SB babies are sometimes born with the spine open to one degree or another. This can be surgically repaired, but nerve damage is permanent. The disease has no cure, though many types of medical treatment can increase the quality of the patient's life. As a parent, I can't imagine too many things more painful to handle.

A pause hung between us—and Bill filled it. "Why don't you call me in about an hour and a half. I have to sit around the hospital for two and a half hours, waiting. We can talk."

I got off the phone feeling many things: compassion for Bill's daughter and family. Admiration and awe for the family: The love that bound them was obvious in Bill's voice. The conversation drove something else home: *Bill's a dad*. He talks about his wife and five kids from the stage—that's no secret. But he's not just a dad; he's a *committed* dad. The kind of dad who sits around a hospital with his child for hours with tons of other things he could be doing. I realized why I'm a Bill Miller fan. It's not just his music, or his art, or his message: It's about values.

We make a big noise about family values. "Family values" are invoked to mean anything from walloping the tar out of your kids for anything you don't like, to caring enough about them to become the kind of person your children would want to model themselves after. To me, family values are about commitment. That means, I am committed enough to my kids, husband, and self. I will do what I must to keep us together, whatever happens.

While I waited to call Bill, I thought about what his life must be like. What is it like to be a celebrity and have people wanting things from you all the time? To have to be entertaining, even if you don't feel like it? I thought about a little girl who needed tests. Memories from the time when my kids were home came to me: standing on soggy lawns on dozens of Saturday mornings, shivering while a pack of little girls kicked a ball around a soccer field. Staying up past midnight to help finish science projects, then picking glue off my fingers for days. And hanging around hospital corridors, worried sick.

At the appointed time, I called Bill. We went through the same ritual. "Hello?"

"Is this Bill Miller?" (Of course, Sandy. It's his cell phone. Whom did you expect?)

"Yeah."

We started to talk. I said something about how much he had to do and what his life must be like.

He laughed. "If people only knew." He went off about schedules and tours and kids. "Sometimes my wife is teaching over on the other side of town, and I ... " I was getting tired just hearing about it. There was a noise in the background and Bill said, "Sandy, a doctor just walked in." He chuckled, "The third one. Could you call me back in twenty minutes? All this will be over."

I was amused, because isn't this how life is? It's a mess. It's a wonder that anyone gets anything done. Interruptions. Problems. The traffic lights of the universe.

Finally, we talked. The material that became "What the Gathering Means to Me" flowed out. And lots more, which we'll get to. After we hung up, I was high as a kite. Inspired. I trotted around the house, chirping happily.

A few hours later, the phone rang again.

"Hi, it's Bill Miller. I thought of some more stuff since I talked to you. I'm standing in line here, waiting to pick my son up at school. I thought we could talk."

So we did. It was wonderful. I could hear kids in the background, other parents talking. Life going by. And what Bill had thought about!

With that, I'll get down to what he said. What I'd like to say is, "Thank you, Bill! Hanging out with you was fun."

⋘◄◉╫►⋙

Bill began talking about a song from his *The Red Road* album that I'd told him my younger daughter loved, "Faith of a Child." The song is about a young girl who grows up with a handicap. "That song came from a verse from Isaiah. That's one of my favorite books of the Bible. I'm sorry, I don't have the exact verse with me." I found the verse on the cover of Bill's CD, *The Red Road*:

> But those who look to the Lord will gain new strength,
> They will grow wings like eagles;
> They will run and not be weary,

*They will march on and never grow faint.*
—Isaiah 40:31

Bill explained, "'Faith of a Child' is actually from some books and that verse of Isaiah. In 'Faith of a Child', a verse says, 'The rain and the snow that fall from the sky do not return to their Creator void.' That's what I teach. When you get into my words and teachings, I say nothing that you do with God will ever return to you void, whatever effort you make. I think that's what the Gathering is about.

"It's a circular thing. In Native culture, nothing is ever wasted. Everything is used. I remember hunting with traditional Menominee elders. I was so shocked when I saw how *everything* from the deer was used. I'd heard about it, but until you see it ...

"The brain was used to tan the hide. The chemicals from the brain were released in the bucket with the hide. The antlers were used for an altar for prayer; the hooves were used for rattles. The hide was used; the meat was used; the bones were used for jewelry. Everything was used.

"One of the things I get out of the Gathering is that every bad thing can be used for good in our lives. *Everything can be used.*

"That is the key that people need to know. That is the way I have made it in my life. Every day, I have to find contentment, no matter what. If it's hellacious, if I'm in a limo or flying in a Lear Jet somewhere, or in the back of a pickup truck on the Navajo reservation. If I'm singing for sixteen people at a Navajo college or at a sold-out show. Or I'm sitting in a broken-down car. I have to find contentment everywhere.

"It's about time; it's about what you do with your time and how you feel about time. It's about *now* rather than, 'It's *going to be* like this' or 'It *was* like that.'

"It's how you feel right *now*.

"Are you confused? Well, deal with it and look at life exactly the way it is. If you don't, you'll miss out on the blessings that happen.

"I mark my life by my diaries. My diaries are pretty much my songs and my art. I encourage people to keep journals. For me, they are like trees, the limbs on trees. My cousins are professional loggers. I remember looking at trees. I can go into the woods and tell you, 'That one is twenty-five years old, that one is thirty-five years old. That's sixty-five, and that one's a hundred. Just by the width, I can sort of tell. But when you look at a tree and you cut it open, you can see the drought period, the fire, and the rain. The thickness and thinness of the rings show how much water it got each year, or if it went through a fire.

"We need to keep track of our lives. That's the only way we will see advancement or be content that we've lived a good life instead of always complaining, 'Hey, I got this. I got that.'

"Hey! You've got a daughter. So what if she's in a wheelchair! Some people can't even have kids!

"You got this, you got that." His tone voiced his irritation. "People don't count the blessings they have. I think Indian culture has always had an accountability. They were always a thankful people who gave thanks for everything they had. Thanksgiving has got to be a daily thing.

"To answer one of your questions," Bill continued—in the original questions, I had asked, "What saved you? How did you get through your upbringing and emerge so normal?"—"it's been a long process to get to where I am. I stayed at the Seven Hundred Club overnight—how did that miracle happen? I am free of alcoholism; I am free of depression; I am free. Life is beautiful. It's a long, long process with a patient God, with patient friends, dear friends who walk slowly with me. Who touch me softly, speak to me softly, and don't abuse my privacy. We need to find people like that in our lives. That is what the Gathering is to me. It's an intimate conference that never gets too big. It accepts.

"So, that's the way I deal with things: on a day-to-day basis, year to year. It's like a golf game: They say, 'Relax man, it's just a game.' Golf is difficult in that you are hitting a stupid ball, and everybody is staring at you. It's not easy to be relaxed.

"Life is like that, too. You've got everything around; you got the IRS chasing you; you got bills, you got to make payments on your mortgage; you got this, this and this, and yet you're supposed to 'Have a good day!'

"You've got to seize what's important to you beyond what's important. You've got to pay the fees, you've got to do that or they will end up biting you: You'll end up in jail somewhere. A complete balance exists in all that.

"I tend to lean the balance toward family and heartfelt feelings. You'll see a lot of people with great credit: 'We got great credit; we got a seven-hundred-and-fifty-million-dollar home. I got six Escalades in front of my house.'

"Well, it's okay, but that's because they are concentrating on numbers. Statistics are just what they are. Numbers. It's the time we spend with each other, the investment there. It does show. It does pay back. Time that you don't invest with your children or your spouse or your friends shows up later, because eventually it comes back to you. You hear your kids saying, 'Hey, you weren't there for my birthday. You weren't there for that football game. You were always mean to Mom.'

"It's about investing, and I'm not saying I have invested right all my life. I have learned how to reinvest into the day, to look up at the sky and know where I am that day, and to try to go to sleep at night and have some peace. Whatever unrest was going on in the day, I am just glad to be alive. I will deal with the rest tomorrow. I can't deal with it now. Now, I've got to hold my child. I did as much as I could this past school day, or this bill-paying day. That's all I've got.

"We beat ourselves up. The key is to learn how to be laid-back, learn how to find contentment and be content. You start seeing things a lot clearer, because when you're erratic and under pressure, your vision gets limited. Pulled in. It's amazing: We do all that without drugs or alcohol. We limit what we see because we are in so much pain. If you throw alcohol in the mix, life becomes a blur. It's tough to focus. *The bills … I can't do this …* Reality is so focused, fixated, that even without drugs or alcohol, people can't see the reality or details. Throw drugs and booze in, all you've got is a blur.

"The reality is that existence is a three-hundred-and-sixty-five-degree view. It's circular vision; it's everything they have to look at: all of it. You cannot cut it up. If you look at it all, you will know where to look—the right, targeted place. You won't miss the mark; you'll see all around you. And you'll be able to take in what you should see. We're built that way. We don't think we can handle it, but we can. We can handle much more than doctors or therapists give us credit for. There's a lot that we can deal with, really.

"Right in front of me"—he's waiting by his son's school—"there's a mom carrying a backpack. She's got one kid on one arm, the Suburban's door is open, and she's looking for her other kids. I'm sure she's going to make supper for her husband and kids, get them all to bed … This woman is doing six things at once—and she's doing it!

"I'm not saying that's the best way to do things, but we can do a lot more than we give ourselves credit for being able to do. We also need to know when to shut it down, when to rest, smile. When to laugh. When to let go.

"Don't let other people tell you how you're supposed to feel. Say, 'No, man. You're not going to tell me to be depressed. You're not going to piss me off. You're not going to beat me at a traffic light, or cut me off and ruin my day. I'm not going to let you wreck my day!'

"People steal our days, our nights, our afternoons, our mornings. Someone always wants to steal our lives, and we have to be aware of it. Like hell you will! You've got to say *no* to them. You're not saying no to drugs, you're saying no to the world stealing your life away. The more we let ourselves be stolen by the world, the more we're bitchy or whiney to our family. You realize what's happening: The traffic was tight, I missed an appointment—and I yelled at my wife because of it. It's not even human beings that do it; it's all these other events that take us away from what we should be."

"What I'm hearing is ... *you*," I say. "A very strong soul that's worked a very great deal to have the understanding you do."

"Yeah. You know, all of us have to work. I see people suffering in different degrees. Like Christ says, 'Sin is sin to God.' All sin is sin to Him; you can't look upon Him. Tragedy is tragedy whether you've had a miscarriage, or were beaten up all your life, or were sexually molested: All of it causes us to go through a lot of painful moments. The fact is, whatever pain causes you to miss out on life, now—that's your choice. I have decided, No! I've had too much taken away from me. I refuse to let anybody take it away from me anymore.

"You've got to draw the line. You can't live in a gray area anymore: You have to see things black-and-white. You deserve better; you deserve the best possible. I'm not talking about money; I'm talking about moments in time.

"Professional athletes have teams of people to take care of them. Tennis players have masseuses and professional-grade equipment and courts. They don't play on broken-up courts with broken bottles all over, with bad shorts and shoes. They play with the best and they work themselves to be the best, too. They have professional trainers, the best trainers.

"Well, how can we get by with three wheels on our cars, one headlight, and no lunch? We are abusing ourselves in order to prove we're good people. *I'm a good man!* Why don't we treat ourselves better?

"You might find a miracle healing in a way. It's very simple in some ways, and there's also a mystical part, too. A part that's the unseen. The faith that we have in God and ourselves and in things around us that add to the equation. They have to be there. The part of the unseen that's the feeling behind the first kiss. It's the feeling when you have your first child, when you see that baby come out into the world. That's the mystical feeling you can't put into words; no author can put it into words. You just gasp. You just cry. You feel it. It has to be there, it has to be important ...

"What I'm saying is that to be disciplined enough to say no to the visible world, the world that would steal you, you need the unseen world.

"The unseen world is bigger than the visible world. Building our bridges to that world is what we are here for, as far as I can see. There are bridges; there are doors, rivers. There are stones to skip on the water, melodies to sing. These are all the openings to the mystical, unseen world. The openings to that world are there; what people don't realize is that we can have an experience of that world. We can go there, for a time. I have had my own teachers, medicine men and people like that. They can help us, they can help people think and find their souls.

"But I still think that skipping a stone in a lake ... " He sounded tender, thoughtful. A roar of released kids came over the phone. "My son's coming now ... "

The interview ended with a boy's voice asking if a friend could come over. "Daddy, can he?"

"You'll have to ask his father," Bill said. And then, into the receiver, "Talk to you later, Sandy."

SECTION SIX

# RESOURCES

Dear Readers,

When you finish this book, I hope you feel elevated and energized—determined to become all that you can be. That was my purpose in writing Stepping Off the Edge. When the initial high goes away, which it will, you may wonder, Where did it go? How can I get that feeling back?

I included the following section to combat that letdown and facilitate your further learning. If you explore the resources here, you can transform your soul and mind. If you immerse yourself in the knowledge contained in these books and other teaching devices, you can have not just a momentary high, but also an unchained spirit.

The material included here offers years of growth opportunity; I've cooked up a feast for the soul. The most important part is diving in. Pick something that appeals to you and imbibe it: Drink it deeply into your being.

You can also read my book again and do the exercises. Work together: step off the edge with a buddy. Or a group of buddies.

If you'd like me to write a workbook to go with this book, or figure out a way of dropping in on your study group, contact me at the Stepping Off the Edge web site. Enough energy can make anything happen.

I offer you my very best wishes on your journey,

Sandy Nathan

# BOOKS AND
# OTHER RESOURCES
# I LOVE

READINGS ABOUT TOPICS PRESENTED in the text appear below. A more extensive list can be found on www.steppingofftheedge. com. Entries are arranged alphabetically by topic and author.

## ALTRUISM: THE POSITIVE USE OF WEALTH

"Wealth before welfare" is an economic adage: Budding economists are taught that a social system must generate sufficient wealth before it is able to address the welfare of its members. Once individuals or a society attain sufficient means, it can be used for any purpose, including helping humanity. The wealthy people below remind us that wealth is a means and that higher impulses can be supported with it.

**Bill & Melinda Gates Foundation,** P.O. Box 23350, Seattle, WA 98102. Phone: (206) 709-3140. Email: info@gatesfoundation.org. The Gates Foundation is funded with $27 *billion* dollars, making it the largest charitable foundation in history. The Foundation's assets are aimed squarely at finding solutions to the world's worst health problems.

**Doug Herthel, DVM, and his wife and business partner, Sue Herthel.** The Herthels founded and own Alamo Pintado Equine Medical Center and Platinum Performance. Alamo Pintado Equine Medical Center, 2501 Santa Barbara Avenue, P.O. Box 249, Los Olivos, CA 93441. Phone: (805) 688-6510, fax: (805) 688-0269, web site: www.alamopintado.com. Very close to my home, Doug and Sue Herthel have purchased land slated for high-density development and are maintaining it in agricultural use. They've insured the rural quality of life for themselves and their neighbors by employing their own creative land use planning.

**The Hewlett and Packard families** led the way in the computer revolution. In Hewlett Packard, they created a corporate culture stressing cooperation, and products that expanded human welfare through technology. Both families created enormous philanthropic foundations, insuring their founders' contributions to society would continue past their deaths.

> The David and Lucile Packard Foundation, 300 Second Street, Suite 200, Los Altos, CA 94022. Phone: (650) 948-7658, web site: www.packard.org

> The William and Flora Hewlett Foundation, 2121 Sand Hill Road, Menlo Park, CA 94025. Phone: (650) 234-4500, fax: (650) 234-4501, web site: www.hewlett.org

**Markkula Center for Applied Ethics,** at Santa Clara University. Mailing Address: Markkula Center for Applied Ethics, Santa Clara University, 500 El Camino Real, Santa Clara, CA 95053-0633. Phone: (408) 554-5319, fax: (408) 554-2373, email: ethics@scu.edu, web site: www.scu.edu/ethics/. Created by one of the founders of Apple Corporation, the Markkula Foundation encourages ethical action in every aspect of society.

**Turner Foundation, Inc.** 133 Luckie Street NW, 2nd Floor, Atlanta, GA 30303. Phone: (404) 681-9900, fax: (404) 681-0172, web site: www.turnerfoundation.org. In addition to his billion-dollar gift to the UN in 1990, Mr. Turner created, and still personally chairs, The Turner Foundation. The Foundation is dedicated to improving environmental quality, maintaining wildlife habitat, and curbing population. The largest landholder in the United States, Mr. Turner has returned thousands of acres to its natural state and encouraged native species to return.

These are but a few of the many individuals and organizations devoting their wealth to serving humanity and bettering their communities.

## ANCESTORS: CAN'T LIVE WITHOUT 'EM

Haley, Alex. *Roots.* Dell, Reissue edition, 1980. This classic book demonstrates how important knowing one's ancestors is.

Sudama Mark Kennedy, M.A. Religious Studies, University of California, Santa Barbara. In addition to leading the shamanic world music band Dreamtime Continuum, Sudama Mark Kennedy practices a form of intuitive healing incorporating Huna Hawaiian, Chinese energetics, and numerous other healing modalities. In 2003, Mr. Kennedy won a "Lifting Up the World" Peace Mediation Award from the United Nations. Web site: www.sudama.com, email: sudama2@cox.net

## BEHAVIORAL ADDICTIONS: SPENDING, COMPULSIVE WORK, AND ON-LINE ADDICTIONS

Schaef, Anne Wilson. *When Society Becomes an Addict.* HarperCollins Publishers, 1991. What happens if you add up the substance addictions, behavioral addictions, and the human glue—such as codependency—that holds them together? Anne Schaef finds the total *is* modern society. This fascinating book combines gender models, addiction treatment theories, and a broad view of addiction.

Benson, April Lane. *I Shop, Therefore I Am: Compulsive Buying and the Search for Self.* Jason Aronson, 2000. Covers every aspect of compulsive spending and recovery. Meant for psychotherapists, this book is still readable. Karen McCall wrote the chapter on treatment. (See The Financial Recovery Institute.)

The Financial Recovery Institute[sm]: Reclaim Your Life[sm], Karen McCall, founder. www.FinancialRecovery.com, Phone: (415) 457-7019, fax: (415) 457-7651. Karen McCall offers financial recovery counseling. Financial problems are not just about money, or lack of budgetary skills. They always have an emotional component that must be understood. Karen's approach takes this into account.

Greenfield, David N., Ph.D., *Virtual Addiction: Help for Netheads, Cyberfreaks, and Those Who Love Them,* New Harbinger Publications, 1999. Dr. Greenfield is a clinical psychologist and pioneer in detecting and treating Internet addiction. He conducted one of the largest surveys on Internet use: the ABC News.com Internet Addiction Survey.

Anti-addiction resources: See www.steppingofftheedge.com for a directory to Twelve-Step Programs.

Want to win on eBay? This series of articles shows you how to win the auctions you want at prices you can afford and how to break free of eBay addiction. See "An Ode to eBay" on *Spurs Magazine,* www.spursmagazine.com. Use the index to reach the series.

## CORPORATE CULTURE AND CHANGE
## WHAT HAPPENED AT ENRON?

We tend to separate our lives into spiritual and worldly realms, acting as if whatever we do in one has no impact on the other. Not so. Each of us earns a living by applying our life force—soul and will—in the material world. Everything that we do in our work and with our earnings expresses and affects our souls and those of others. Here are some contacts offering illuminating and revolutionary insight about business.

**Richard T. Pascale,** Ph.D. I was fortunate enough to be a member of Dr. Pascale's staff when he taught at Stanford University's Graduate School of Business. After teaching at Stanford for twenty years, he is now an associate Fellow at Oxford and an organizational consultant. Richard Pascale continues to transform the world's thinking about business theory and corporate culture. I've included two of his publications here; the rest are shown on www.steppingofftheedge.com.

Pascale, Richard Tanner and Anthony G. Athos. *The Art of Japanese Management.* Warner Books (Reissue edition), 1982.

Pascale, Richard T., Mark Milleman, and Linda Gioja. *Surfing the Edge of Chaos: The Laws of Nature and the New Laws of Business.* Random House, 2000.

A short and readable introduction to Dr. Pascale's thoughts about the relevance of complexity science to management can be found on the www.emeraldinsight.com web site, in the April 2004 edition. You can contact Richard Pascale at: RTPASCALE@aol.com

Bryce, Robert. *Pipe Dreams: Greed, Ego, and the Death of Enron.* BBS Public Affairs, 2002. This readable, entertaining book by a Texas investigative reporter shows what went wrong with Enron. Bryce makes obscure accounting practices understandable, and turns the principal actors into real, if generally repulsive, people.

## HORSES, HIGHER CONSCIOUSNESS, AND HEALING

Was it Mark Twain who said, "The outside of a horse is good for the inside of a man"? People associated with horses have been aware of their healing influence for thousands of years.

Rancho Vilasa Peruvians, Barry & Sandy Nathan, www.ranchovilasa. com. Our family has bred Peruvian Paso horses for almost twenty years. Peruvian horses continue to amaze us with their curative and intuitive ways. In addition to featuring beautiful photos, our ranch web site keeps you up-to-date with ranch news.

Our web sites, *Spurs Magazine* and *Equines & Heart Strings*, www. spursmagazine.com and www.equinesandheartstrings.com, offer articles about owning, training, and loving horses.

Sr. Jorge de Moya of Narrawin Stud and Olivaylle Pty. Ltd. of Victoria, Australia, purchased our stallion and two mares. Jorge is creating a first-class olive plantation and eventually will add an equine-themed resort. His innovative breeding program seeks to reconnect modern gaited horses with the roots of Spanish horses in the New World. www.olivaylle.com.au

Two books by professionals who have thoroughly examined the relationship between horses and health:

McCormick, Adele, and Marlena McCormick. *Horse Sense and the Human Heart.* Health Communications, 1997. The Drs. McCormick are experienced psychotherapists who have used Peruvian Paso horses in their therapeutic regimen for many years.

McCormick, Adele von Rust, Ph.D., Marlena Deborah McCormick, Ph.D., and Thomas McCormick, M.D. *Horses and The Mystical Path: The Celtic Way of Expanding the Human Soul.* New World Library, 2004. Exhaustively researched, the sequel to *Horse Sense and the Human Heart* traces the deep connection between the equine species and human spiritual experience.

## PHILOSOPHIC PERSPECTIVES FROM INDIA & ASIA

Swami Kripananda. *Jnaneshwar's Gita: A Rendering of the Jnaneshwari.*
State University of New York, Albany, 1989. This rendering of the
*Baghavad Gita* presents the original text and a complete commentary
by the thirteenth century Indian saint, Jnaneshwar. Chapter 16 of
the *Gita* gives the clearest exposition of the demonical state in a
human that I have seen; Janeshwar's comments expand the definition.
For a briefer rendition, see *Pocket Bhagavad Gita*, Winthrop Sargeant,
translator, State University of New York Press, Albany.

Swami Shantananda with Peggy Bendet. *Splendor of Recognition:
An Exploration of the Pratyabhijñā-hṛdayam: A Text on the Ancient Science
of the Soul.* Siddha Yoga Publications, 2004. Includes a Sanskrit
pronunciation guide CD. *The Pratyabhijñā-hṛdayam* is one of the most
important texts of Kashmir Shaivism, an ancient school of Indian
thought. Swami Shantananda, a highly experienced scholar and
monk, illuminates this ancient text with good humor and insight.

Sogyal Rinpoche. *The Tibetan Book of Living and Dying: The Spiritual
Classic & International Bestseller.* Revised and Updated Edition, Harper
SanFrancisco, Reprint edition, 1994. A classic book not only on
conscious dying, but also Buddhism.

Thich Nhat Hanh. *Living Buddha, Living Christ.* Riverhead Books, 1997.
A compassionate look at two of the world's great religions.

## PSYCHOSYNTHESIS

The theoretical structure that meant most to me in graduate school,
psychosynthesis is a living discipline, best learned through trained
practitioners. It depends strongly on personal interaction, visualizations,
and exercises. See www.steppingofftheedge.com for additional readings.

Organizations promoting psychosynthesis in the United States:

The Association for the Advancement of Psychosynthesis, A North American psychosynthesis membership organization dedicated to furthering psychosynthesis. Address: AAP, P.O. Box 1510, NY, NY 10028. email: ebrent54@excite.com. Phone: (646) 320-3914, web site: www.aap-psychosynthesis.org

The Synthesis Center, 274 North Pleasant Street, Amherst, MA 01002-1725. Phone: (413) 256-0772, web site: www. synthesiscenter.org, email: admin@synthesiscenter.org. Many psychosynthesis books and related materials are hard to find. The best place to find books, monographs, and materials is through Synthesis Distribution at The Synthesis Center, www.synthesiscenter.org.

Classic and contemporary readings in psychosynthesis:

Assagioli, Roberto, M.D. *Psychosynthesis: A Collection of Basic Writings*. The Synthesis Center, 2000. www.synthesiscenter.org. This book contains the core of Assagioli's thought. His theory dovetails with some of the Buddhist and Hindu models of the mind, which were developed from the contemplations of ancient sages.

Assagioli, Roberto, M.D. *The Act of Will*. Viking Press, 1971. www.synthesiscenter.org.

Brown, Molly Young. *Unfolding Self: The Practice of Psychosynthesis*. Helios Press, Allworth Press, NY, 2004.

Firman, John, and Ann Gila. *Psychosynthesis: A Psychology of the Spirit*. SUNY Press.

## SAINTS AND HOLY MEN AND WOMEN WRITE ABOUT THEIR EXPERIENCE AND SPIRITUAL LIFE

Black Elk, John Gneisenau Neihardt (Preface), Nicholas Black Elk. *Black Elk Speaks: Being the Life Story of a Holy Man of the Oglala Sioux*. Bison Books Corp., 2003.

Demallie, Raymond J., *The Sixth Grandfather: Black Elk's Teachings Given to John G. Neihardt*. University of Nebraska Press, 1985. This book reportedly has Black Elk's interviews verbatim, reducing the translator's influence.

Swami Chidvilasananda. *My Lord Loves a Pure Heart: The Yoga of Divine Virtues*. Siddha Yoga Meditation Publications, 1995.

Lame Deer, John (Fire) and Richard Erdoes. *Lame Deer, Seeker of Visions*. Simon & Schuster (Revised Edition), 1994.

St. John of the Cross. *The Collected Works of Saint John of the Cross*. Kavanaugh & Rodriques, Trans., I C S Publications, Institute of Carmelite Studies, Revised edition, 1991.

Swami Muktananda. *Play of Consciousness: A Spiritual Autobiography*. Siddha Yoga Meditation Publications, thirtieth anniversary edition, 2000.

Padilla, Stan. *Chants and Prayers: A Native American Circle of Beauty*. The Book Publishing Company, 1995. The quotation from Black Elk in the text is found on page 78.

Saint Teresa, Otilio Rodriguez (Translator). *The Collected Works of St. Teresa of Avila*. ICS Publications, 1976.

Teresa of Avila, E. Allison Peers (Translator). *Interior Castle*. Image, Reissue edition, 1972.

Mirabai. *Mirabai: Ecstatic Poems*. Bly, Robert (Translator). Jane Hirshfield (Translator). Beacon Press, 2004.

Rumi. *Essential Rumi.* Coleman Barks (Translator). Harper
SanFrancisco, 1997.

## CONTACTS

Contact information for people and places mentioned in the text is
found here.

Swami Chidvilasananda is my meditation teacher. I was also a
student of her predecessor, Swami Muktananda, until his death in
1982. Information about Swami Chidvilasananda and Siddha Yoga
Meditation can be found at www.siddhayoga.org. SYDA Foundation,
P.O. Box 600, 371 Brickman Road, South Fallsburg, NY 12779-0600.
Phone: (845) 434-2000

The Country Music Hall of Fame® and Museum. 222 Fifth Ave. S.,
Nashville, TN 37203. Web site: www.countrymusichalloffame.com.
Phone: (800) 852-6437, email: eblast@countrymusichalloffame.com.

Coker Creek Village Adventure and Retreat Center, A Christian
Facility. Coker Creek Village, site of the Gathering. The Village offers
year-round retreat and adventure opportunities. Retreats can be quiet
and contemplative, or action-packed. 12528 Highway 68, Coker
Creek, TN 37314. Phone: (800) 448-9580 or (423) 261-2310. Email:
info@cokercreekvillage.com. Web site: www.cokercreekvillage.com

The Gathering. The Gathering is a spiritual retreat sponsored by the
Holston Conference of Native American Ministries of the United
Methodist Church. Web site: www.thegathering.us. Check the web
site for information on future Gatherings and to contact organizers.

John Friend, founder of Anusara Yoga, is one of the most respected
hatha yoga instructors in the country. He provides comprehensive
instruction and an inclusive on-line store featuring books and yoga
supplies. Contact: Anusara Yoga, 9400 Grogans Mill Rd., Ste. 200,

The Woodlands, TX 77380. Toll-free phone: (888) 398-9642, local phone: (281) 367-9763, fax: (281) 367-2744, web site: www.anusara.com, email: oneyoga@anusara.com.

Sally Kempton, author of *The Heart of Meditation*, gives meditation retreats and instruction. See her web site, www.sallykempton.com, for her schedules.

Bill Miller: Native American Musician, Artist, and Speaker. Bill Miller's music and concert schedule can be found on his web site, as can booking information. www.billmiller.net

Lily Nathan: Information on Lily Nathan's writing and art may be found at www.lilynathan.com.

Powwow Dancers and Workshop Presenters at the Gathering: To contact dancers or workshop givers at the Gathering, see www.thegathering.us.

School of Education, Counseling Psychology, and Pastoral Ministries, Santa Clara University. I earned my MFCC at Santa Clara University. Department of Counseling Psychology, Santa Clara University, 500 El Camino Real, Santa Clara, CA 95053. Phone: (408) 551-1603, fax: (408) 554-2392, web site: www.scu.edu/cp.

## DEATH & DYING, GRIEF, & CHRONIC ILLNESS

Topics none of us can dodge. These are my favorite resources.

Becker, Ernest, Sam Keen (Foreword). *The Denial of Death*. Free Press, 1997. Becker wrote this Pulitzer Prize–winning book as he faced his own death. He finds our failure to acknowledge our own deaths as the cause of limited and fear-ridden lives. Rather than fully living, we construct monuments to fool ourselves into thinking we're immortal.

Levine, Stephen and Ondrea. *Who Dies? An Investigation of Conscious Living and Conscious Dying.* Anchor, Reissue edition, 1989. The Levines are known as among the best grief counselors in the country. They've authored many books about conscious dying; this may be the most famous.

Levine, Stephen and Ondrea. *The Grief Process: Meditations for Healing,* Sounds True, 2000. Audiotape set. I found this invaluable when my mother died.

Levine, Stephen. *Merciful Awareness: Natural Pain Management.* Sounds True, 1999. Audiotape set. This was invaluable when I had my knee replaced.

Minar, Barbra Goodyear. *Walking into the Wind: Being Healthy with a Chronic Disease.* Xlibris Corporation, 1st edition, 2000. Despite living with chronic illness for thirty years, Barbra Minar has created a full and gracious life. She shares her secrets in this intimate book, writing from a Christian perspective.

Ram Dass. *Still Here: Embracing Aging, Changing, and Dying.* Riverhead Books, Reissue edition, 2001. Ram Dass wrote this book after suffering a massive stroke. He credited that stroke with teaching him humility. Ram Dass writes from a Hindu/Eastern perspective, though he is a trained Western psychologist.

Bauby, Jean-Dominique. *The Diving Bell and the Butterfly: A Memoir of Life in Death, Vintage.* Reprint edition, 1998. In 1992, the author suffered a massive stroke that left him completely paralyzed. He could blink his left eye—that's it. To write this book, Bauby blinked as a reader read a special alphabet aloud. A blink meant, "Write that *letter.*" This is a lovely, haunting memoir of a man who used his mind to entertain and delight himself when that's all he had.

## EVIL: HOW TO COPE WITH IT

Peltier, Leonard. *Prison Writings: My Life Is My Sun Dance*. St. Martin's Press, NY: 1999. Written from prison, this book is an eye-opener.

Swami Muktananda. "Only One Self Resides Within Everyone." *Darshan Magazine #150*, September 1999, page 37. Published by SYDA Foundation, 371 Brickman Road, P.O. Box 600, South Fallsburg, NY 11788-0894. www.siddhayoga.org. This article is quoted in the text and provides a definition of evil and what to do about it.

Becker, Ernest. *Escape from Evil*. Free Press, Reissue edition, 1985. A timeless book focusing on human darkness.

Peck, F. Scott. *People of the Lie*. Touchstone, 2nd edition, 1998. I like this book for its depiction of how "dirty lenses"—our distorted perceptions—create evil. Those who do evil, the People of the Lie, choose their distorted view over reality.

_____. *The Road Less Traveled*. Touchstone, Twenty-fifth anniversary edition, 2003. The classic book that defined a generation's spiritual search.

Mirabal, Robert. *Taos Tales*. Silver Wave Records, 1999. The CD jacket provides food for contemplation, as does the music.

## EVIL & PSYCHOPATHOLOGY AS PRESENTED BY TRADITIONAL PSYCHOLOGY

Cash, Adam, Psy.D. *Psychology for Dummies*. Dummies Press, 2002. An easy-to-read overview of Western psychology, this guide covers all the bases, including schools of psychology, how to pick a therapist, *and* psychopathology. The author is a forensic psychologist working with mentally disordered criminal offenders.

Hare, Robert D., Ph.D. *Without Conscience: The Disturbing World of the Psychopaths Among Us*. The Guilford Press, 1999. Provides a deeper and more disturbing look at those with ASD, antisocial disorder.

Pennington, Bruce F., Ph.D. *The Development of Psychopathology: Nature and Nurture*. The Guilford Press, first edition, 2002. Critically acclaimed, this book reflects the latest neuroscientific perspective of the development of psychopathology.

Freud, Sigmund, Peter Gay (Introduction). *The Psychopathology of Everyday Life*. W. W. Norton & Company; New Edition, 1971. In this book, Freud discusses "Freudian slips," those not-so-innocent mistakes, misinterpretations, and bits of forgetfulness that reveal deeper motivations. Unabridged republication of the classic 1914 edition.

## SCIENCE & HUMANITY'S SEARCH FOR MEANING

Newberg, Andrew B., M.D., D'Aquili, Eugene G., M.D., and Vince Rause. *Why God Won't Go Away: Brain Science and the Biology of Belief*. Ballantine Books, 2002. This book is based on a scientific investigation of humanity's search for meaning. Shows how our spiritual quest is based on brain function and structure.

Sacks, Oliver. *Awakenings*. Vintage, Reprint edition, 1999.

————. *An Anthropologist on Mars: Seven Paradoxical Tales*, Vintage, 1996.

Two readings on consciousness and neuroscience by a pioneer.

Kant, Immanuel, Ellington, James W. (Translator). *Prolegomena to Any Future Metaphysics That Will Be Able to Come Forward As Science with Kant's Letter to Marcus Herz, February 27, 1772: The Paul Carus Translation*. Hacket Publications, 2nd edition, 2002. The famous philosopher shows we can never know anything in itself.

*What the Bleep Do We Know?* Don't like to read? Get the message in film form. http://www.whatthebleepdvd.com. This amazing movie presents quantum physics and the biology of consciousness for everyone as presented by famous scientists. The New Renaissance Bookshop, 1338 NW 23rd Ave. at Pettygrove, Portland, OR 97210, has a page on their web site, http://www.newrenbooks.com/books/bleep1.html, featuring books by all the scientists in *What the Bleep*.

## WORKING WITH THE MIND TO DEVELOP EMOTIONAL AND COGNITIVE CONTROL

Here are a few examples from a number of traditions showing ways to control, or at least rein in, one's mind. In the process, we can gain greater happiness and self-control.

Swami Anantananda. *What's on My Mind: Becoming Inspired with New Perception.* SYDA Foundation, 1996. This book contains my favorite exercises on controlling "the thieves of the heart," emotions like envy, fear, greed, pride, and infatuation. *What's on My Mind* is written from a yogic perspective and contains practical tips anyone can use.

Assagioli, Roberto. *Psychosynthesis: A Collection of Basic Writings.* The Viking Press, 1971. Assagioli clearly sets out the usefulness of mental images in creating a desired future in "Technique of Ideal Models," pp. 166-177. More on psychosynthesis can be found in a separate section.

Albert Ellis is the father of Rational Emotive Therapy (RET). He has written books about overcoming almost every psychological malady. RET works, according to my experience in graduate school, but it is very brisk: "Ninety percent of human suffering is due to whining," an old Albert Ellis-ism I recall.

Ellis, Albert. *A New Guide to Rational Living.* Prentice Hall Trade, 1975. The masterwork by the King of RET. In print since 1975:

a long time to stay in print in this publishing world. It works.

—————. *How to Stubbornly Refuse to Make Yourself Miserable About Anything—Yes, Anything.* Lyle Stuart Hardcover, 1988. The title says it all.

Swami Durgananda (Sally Kempton). *The Heart of Meditation: Pathways to a Deeper Experience.* SYDA Foundation, 2002. With twenty-eight years of meditation, twenty-two of them as a Saraswati monk, Swami Durgananda has the expertise that many writers struggle to establish. Durgananda has left monastic life, going back to her earlier name, Sally Kempton. This is a beautiful, superbly written book.

Abraham Maslow is considered one of the founders of humanistic and transpersonal psychology. Here are three classic books in which he sets out his ideas.

Maslow, Abraham H. *Religions, Values, and Peak Experiences.* Penguin Books, 1994. Originally copyrighted in 1964, this is one of the early classics in the psychology of mysticism. Maslow defines the peak experience here and outlines its function in human life.

—————. *The Farther Reaches of Human Nature.* (An Esalen Book) Penguin Books, Reprint edition, 1993. This work was compiled after Maslow's death and is a synthesis of his ideas. He discusses biology, cognition, creativity, self-actualization, and the hierarchy of needs.

—————. *Maslow on Management.* Wiley, Revised Edition, 1998. Originally written in 1962 after Maslow spent the summer at a factory, this book presents Maslow's ideas on humane management. This book has become the sourcebook for ideas on enlightened management.

Ward, Francine. *Esteemable Acts: 10 Actions for Building Real Self-Esteem*. Broadway, 1st edition, New York, 2003. I call this book behaviorist because its author emphasizes the actions we need to take to develop true self-esteem. Ward's book takes into account spiritual factors, dreams, and imagination, but it's facing fear that produces the payoff. Contact: Francine Ward, J.D., Esteemable Acts web site: www.esteemableacts.com, email: francine@estimableacts.com. P.O. Box 1239, Mill Valley, CA 94942.

## WRITING & PUBLICATION

Some of my favorite resources for writing and publication:

King, Stephen. *On Writing: A Memoir of the Craft*. Pocket Books, 2002.

Lamott, Anne. *Bird by Bird: Some Instructions on Writing and Life*. Anchor, 1995.

Browne, Renni and Dave King. *Self-Editing for Fiction Writers: How to Edit Yourself into Print*. Quill, an imprint of HarperCollins Publishers, 1993.

Mark Victor Hansen's Mega Book Marketing University, M.V. Hansen & Associates, Inc., P.O. Box 7665, Newport Beach, CA 92658-7665. www.megabookmarketing.com. Mark Victor Hansen's Rich Results Newsletter delivers free positive thinking exercises to your inbox for a year. www.markvictorhansen.com/rich_results.php

Poynter, Dan. *The Self-Publishing Manual: How to Write, Print, and Sell Your Own Book*. Para Publishing, 14th edition, 2003. This book is known as the bible of self-publishing.

The Writers' Corner, www.spurswriterscorner.com. I offer a series of articles for writers on my 'zine, *Spurs Magazine*. My focus is on getting below the surface of your psyche and producing something worth writing, as well as mobilizing the drive to complete a project.

# ABOUT THE ILLUSTRATIONS AND COVER ART

I USED A MULTI-STEP PROCESS in producing the illustrations. Starting with photographs, I selected an image or images, sometimes producing collages to create the effect I wanted. After that, I made pencil sketches for each illustration. From those, I made a pen-and-ink drawing. Scanning the drawing into Photoshop, the fun began as I worked and reworked the images electronically for the high resolution needed for publication. This meant ironing out bulges and flaws with Photoshop's paintbrush, doing such picky detail work that I amazed even myself. It took a long time.

The only time I really got hysterical was when I clicked the paint bucket tool in the wrong place and turned my aunt Nona's *finished* portrait into a blank white page. The Undo command didn't work, having been used probably a zillion times in that session. (I assumed it was being stubborn.) Panicking, I thought that the screen would go back to what it was before the disaster if I closed Photoshop without saving the image.

It did: The image went all the way back to the original scan, which had been last seen long hours of tedious work before. Arggh! There's no auto save on *our* Photoshop.

Only then did I remember the History key. I could have just clicked it before the dreadful accident, instead of having to do the portrait again. Which is what I did.

This story demonstrates that the number of computer-related heart attacks and deaths is probably lower than it should be, given the emotion aroused.

Despite all this, the drawings were finished. While I produced the illustrations, other people were involved along the way. Photographers played a part. Georgia Dennis took the photographs of the Native Americans. My daughter Zoë was responsible for the photographs of horses. I took the photos that went into the drawing of my aunt Nona Reed.

While the finished product sometimes didn't look much like the original photo or person in the photo, real people formed the bases of the illustrations. *Stillness* is based on a photo of Louella Lane, a Gathering participant. *The Hoop Dancer* depicts Lowery Begay dancing at the Gathering. *Horse and Rider* shows Corcovado BSN and my husband, Barry. *Nona Reed, Redbird Woman*, portrays my aunt Nona. *Angels Don't Leave* is based on a photo of Bill Miller at the Gathering. The spectacular angels behind him were based on images from Bill's paintings. *The Drum* depicts drummers at the Gathering's powwow. A number of people were worked into these figures, including Lowery Begay, Ben Sanchez, and Stanley Bell. The drawing *Twiggy* came from a photo of Twiggy taken at a horse show by my daughter Zoë.

Cover images came from a number of sources. The horse is Azteca de Oro BSN, a Peruvian Paso gelding bred by our ranch, Rancho Vilasa, and photographed by Zoë Nathan. The oil portrait of Bill Miller is by Lily Nathan, taken from a photo of Bill by Georgia Dennis. Georgia Dennis photographed the Men's Traditional Dancer, Stanley Bell.

I deeply appreciate the use of your images.

Several of the dancers and drummers are available professionally. I invite you to check the Gathering web site, www.thegathering.us, for contact information. You may book Bill Miller through his web site, www.billmiller.net.

# NOTES

[1] eBay claims trademark rights to this mark.

[2] Weight Watchers claims trademark rights to this mark.

[3] Swami Muktananda, "Only One Self Resides Within Everyone," *Darshan Magazine* 150, (1999): 37. Reprinted with permission of the SYDA Foundation.

[4] Roberto Assagioli, *Psychosynthesis: A Collection of Basic Writings* (New York: Viking Press, 1965): 19. Assagioli names Bucke, Ouspensky, Underhill, Jung, Deoille, various yogic practitioners and yogis, and philosophers such as Kant and Herbart as individuals or theorists who describe a Higher Self in their writings.

[5] Stan Padilla, *Chants and Prayers: A Native American Circle of Beauty* (Summertown, Tennessee: The Book Publishing Company, 1995): 78.

[6] Adrian Raine, DPhil; Todd Lencz, Ph.D.; Kristen Taylor, Ph.D.; Joseph B. Hellige, Ph.D.; Susan Bihrle, Ph.D.; Lori Lacasse, B.Sc.; Mimi Lee, B.Sc.; Sharon Ishikawa, Ph.D.; Patrick Colletti, M.D.; "Corpus Callosum Abnormalities in Psychopathic Antisocial Individuals"; *Archives of General Psychiatry*; 60, no. 11, (2003):1134-1142.

[7] According to the first major statistical survey attempting to determine the prevalence of personality disorders in the United

States, perhaps 30.8 million American adults (14.8 percent) met diagnostic criteria for at least one personality disorder as defined by the DSM-IV. Prevalence, Correlates, and Disability of Personality Disorders in the United States: Results from the National Epidemiologic Survey on Alcohol and Related Conditions. [CME] Bridget F. Grant, Deborah S. Hasin, Frederick S. Stinson, Deborah A. Dawson, S. Patricia Chou, W. June Ruan, and Roger P. Pickering. *Journal of Clinical Psychiatry,* 65, no. 7 (2004). DSM-IV is the American Psychiatric Association's Diagnostic and Statistical Manual of Mental Disorders, Fourth Edition.

[8] Mirabal, Robert, Taos Tales, Silver Wave Records, 1999. The CD jacket provides food for contemplation, as does the music.

[9] In the text, I'm hard on the materialistic aspects of Silicon Valley's culture. The evil, heartless capitalist; the shallow, vain woman of means; and the greed-consumed businessman are stereotypes that prevent us from appreciating our common humanity. "Books and Other Resources I Love" presents information about capitalists who have used their wealth to further the well-being of others.

# INDEX

## A

abstinence, 44–45, 64–65, 226
abuse, 181–183, 191–192, 210–211, 261
achievement, 217
*Act of Will, The*, 86–87
Addict, the, 56–65, 81, 87, 224
addiction
   abstinence and, 64–65, 226
   behaviors of, 154
   behaviors, typical, 58–59
   benefits gained through experience,
     68–69
   carrots and, 235
   coping with, 176–177
   costs of, 66–67
   development of evil and, 198
   Devil and, 205–206
   negative consequences of, 56–57
   recovery from, 57–65, 210, 216, 257–258
   self-assessment and, 53–56
   as a spiritual obstacle, 43–49
   subpersonalities and, 81
   surviving, 184–185
   twelve-step programs and, 56
   types of, 9
   work, 116, 154, 217, 221
AIDS, 182
Allen, Woody, 187
American Indians. *see* Indians
ancestors, 91–93, 96
angels, 224–225
*Angels Don't Leave*, 166
anger, 193–194
antisocial personality disorder (APD), 196
anxiety, 133–134
APD (antisocial personality disorder), 196
appearances, 171, 201
art, 37–39, 43, 209–210. *see also* illustrations
*Art of Japanese Management, The*, 148
Assagioli, Roberto, 81, 86, 88, 189
athletes, 269
attachment, need for, 28
awareness, 62–63

## B

Beatles, the, 144
*Beautiful Mind, A*, 183
Becker, Ernest, 161
Begay, Emerson, 145, 167–171

Begay, Ida, 145
Begay, Lowery, 145, 167–171
behaviorism, 153, 171
belief, 82–85
belonging, need for, 28
benefits gained through experience with
   addiction, 68–69
*Bhagavad Gita*, 41, 68
Bigay, Danny, 145, 167–171
biological needs, 28
birth, 132
Black Elk, 88
*Black Elk*, 190
*Black Elk Speaks*, 88
blame, 58, 194
blowguns, 175
boating, 228–231
borderline personality disorder, 194
Bordewich, Fergus, 195
brio, 100
Buddhism, 21, 79, 163
Bybee, Ethel, 111
Byler, Clara Ella, 111

## C

Cachuma, Lake, 247
cancer, battle with, 160–165
ceremonies, 176–177, 179
Cherokee Nation, 126, 145, 256
*Chicken Soup for the Soul*, 24
Choctaw Nation, 145
Christianity, 79, 143–144, 180–181
Christmas, 233
chronic pain, 141–144, 159, 249
Chumash spirituality, 92–93, 155
churches, 143–144
cognitive dissonance, 113
cognitive needs, 28
Coker Creek, TN. *see* Gathering, the
*Collected Works of Saint John of the
   Cross*, 87
*Collected Works of St. Teresa of Avila,
   The*, 87
Collins, Vicki, 136–138, 175–176, 257–258
compassion, 68
compulsions, 116
consciousness, 86–89
Consciousness, Lizard, 121
contemplation, 16

contentment, 174–175, 267
control, 59, 161
corruption, 8
cost/benefit analysis, 65–70
costs of addiction, 66–67
Country Music Hall of Fame, 122
Crisp, Scott, 145, 175
cults, 9
culture, 95, 220–221, 266

**D**

*Daddy-O*, 228–231
death
    Buddhism and, 163
    denial of, 161
    God and, 242
    process of, 132
    suicide and, 208–209
    Twiggy's story, 235–240, 246
Debtors Anonymous, 62
defense mechanisms, 194–196
deletion, 196
denial, 58, 195
*Denial of Death*, 161
depression, 261
Depression, Great, 218–220
Devil, facing, 205–212
Dickens, Charles, 23
disidentified consciousness, 87
distortion, 196
distractions, 139
Divine, defined, 9
divine spark, 202–203
Doestoevsky, Fyodor, 23
Dreamtime Continuum, 122
Drum, The, 172
Durgananda, Swami, 169

**E**

eagles, 247
earthquakes, 245–248
eBay. *see* addiction
education, 210, 218, 228
ego, 89–90, 131
Emancipation Proclamation, 182
Empty Nest Syndrome, 115
enlightenment, 133
environment, 153
esteem, need for, 28
esthetic needs, 28
evil
    abuse and, 203
    choice of, 204

development of, 193–197
Devil and, 205–212
embracing, 209–210
experiences and, 198–199, 202
good and, 200–201
Man, I've Had It with Evil exercise,
    197–198
nature of, 188–191
overcoming, 104
rules against, 212
semantics and, 212
sin and, 269
evolution, social, 183
exercise, addiction to, 154
exercises
    control of feelings, 161
    cost/benefit analysis, 70
    experiences of evil, 202
    faults, 165
    goal setting, 151
    How to Succeed on Retreat, 138–140
    Man, I've Had It with Evil, 197–198
    Maslow's Hierarchy of Needs, 30
    materialism, 61
    Self-development, 90
    subpersonalities, 114
    transpersonal qualities, 39–40
    What do I really want?, 6–7
Exploration of the *Pratyabhijña-hrdayam*, 87

**F**

faith, 82–85. *see also* God
"Faith of a Child", 265
false identification, 81
family, 115, 123–127, 262–263
faults, 161–165
fear, 68, 150–151, 156, 161–162
Feather, Jonathon, 145, 167–171
feelings, controlling, 161
financial sobriety, 71–73
First Nations' People. *see* Indians
food, 135
freedom, 205
Freud, Sigmund, 81, 115
fun, commandment for, 222

**G**

Gamblers Anonymous, 62
gambling, addiction to, 154
gardening, 251
Gathering, the. *see also* Miller, Bill
    call to, 109
    ceremonies of, 176–177, 187

Coker Creek, TN, 110, 133–138, 142
importance of, 64
invitation to, 257–258
"Invitation to the Gathering, An",
257–258
Native Americans and, 177–180
powwow at, 155–157
"What the Gathering Means to Me",
255–256
generalization, 195–196
genocide, 182, 211
GI Bill, 218
goal-setting, 151
God
belief in, 82, 181, 208
death and, 242
defined, 9
delusions of, 211–212
experiencing, 84, 88, 112
fighting evil and, 208–209
offering of, 241
One-Step program, 217
power of, 216–217
Process of, 225
relationship with, 96–97
spiritual development and, 224–225
trust in, 163–164
unity with, 137
goodness, essence of, 189, 200–201
grace, 148, 185, 208
Great Depression, 218–220
greed, 13
grieving, 160
growth opportunities, 31, 44–45

H

Haley, Alex, 94
Hansen, Mark Victor, 24–26, 149
hardships, overcoming, 183–185
Hawaiian healing, 94
Heart of Meditation, The, 167
heaven, 189
hell, 189
Higher Self, 88–90, 189–190
hindrances to spiritual growth. see obstacles to
spiritual growth
Hinduism, 79, 137
Hitler, Adolph, 194, 212
Holocaust, 211. see also genocide
Hoop Dancer, The, 76f
Horse and Rider, 99f
Horse Book, The
inspiration and, 161

publishing industry and, 26, 149–150
significance of, 249
writing of, 215
horses
love of, 226–227
selling, 174
"serviceably sound", 192
showing, 155–156
Spirit Ride and, 174
Twiggy's story, 235–240
How to Succeed on Retreat, 138–140
Huna healing, 94
hunting, 175
hurting others, 189

I

illustrations
Angels Don't Leave, 166
Drum, The, 172
Hoop Dancer, The, 76f
Horse and Rider, 99f
Nona Reed, 129f
Stillness, 17f
Twiggy, 243
immortality, 10
Indians
accountability and, 266
ceremonies, 176–177, 179
Cherokee Nation and, 126
discussion of, 177–178
Gathering, the. see Gathering, the
Killing the White Man's Indian, 195
music and, 167–171
Native American Ministries of the
Holston Conference of the United
Methodist Church, 180
powwows, 155–157
religion and, 79
spirits and, 92–93
indigenous people. see Indians
infatuation, 35–39
inferiority, 219–220
inner voice, 112–116, 121, 133–134
insurance, medical, 183
interview with Bill Miller, 261–270
intoxication. see addiction
"Invitation to the Gathering, An", 257–258
Isaiah 40:31, 264–265

J

Jesus Christ
birth of, 233, 241
healing and, 143–144

reality of, 85
    as the Savior, 241
    sin and, 269
    spiritual path and, 21
John 8:32, 205
John, Saint, 87
Joplin, Janis, 157
Juckett, Mona, 167–171
Jung, Carl, 33–34

### K

Kant, Immanuel, 79, 83–84
Kantian dilemma, 84
Kennedy, Sudama Mark, 94
killing, 180–181
*Killing the White Man's Indian*, 195
kindred spirits, 137
Krishna, 21, 97

### L

Lake Cachuma, 247
Lenny's story, 200–201
Levine, Ondrea, 184
Levine, Stephen, 184
Lincoln, Abraham, 182
listening, 104
*Living Buddha, Living Christ*, 97
Lizard Consciousness, 121
loss, 235–240
love, 185, 208
lust, 68–69
Luther, Martin, 98

### M

Man, I've Had It with Evil exercise, 197–198
mantras, 101–103
Mark 10:21, 222
Maslow, Abraham, 27–29, 88, 190, 218
Maslow's Hierarchy of Needs
    enlightenment and, 88–89, 190
    exercise, 30
    Great Depression and, 218
    table, 28
materialism, 61–62, 95
medical insurance, 183
meditation. *see also* prayer
    ancestors and, 94
    chronic pain and, 144, 157, 159
    fighting evil and, 209
    music and, 169–170
    renewal and, 162
    as spiritual practice, 120–121
mental illness, 183, 194, 198–199

Methodism, 180
Miller, Bill
    abuse and, 261
    addiction and, 261, 266
    art of, 43
    Christianity and, 180
    contentment and, 267
    discovery of, 33–35
    "Faith of a Child", 265
    family and, 262–263, 270
    at the Gathering, 109, 146–157
    horses and, 174
    interview with, 162, 173, 261–270
    music and, 122, 167–171, 264–265
    notetaking and, 215–216
    past of, 184
    "What the Gathering Means to Me",
        255–256
Mirabai, 88
Mohammed, 21
moral superiority, 199
mores, 6
Moses, 21
Mother Teresa, 201
motivation, 191
mourning, 160
Moya, Jorge de, 147–148
Muktananda, Swami, 67, 188–190
music, 34, 122, 122–123
*My Lord Loves a Pure Heart: The Yoga of Divine
    Virtues*, 102–103

### N

Nakai, R. Carlos, 147
Nash, John, 183
Nathan, Barry, 99, 225
Nathan, Lily, 37–39
National Geographic, 182
Native American Ministries of the Holston
    Conference of the United Methodist
    Church, 180
Native Americans
    accountability and, 266
    ceremonies and, 176–177, 179
    Cherokee Nation and, 126
    discussion of, 177–178
    Gathering, the. *see* Gathering, the
    *Killing the White Man's Indian*, 195
    music and, 167–171
    Native American Ministries of the
        Holston Conference of the United
        Methodist Church, 180
    powwows and, 155–157
    religion and, 79

spirits and, 92–93
Natives. *see* Indians
Navajo Nation, 145
Needs, Maslow's Hierarchy of, 28, 30
Neuro Linguistic Programming, 34
nirvana, 138
Nobel Prize, 183
notetaking, 215–216
nuomenon, 83

**O**

obstacles to spiritual growth, 35–39, 43–49
*Oliver Twist*, 23

**P**

pain, chronic, 141–144, 159, 249
Pascale, Richard, 148
Peace Corps, 37
Peltier, Leonard, 188
people, indigenous. *see* Indians
perception, 195
personal needs, 28
personality theories, 79–81
personas. *see* subpersonalities
physiological needs, 28
pilgrimages, 110, 111–112, 116, 123–127
powwows, 155–157
Poynter, Dan, 25–26
practice. *see* spiritual practice
*Pratyabhijña-hrdayam*, 87, 137
prayer. *see also* meditation
    fighting evil and, 209
    music and, 169–170
    as spiritual practice, 101
    unanswered, 63
    worship and, 98
*Prison Writings: My Life Is My Sun Dance*, 188
projection, 194–195
*Prolegomena to Any Future Metaphysic, A* 84
Psalm 19, 142–143, 162–164, 246
psychosynthesis, 80–81, 86
publishing industry
    agents and, 149
    desire to publish and, 115
    frustrations with, 22–27, 41–42, 249–251
    self-publishing and, 25–26
    self-will and, 164
    as a spiritual journey, 30, 222–224

**Q**

qualities, transpersonal, exercise, 39–40

**R**

racism, 181–182, 194, 202. *see also* genocide
rape, 182
recovery from addiction, 53–65
*Red Road, The*, 264–265
Reed, Nona, 129f
rejection, 22–27
rejuvenation, 119–120
relationships, 36–39, 47–49
religion
    Buddhism, 21, 79, 163
    Christianity, 143–144
    cloistered lifestyle, 133
    damage from, 9
    development of evil and, 194
    Hinduism, 79, 137
    message of, 91
    moral superiority and, 199
    similarities of, 79
roadblocks to spiritual growth. *see* obstacles
    to spiritual growth
roles of people, 81, 86
Rumi, 88
Russo's Harbor, 229

**S**

Sacks, Oliver, 83
Sacramento, CA, 229
safety, need for, 28
Saint John, 87
Saint Teresa of Avila, 87
saints, 87–88
San Francisco, CA, 218–221
San Joaquin River Delta, 229
Sanchez, Ben, 145
satisfaction, 174
schizophrenia, 183
self-actualization, need for, 28
self-awareness, 58
    conflict and, 195
    denial and, 78–79
    evil and, 189
    fighting evil and, 210
    Higher Self, 88–89, 189–190
    recovery and, 62–63
    spiritual journeys and, 111
    subpersonalities and, 86–87
    writing and, 231
self-doubt, 131
self-esteem, 210
self-publishing, 25–26. *see also* publishing
    industry
Self, the, 9, 87, 89, 189–191

self-will, 164
Seligman, MO, 123–127
semantics, 212
September 11, 2001, 110
"serviceably sound", 192
Shakespeare, William, 78–79
Shakti, 97
shopping, addiction to, 154
Silicon Valley, 218–221, 226
sin, 269
Sioux Nation, 145
skill-building, 210
slander, 187–188, 226
social mores, 6
society, 13
sociopathy, 199, 211–212
solitude, 115, 117–119, 133
Solvang, CA, 33
soul, 8, 10
Spanish Inquisition, 212
spending, addiction to, 154
Spinal bifida, 262
spirit
    defined, 10
    existence of, 91–93
    force of, 21
    growth opportunities of, 31, 90
    relationship with God and, 100
Spirit Ride, 174
spiritual journeys. see pilgrimages
spiritual practice
    cycle of, 27
    defined, 14
    gardening and, 251
    importance of, 10–11, 97
    mantra, 101–103
    prayer, 101
    relationship with God and, 100
    spiritual journeys and, 113
Splendor of Recognition, The, 87
Spurs Magazine, 54, 154
Stalin, Joseph, 212
stereotypes, 6
stickball, 175
Stillness, 17f
subpersonalities
    development of evil and, 193–194
    mapping, 114
    messages and, 152
    self-awareness and, 86
    spiritual journeys and, 112–113
    spiritual nature of, 91
    strength of, 81

success, fear of, 150–151, 156
suicide, 208–209
sundance, 188
support, 62
survivors of abuse, 181–185
synchronicity, 137, 148

T
technology, 139
temptation, 8–9
Ten Commandments, 212
Ten Ways of Achieving Nirvana Today, 138
Teresa, Mother, 201
Teresa, Saint, 87
therapy, 210
Tibetan Book of Living and Dying, 79
Tolstoy, Leo, 23
training, 153
transcendent needs, 28
transpersonal qualities, 39–40
traveling, 116–119, 133–138
trees, 266
truth, 205
twelve-step programs, 56, 217
Twiggy, 235–240, 243

U
United Methodist Church, 180

V
voice, inner, 112–116, 121, 133–134

W
What do I really want?, 6–7
"What the Gathering Means to Me", 255–256
will, the, 87–90
Witness, the, 56, 58, 86, 88, 96
work, compulsion for, 116, 154, 217, 221
World War II, 218–219
worship, 97–98
worth, 226
writer's block, 150, 249
writing, 209–210, 231, 233–234. see also
    publishing industry

Y
yoga, 102–103, 160
Yoginis, 160
youth, 174